FOURTH EDITION

a guide book of
MEXICAN COINS
1822 to date

by: T.V. BUTTREY
and: CLYDE HUBBARD

Special Contributors
To This Edition:
Donald E. Bailey, John L. Cobb, Gregory J. Franke
Javier Lopez de Lerena, Lennert E. Philipson
Gabriel Gomez Saborio, Anna Maria Cross de Torres
Claudio Verrey, Jeffery Zarit

**krause
publications**
IOLA, WISCONSIN 54990

ACKNOWLEDGMENTS

Our sincere thanks and appreciation go to the following individuals and organizations for their assistance and contributions to previous editions of this volume:

Stephen Album

American Numismatic Society

Don Bailey

Banco de Mexico, S. A.

Hal Birt, Jr.

Kenneth E. Bressett

Colin R. Bruce II

Edward Busse

Amon G. Carter, Jr.

Henry Christensen

William W. B. Christensen

Federico Clavería

John Cobb

David Conkle

Jacobo Dultzin

Carlos Gaytán

Lawrence S. Goldberg

Antony J. H. Gunstone

José Luis Herrera S.

Pat Johnson

Andrew Kornafel

Javier de Lerena

Richard A. Long

Alberto Mendez

Mrs. Sonya Morillón

Miguel L. Muñoz

Hitoshi Nagai

Mr. and Mrs. R. Henry Norweb

Pat L. Pace

Dr. A. F. Pradeau

Toby L. Qualls

Hank Rodgers

Neil Shafer

James C. Shipley

Arnold Silverstein

Smithsonian Institution

José M. Sobrino

R. C. Soxman

Hans Stettler

Richard D. Thompsen

Sergio Torres Martinez

Moises Verjovsky

Holland Wallace

Randolph Zander

Library of Congress Catalog Card Number: 76-49264

ISBN: 0-87341-089-0

TABLE OF CONTENTS

1 | INTRODUCTION AND HISTORICAL BACKGROUND

Coinage Under Spanish Rule

Hernán Cortés finally captured the Aztec city of Tenochtitlán in 1521. It became the capital of New Spain and was renamed México, or in English, Mexico City. (Throughout this volume, the unaccented "Mexico" will refer to the nation, and the accented "México" to the city and the mint of the city.) Cortés had found in Mexico a variety of Indian tribes, some enjoying a sophisticated civilization but none using coined money. As the Spaniards settled the land to stay, they soon found that the Indian exchange of copper ingots or cocoa beans was highly inconvenient, while the gold and silver which were the first source of wealth in New Spain could most easily be exported in the form of coin. For these reasons petitions were directed to the king in the early days of Spanish rule, requesting the establishment of a mint at México. Finally in 1536, after many delays, the mint was opened. The initial coinage consisted of silver ¼, ½, 1, 2, 3, and soon 4 *reales;* and copper 2 and 4 *maravedises.* The México mint was the first, and is today the oldest, of the mints of the Western Hemisphere.

The coinage system introduced from Spain was based on the *real,* which had originally been a medieval Italian gold coin. Like all monetary units in history the *real* slowly lost its value, until in 1536 it was defined as about 3.43 grams of silver 93.05% pure. Of the coins struck on this system at México, the copper coins and the 3 *reales* were quickly discontinued, and the ¼ *real* was struck only sporadically. The important denominations were the ½, 1, 2, 4, and after some years the 8 *reales.* The gold coinage of colonial Mexico was similarly organized. The unit was called the *escudo;* the coinage was in pieces of ½, 1, 2, 4, and 8 *escudos.* The gold ½ *escudo* equalled the silver 8 *reales;* or, sixteen of any denomination in silver exchanged for one of the same module in gold. This coinage defined a silver to gold ratio of 16.5 to 1 rather than the apparent 16 to 1 because of the slightly differing alloys of the gold and silver coinages, and established at least in theory a bimetallic coinage throughout the nation.

During the centuries that followed its opening the México mint poured out a flood of coinage, especially in silver. By far the most popular and famous coin was the 8 *reales.* The "piece of eight" probably enjoyed wider circulation than any other coin in history. Its exportation to Europe encouraged the striking there of large silver pieces, the *thalers, scudi,* pieces of 5 *francs* or 5 *lire* in which the coinage of Europe abounded for several centuries. In the Far East the "piece of eight" was the standard of value. As early as the 16th Century, Spanish trade with the East moved through Mexico via the ports of Veracruz and Acapulco. Exotic goods from China and the Philippines were paid for by the exportation of coined money from Mexico.

The most important fact of mint organization under colonial rule is that there was only one mint in operation until the last decade of Spanish dominion. The México mint alone supplied all the coin of the country. But the revolution which first broke out in 1810 eventually brought such uncertainty to the country that normal communications were disrupted. On many occasions the supply of coin at one point or another would fail, without there being any possibility of transporting more from the México mint. Consequently the viceregal government permitted the opening of branch mints, some of which never closed and continued to strike after 1823 as mints of the Republic.

Events of 1810-1823

The revolution against Spanish rule, which had begun in 1810 as an uprising against privilege, was finally successful in a surprising way. The break from Spain was ultimately engineered by the very groups against whom the revolution had been aimed: the propertied classes, the clergy, the military. Some elements in these groups, fearful of their shaky position in the face of the liberal Spanish Constitution of 1812 and the unstable Ferdinand VII, determined to solidify their positions by establishing in 1821 a conservative Mexican Empire. In June, 1822, the head of the regency, Agustín Iturbide, was crowned Emperor.

Under the Empire gold and silver was struck with the portrait of Agustín at the México mint, to the same module as the Spanish coinage before. The branch mints continued to operate, turning out coins from predated dies bearing the bust of Ferdinand VII. No national copper was struck anywhere, although an issue was authorized for México. There was a small issue of coppers for regional use in the province of Nueva Vizcaya.

The Republic

In 1823 the brief Empire came to a well-deserved end, and the Republic was declared. As far as the coinage was concerned the mints continued to strike the same denominations, of the same gold and silver fineness, as they had under the Colonial or Imperial governments, but the types were altered to appropriately Republican symbols and the language of the legends changed from Latin to Spanish. The number of mints gradually expanded during the 19th century, finally reaching a total of fourteen. As several of them operated only briefly, in no given year did more than eleven issue coins.

So many mints were not needed to produce the coins of the Mexican Republic. Far from serving a useful function in the monetary system, some came into being as a device to wring fees from the mines, which otherwise might have exported raw metal. Others were opened by state or Federal authority for the enrichment of individuals prominent through influence or bribery. Finally, the mints were involved in the question of the very nature of the Mexican constitution. During the first forty years of the Republic one of the most pressing political problems was that of the sovereignty of the states: was Mexico to be a Federal Republic, that is, an association of free states, or a Central Republic in which the states were only departments of the central government? A mint, as a symbol of sovereignty, was occasionally created by state authority simply to prove that it could be done. Further, the coinage of state-issued copper was soon discovered to be an enormous source of revenue for these governments, normally in a state of bankruptcy.

Throughout the 19th century the Mexican mints, regardless of how they first came into being, were usually leased to individuals or corporations, often against an initial loan to the government which was to be recouped through the assessment of mint fees. The various terms of the leases, the competition for coinage rights, and the normally penurious condition of both Federal and state governments (and their officials) were easy inducements to fraud. Any mint was liable, in addition, to the depredations of bandits or rebels, or even of the government itself in times of extraordinary need. The public finances of Mexico were regularly chaotic, a situation reflected in its monetary policy.

MEXICO
IN 1822-1823

TERRITORY
LOST 1836-1852

MEXICO SINCE 1852

TERRITORY
HELD 1822-1823

SAN FRANCISCO
CARSON CITY
DENVER
PHOENIX
EL PASO
OKLAHOMA CITY
LOS ANGELES
CHIHUAHUA
SAN ANTONIO
SAN LUIS POTOSI
MEXICO
GUADALAJARA
GUATEMALA
COMAYAGUA
TEGUCIGALPA
PANAMA
CHICAGO
NEW YORK CITY
WASHINGTON, D.C.
ATLANTA
NEW ORLEANS
MIAMI
HAVANA
BOGOTA
QUITO
LIMA

Coinage Production

As to the coinage itself, the basic machinery varied from mint to mint, and central control over the mints was inadequate. The result was that the nation's coins often showed marked variation in style, fabric, and even fineness. Flans were not always exactly round, nor the metal pure. As late as 1849, for example, the San Luis Potosí mint still had no machinery for the cutting of planchets from rolled sheets of metal. Instead it had to cast its flans, whose porosity and frequent slight concavity after striking made a poor showing when set against the more modern productions of the other mints. Variations in fineness depended on care, or on the honesty of the mint lessee. As an example of an extreme, some of the silver struck at Durango in the late 1840's was alleged to contain as little as 46% pure metal. Therefore, when weights and dimensions are given in the catalog, they are to be understood as theoretical, except in the case of some of the state coppers where they are given as observed; considerable variation occurred in practice.

The mints of the Republic, whatever their origin, struck all gold and silver in general conformity with the standard Federal types. However, since the

| 1829 Zacatecas | 1832 Durango | 1833 Guanajuato |

The obverses of these three 1 *real* pieces, all struck within a five-year period, illustrate typical variations in style.

dies were not always cut from the matrices provided by the central mint at México, and some letter and number punches were used to add details locally, the style of a given type will often vary from mint to mint and period to period. Copper was another matter. Only the México mint struck strictly Federal copper, while the branch mints produced various types for their respective states, usually without even a reference to the Republic in the legends. These state coppers were struck in denominations of ¹⁄₁₆, ⅛ or ¼ *real,* but were generally quite different in their respective alloys, sizes, and designs. They were often issued in quantities far beyond what the circulation could absorb, and in any case were an object of distrust on the part of those who put their faith in intrinsic value. Periodic revaluations, or the wholesale calling in of an issue, completed the confusion. Throughout the first forty-five years of the Republic, the small change was in constant chaos.

Beginning of the Decimal System

The Republican government, eager to make the best impression abroad, especially in Europe, was always conscious of the deficiencies of its coins in execution, in alloy, and in the system of denominations which no longer obtained even in Spain. To modernize the coinage, in the context of a general move to metric weights and measures, a decree was issued in 1857 altering the valuation of the coins from the *real* to the decimal system. However no decimal coin was issued until 1863, when the large centavo appeared; the same year 5¢ and 10¢* silver were also issued. The Maximilian regime, during its brief term in power, introduced a complete decimal system in the Imperial

---

*In México the symbols $ and ¢ denote *peso* and *centavo* respectively. Where used in the text they represent only the denominations *peso* and *centavo*, never U. S. dollars and cents. On the other hand, catalog values are always given in U.S. dollars.

coinage, although it is known that several mints under its control continued to strike *real* coinage with the Republican designs.

After the fall of Maximilian the coinage was in a very awkward state. Both *real* and decimal coin, both Republican and Imperial (there was some attempt to withdraw the latter), both Federal copper and state or local issues were in use. Consequently it was determined that all mints should strike the same types and decimal denominations, and that state copper be withdrawn. Except for one detail the new system quickly came to be accepted. The exception was the balance scale peso of 1869-1873. This coin had exactly the intrinsic value of the earlier Republican 8 *reales*. Its type was introduced to signify the change in monetary system, the design being identical with that of the new 50¢ and 25¢. But the change in type, plus the unfortunate fact that the scale peso was two millimeters smaller than the 8 *reales*, counted against it in the China trade in spite of its unaltered value. Since the export of coined silver accounted for a substantial part of Mexico's foreign trade, rejection of the new peso abroad made its withdrawal imperative. In 1873 the old type, reading "8R," was reinstated. The alteration was necessary to satisfy foreigners, not Mexicans. The coinage system was still in fact decimal; the 8 *reales* coin was simply thought of as divided into 100 centavos.

For the next thirty years the coinage system remained fundamentally unchanged. A brief and unsuccessful attempt was made in 1882-1883 to introduce a more practical copper-nickel coinage of 1¢, 2¢ and 5¢.

The 50¢ and 25¢ were dropped in the 1890's, and the 20¢ introduced. In 1898 the obverse of the copper and silver coins was redesigned, and the 8 *reales* renamed the "Peso." In 1899 the small bronze centavo replaced the larger copper piece. The gold coinage remained unaltered, although the $2½ was not struck after 1893. These adjustments were superficial; the intrinsic value of the gold and silver was not altered. This continuity from a numismatic point of view conceals the fact that the coins were becoming less satisfactory in trade. The great economic problem of the last quarter of the century, in the United States as well as in Mexico, was the falling price of silver. Mexico had traditionally produced vast amounts of silver, and counted on the metal as the first of her exports. The country was on a silver standard and free coinage was permitted. Abroad, however, silver was in oversupply. Several important silver consuming nations turned to the gold standard. As the price of silver began to fall in the 1870's the peso came to be worth less and less. In trade with other nations on the gold standard the peso could only be tariffed at its bullion value. The result was a vicious circle: as less silver could be exported the value fell; more silver was brought to the mint to be coined, since that was all that could be done with it; as a result the currency was inflated and the value of silver fell still more.

The effect on the gold coinage is obvious: it ceased to circulate. That there is a great variety of 19th century decimal gold should not obscure the fact that it finally could not be used as coin. For that reason later dates are usually found in rather nice condition. Anyone could have had gold struck at the mint, but no one would have spent it except at a premium calculated against the daily value of the silver peso. The relatively large amounts of gold struck in the 1890's and 1900's, especially the $1 and $20, probably represent coins struck for jewelry, or gifts, or just for convenience in the handling of bullion.

The Monetary Reform of 1905

By 1905 the coinage was entirely out of line with reality. Silver, especially the $1, was overproduced and falling in value, while gold did not circulate at all. A $20 gold piece was actually worth $39.48 in silver. The reform of 1905 changed almost everything. Gold coins were reduced in size by almost 50%, and the alloy of .900 gold, .100 copper was introduced in keeping with modern usage. Coinage of the silver $1 was suspended and the 50¢, 20¢, and 10¢ silver reduced in both weight and fineness. The 5¢ piece became nickel, easier to handle and more resistant to wear than the earlier 5¢ silver. A 2¢ bronze was introduced and the 1¢ bronze redesigned. The purpose of all this was to contrive a really useful minor coinage, and to eliminate silver as a standard of value. The silver $1 was to become scarcer and subordinate to gold, the minor silver to be in effect fiduciary. Owing to the coincident rise in the price of silver bullion toward the end of 1905 the reform was a success. Some 70 million silver pesos were exported by the government to be exchanged abroad for gold; by mid-1906 the new gold $5 and $10 represented fully 45% of the monetary circulation of Mexico. In 1908 and 1909 it was possible to strike the old silver peso again without fear that it would lose its value.

Mexican gold coinage has not been changed intrinsically since 1905, although today its value vis-à-vis silver is again much higher than the denominations indicate. In 1943 the $50 gold omitted the mark of value in recognition of this fact, but the gold coined since then still carries the old denomination. The silver coinage, however, has been adapted to the times. The fluctuating values of silver bullion, and of the peso in foreign exchange, forced several redefinitions of the silver content of the peso. With only one exception every alteration was in the direction of smaller silver content. First in 1918 the peso was reduced in size, and in fineness to .800, the level of the minor coins. In 1919 the fineness fell to .720. (On coins of this type and silver content, "0.720" appears on the obverse beside the eagle's head.) In 1935 the rise in the price of silver again required an adjustment. Coinage of the peso was halted, and a great quantity of 50¢ pieces dated 1935 appeared in a low silver content of only .420 fine. In 1937 the .720 content was resumed. By 1947 the peso had to be reduced to .500 fine, by 1950 to .300, by 1957 to .100. From the beginnings of the Republic to today the fine silver content of the peso fell from 24.4 to 1.6 grams, and then to nothing as the copper-nickel peso was introduced in 1970.

Because of the falling intrinsic value of the peso, larger denominations in silver were introduced to preserve public confidence in the coinage. The first was the $2 of 1921, struck in .900 fine silver. It is easily calculated that the coin contained no more silver than two pesos of .720 fineness; the effect of a larger coin, struck with a higher percentage of silver, was only psychological. In 1947 the silver $5 was introduced. This too was later reduced in fineness, then in size so that the silver $10, .900 fine, appeared in 1955. As of 1960 Mexican silver coinage presented a curious picture: three denominations, each struck to a different fineness. No large denomination silver was issued from 1960 to 1968, when the $25 first appeared. Struck in .720 fine silver, it is slightly smaller and lighter than the $10 of 1955-60. After another issue in 1972, the 25 pesos was abandoned in favor of a .720 fine 100 pesos coin in 1977; this came on the heels of a severe devaluation of the peso in foreign exchange during 1976.

Minor silver coins suffered the same misfortune as the peso, and one by one ceased to be silver altogether. The process has been slow, complicated by the changing values of the other coinage metals — copper, nickel, tin and zinc. The mint has been willing to experiment in alloys and flan sizes, so that the minor coinage does not have the continuity of that of the United States, for example. It has been common to find coins of two or more flan sizes or alloys in circulation representing the same denomination.

BRIEF CHRONOLOGY
OF INDEPENDENT MEXICAN COINAGE

1822 First Imperial Coinage — Under Agustín I the México mint produced a coinage in gold and silver bearing the Emperor's head, in the Spanish manner. The reverse type was entirely Mexican: the eagle, in this case crowned, perched on the *nopal*. The denominations, while not forming a full series, continued in the Spanish system so that intrinsically the coinage remained unchanged.

1823 First Republican Coinage — After the fall of Emperor Agustín I, the mint at México began the coinage of 8 *reales* and 8 *escudos* bearing the Republican type of eagle. This eagle, perched on a cactus and holding a snake in its talon and beak, is seen from its left and is known as the "hooked neck eagle." The design was discontinued in mid-1825 and was not used again for nearly a century. It reappeared on the gold $20 in 1917, and on the commemorative silver $2 of 1921. Since 1936 it has been reintroduced gradually on all coinage except gold.

1824 Facing Eagle — The hooked neck eagle coinage was struck at branch mints as late as 1825, but in 1824 the México mint adopted for national use a rendition of the eagle facing. This type persisted, with stylistic variation, until 1949 on the coins struck for circulation (the 1949 1¢ is the last to bear it), and until this day on all gold except the $20.

1842 Silver Quarter *Real* Revived — After considerable unhappiness had arisen over the quantity and quality of the minor copper in circulation, it was decided to revive the ¼ *real* in silver. This denomination was frequently produced in colonial days but had never before been struck under the Republic.

1863 First Republican Decimal Coinage — The México and San Luis Potosí mints both issued 1 centavo copper coins, and the latter mint produced silver in 5 and 10 centavos denominations.

1864 Maximilian Coinage — The regime of Emperor Maximilian introduced a complete decimal system. Copper 1¢, silver 5¢, 10¢, 50¢, $1, and gold $20 were actually struck. Many of the branch mints under Imperial control, however, were compelled to continue the striking of Republican *real/escudo* types for want of Imperial dies.

1872 Last Subsidiary Coinage of *Reales* — The Alamos mint struck an issue of 2 *reales* coins in 1872. This was the last such issue other than the deliberate restoration of 8 *reales* coinage from 1873 to 1897.

1873 Last Non-Decimal Gold Coinage — In 1873, the Hermosillo mint issued an 8 *escudos* gold coin. This was the last issue of non-decimal gold in Mexico.

1873 8 *Reales* Restored — Because of objections raised in the Orient, the new 1 peso balance scale silver coinage was suspended and the old-style 8 *reales* substituted during 1873.

1898 Silver 1 Peso Reinstated — The 1 peso silver coin was again issued in 1898 as a final replacement for the 8 *reales* coinage, but the general design of the piece remained the same as the 8 *reales*.

1905 General Monetary Reform — On March 25, 1905, a sweeping monetary reform was promulgated. The free coinage of gold and silver was terminated, and the remaining branch mints were closed permanently. The gold standard was introduced, with a gold coinage redesigned and diminished in size by roughly 50%. The silver peso was suspended, and minor silver of 50¢, 20¢, and 10¢ was authorized at a fineness of .800. The silver 5¢ was abandoned for a nickel piece, and a new 2¢ bronze introduced. The obverse eagle was redesigned for the entire coinage. The bust of Hidalgo appeared as the main reverse device for the new $5 and $10 gold pieces, marking the first time that a portrait of a Mexican patriot was used on regular issue coinage.

1918 First General Reduction from Standards of 1905 — The first of a number of downward changes and adjustments from the standards of 1905 occurred in 1918.

1970 First non-Silver Peso — A copper-nickel peso was introduced, the first time in the history of Mexico that the denomination was struck at an official mint without some precious metal content.

THE MINTS AND MINT MARKS

Normally the mint mark is an abbreviation of the mint name, composed of its first and last letters, the latter often raised — thus M^o for México, Z^s for Zacatecas. Occasionally the second letter is superscript, or omitted altogether. In the early coinages of Guanajuato and Oaxaca the last letter is found within the circle of the first — G, ⊕.

In the catalog sections of this book every effort has been made to show mint marks in the form used on the coins. Because of typographical limitations, however, the dot or dash under the small superscript letter is omitted. Thus the mint mark M^o on a coin appears simply as M^o in the text. For the same reason, superscript letters of copper centavos 1869-98 have been placed at the side, although on the coins they appear *above* the large letter, with the exception of G^o for Guanajuato. For example, a centavo bearing the mint mark $\overset{N}{C}$ or $\overset{I}{P}$ is listed herein as C^N or P^I.

In the case of a few issues in the *real/escudo* system it has not been possible to determine the exact form of mint mark used. Such pieces from Hermosillo and Oaxaca in the 1860's are noted in the listings. In addition, the omission of the superscript letter, notably on small silver of Guadalajara, San Luis Potosí, and Zacatecas, has not always been ascertained.

Alamos (A, $\overset{s}{A}$, A^s), a mining town in northwestern Mexico, in the state of Sonora. Once the extremely wealthy capital of the state of Occidente (separated in 1830 into the two states of Sonora and Sinaloa), in this century it has deteriorated into a backwater. In 1828 and 1829 copper ⅛ *reales* were struck in Alamos for the state of Occidente, but it was not until 1862 that a mint was opened for the coinage of Federal gold and silver. The coinage of 1862-63, and of all fractional silver of the *real* system save the 2 *reales* of 1872, is virtually unknown. (The 2 *reales* of 1872 is the last issue of silver coinage in that system to have been struck by any Mexican mint.) The gold 8 *escudos* was struck at Alamos, but no fractions.

Contrarily, the introduction of the decimal system elicited many issues of fractional silver at Alamos. While the issues tended individually to be small, more than 50 varieties of the 5¢, 10¢, 25¢, and 50¢ are known. The 8 *reales* was struck with annual regularity, even to the exclusion of the balance scale peso type issued by most other mints from 1869 to 1873. A pair of unused matrices for the peso was found during an inventory in 1876; the reason for their never having been put to use is not known.

All denominations of decimal gold were struck at Alamos, but the $1, $2½, and $5 were each minted on only one occasion and are rare.

The Alamos mint was closed in 1895.

HERMOSILLO

CHIHUAHUA

GUADALUPE
Y CALVO

ALAMOS

CATORCE

SAN LUIS POTOSI

CULIACAN

MEXICO

DURANGO

ZACATECAS

GUADALAJARA

GUANAJUATO

TLALPAM

OAXACA

Catorce (C^E), formerly *Real del Catorce,* a village in the state of San Luis Potosí. Although a provisional mint there had issued a crude emergency coinage under Spanish authority in 1810-11, no Republican mint was authorized at Catorce for another half century. Owing to the unflagging efforts of a local entrepreneur a mint was established in 1863, but the competition was deeply resented by the inhabitants of the state capital, which had its own much more important mint. Grave irregularities in both the original contract and the operation of the mint brought coinage at Catorce to a relatively quick end. Although there is some evidence that coins were produced as late as 1869, the entire coinage of Catorce, as far as is known, consists of the 2, 4, and 8 *reales* all dated 1863.

Chihuahua (C^A, CH, CH^A), capital of the northern state of Chihuahua· Here, as at Catorce, a secondary Spanish colonial mint operated during the first Mexican revolution. The Republican mint was established in 1831. Under the *real/escudo* system both the 8 *reales* and 8 *escudos* were produced with regularity, but the fractional *reales* are quite scarce and fractional gold is unknown.

On changing over to decimal coinage in 1868 the Chihuahua mint took up the wreath type 5¢ and 10¢ first struck at San Luis Potosí in 1863, and was the only other mint to issue the type. Generally, fractional silver was regularly struck only during the last decade of the life of the mint, and only then in any sizable amounts. The $20 gold was the usual denomination of the mint; the only fractional gold known is a small issue of $1, $5, and $10 struck in 1888. Of all decimal denominations, only the 1¢ copper was never struck.

The Chihuahua mint was closed in 1895.

Culiacán (C, C̀, Cᴺ), in northwestern Mexico, capital of the state of Sinaloa. Although agitation on the state level since the earliest days of independence had brought about the tardy construction of a building and the purchase of necessary machinery, the mint began to function only in 1846 through a Federal decree as an offshoot of the mint of Guadalupe y Calvo. All denominations were struck in gold and silver under the *real/escudo* system, but some varieties are decidedly scarce and the 4 *escudos* is rare.

The change to the decimal system meant no alteration of the policy of producing the spectrum of denominations: all are known from Culiacán and many are quite common. The scarcest is the gold $2½ piece, which was apparently struck only once, in 1893.

During the last years of the branch mints, Culiacán was the only mint other than México to strike the small bronze 1¢. The mint was closed in 1905.

Durango (D, Ď, Dᵒ), center of a rich mining area, capital of the state of Durango. Here too a mint was opened in 1811 for the emergency production of Spanish colonial coin. In this case the mint remained open to strike for the young Republic following its independence. Durango was an early and important mint for the production of 8 *reales,* although coins of this series are harder to find from the 1840's on — perhaps an indication of a larger export to the Far East. Fractional silver, save the 4 *reales,* was struck frequently, but usually in small quantities. *Escudo* system gold is sporadic and mostly scarce.

During part of the 1830's and 1840's the Durango mint employed dies which had been manufactured in Europe. The style is much finer than that usually found, the lettering smaller and more precise, and the eagle quite different in execution from any others (see illustration on page 7). The dates, however, are frequently overcut with great crudity, even to the point of being rendered illegible on the die.

Under the decimal system all denominations were struck in silver, those of earlier date tending to be the scarcer. Decimal gold is uncommon.

The Durango mint was closed in 1895.

Estado de México (EᵒMᵒ), a mint situated in Tlalpam, then the capital of the State of México, now part of the Federal District. Established in 1828 as a source of revenue for the state, the mint was ill-managed and never succeeded in attracting the business of the silver mines. The fiasco was soon apparent and the mint was closed in 1830. Several denominations in both gold and silver are known, all scarce or rare.

Guadalajara (G, Ǵ, Gᴬ), capital of the state of Jalisco. Coinage began under Spanish colonial rule and continued without a break into the Republic, although the earliest Republican pieces are dated 1825. The coinage of 8 *reales* was regular, but fractional silver did not appear in large quantities until the 1840's. Gold was struck sporadically in all denominations; many varieties, especially the 4 *escudos,* are quite scarce.

In the decimal series the fractional silver is more common, although fewer of these issues were struck at Guadalajara than at any other mint save Oaxaca. No 50¢ piece was struck, and decimal gold appears in the $10 denomination only.

One feature of the Guadalajara coinage is the scarcity of $1 silver and 8 *reales* when set against the mint statistics. Presumably these were exported to the Far East in proportionately greater quantities than pesos of the other mints.

The mint was closed in 1895.

Guadalupe y Calvo (GC), a small mining town in the state of Chihuahua, came into being as the result of the opening of gold and silver mines in the mid-1830's. The mint was established in 1843 to take advantage of the ores immediately at hand. The annual average total of coinage was approximately $650,000, about half again as much as the production of the mint at the state capital, Chihuahua, during the same period. But the ore soon began to give out and the mint was closed in 1852. All denominations of the *real/escudo* silver and gold were struck at Guadalupe y Calvo, but many varieties are quite scarce.

Guanajuato (G, Ǥ, G⁰), capital of the state of Guanajuato, this city too lies in a rich mining area. First a rebel mint, established by Hidalgo in 1810, it saw operation as well under the Spanish authorities. With the establishment of the Republic the Guanajuato mint became one of the most important in the nation, with a large and regular production in gold and silver. Along with Zacatecas, Guanajuato was responsible for the coinage of by far the largest part of the silver (of all denominations) in circulation during the first half century of the Republic.

Production was uninterrupted during the occupation of the city by the Imperial forces of Maximilian, 1864-67, but inasmuch as dies appropriate to his reign were not available, most of the coin produced in this period was struck from predated Republican dies and cannot be distinguished. One rarity dating from the occupation is the silver $1 of 1866 bearing the head of Maximilian. The coinage figure is not known but the number of specimens available is very limited.

In the period of Republican decimal coinage the Guanajuato mint again produced very large quantities of silver in all denominations. In gold only the $20 piece was regularly struck, the other denominations appearing sporadically. Only in 1888 was the complete series in gold minted. The Guanajuato mint was closed in 1900.

Hermosillo (Ĥ, H⁰), capital of the northwestern state of Sonora. State copper was struck at Hermosillo during the years 1832-36. An attempt to produce silver as well was a failure. A small issue of 8 *reales* was struck in 1835-36 and 1839 from dies cut independently, not from the official matrices made in Mexico City. As a result the Federal Government demanded that this coinage cease and that the examples already struck be retired from circulation. Today they are of the greatest rarity.

Coinage in gold and silver was not issued regularly from a mint at Hermosillo until 1861. The fractional *real* silver is scarce, as is the fractional gold. The 8 *escudos* of 1873 was the last non-decimal coin issued by a Republican mint.

The Hermosillo mint, like that at Alamos, never struck the balance scale peso, although an inventory in 1876 disclosed that there were matrices of the proper types in storage. Fractional silver was struck with some frequency, but decimal gold is mostly rare.

The Hermosillo mint was closed in 1895.

México (M, Ṁ, M⁰), the national capital. The earliest Republican coins were struck here by the mint which had historically been the first, and for most of the colonial period the only, mint in the country. During the period of the *real/escudo* system the México mint was not actually the most active of the Mexican mints, but it did oversee some of the technical operations at the branch mints and was supposed to provide the matrices for Federal dies employed everywhere. Although it struck great quantities of copper in 1829-37, and again in 1841-42, in silver it ranked a poor third behind Guanajuato and Zacatecas. Production of gold was, as usual, irregular, but some varieties are common.

The attempt to introduce a decimal coinage, in conjunction with the establishment of the metric system in all manner of measures throughout the country, was slow in succeeding. In the years between the first decimal edict of 1857 and the French occupation in 1863, the México mint had produced but a single decimal denomination, the 1¢ copper. The coinage of Maximilian was entirely decimal, although it was short on denominations, there being no 20¢ or 25¢ silver and no gold other than the $20 piece. After his fall the Republican coinage was resumed at México and remained decimal in fact if not at first in the letter of the law. No *real* system silver smaller than the 2 *reales* was struck, and this coin along with all larger *real/escudo* denominations could be expressed decimally (2 *reales* = 25¢, etc.). In 1869 a complete decimal coinage was introduced at México, then was gradually adopted at the various branch mints, finally overcoming the *real/escudo* system in 1873. (Although the continuing issue of 8 *reales* until 1897 was apparently an exception, this coin was simply the equivalent of the decimal peso and was struck because of its great popularity in Oriental trade.)

Now too the México mint emerged as a strong competitor to the branch mints in the quantity of production. It led by far in the production of 1¢ copper; it alone struck the copper-nickel 1¢, 2¢, and 5¢ of 1882-83; and it produced more than half the known issues of the smaller denominations in gold ($1, $2½, $5).

Since the closing of the last branches in 1905 México has been the only Federal mint in operation. Issues too extensive for it to handle have been contracted out to foreign mints in lieu of re-establishing any other Federal mint.

Oaxaca (O, ☉, Ȏ, Oᴬ), a Spanish colonial city in southeastern Mexico, capital of the state of Oaxaca. Coin had been struck there during the revolt from Spain, by both colonial and revolutionary forces. The Federal mint was opened in 1858, closed in 1893. In spite of a regular coinage in gold and silver, the mint produced far less than any other of the Republic in proportion to its length of life. For example, the total of $1 silver and 8 *reales* struck in its entire life of 35 years, just over $5,000,000, is roughly equal to a single year's production at the México mint alone.

A notable feature of the coinage at Oaxaca was the reluctance to strike fractional denominations. Under the *real/escudo* system a single fractional issue in silver is known, and but one in gold, the 4 *reales* and 4 *escudos* of 1861. No state copper was struck (an 1833 copper issue is documentarily attested but apparently does not exist).

Under the decimal system the centavo was briefly produced in very small quantities, and today is very rare. The only fractional silver were the 5¢ and 10¢ produced in 1889-90, which are quite scarce. Some of the decimal gold, however, is not particularly rare.

San Luis Potosí (P, P̄, Pᴵ, S.L.P.), capital of the state of the same name. The mint opened in 1827, striking only the 8 *reales* in any quantity. Fractional silver of the *real* system is known in all denominations but tends to be scarce outside the decade of the 1840's. No gold was struck.

Under the decimal system the fractional coinage was much more frequently issued — San Luis Potosí stands next after México, Zacatecas, and Guanajuato — and many varieties are fairly common. No decimal gold is listed in the mint reports, but a $10 gold piece of 1888 is known (listed in this catalog as a trial strike). The National Museum in Mexico City has a set of silver trial strikes of that year covering all five gold denominations.

The San Luis Potosí mint was closed along with that of Oaxaca in 1893.

Zacatecas (Z, Ž, Zˢ), another mining city, capital of the north central state of Zacatecas. The mint first opened in 1810, striking colonial silver of a crude local type. The quality of the coinage soon improved and the mint continued to strike into the Republic. Under the *real* system the mint was notable for its large and fairly regular production of silver, especially the fractional denominations. These are by and large among the commonest coins of 19th century Mexico. No *escudo* system gold was struck until the late 1850's, however, and the fractional denominations are scarce.

Under the decimal system the Zacatecas coinage remained very extensive in silver but infrequent in gold save for the $10 piece.

The Zacatecas mint was finally closed in 1905.

COIN LEGENDS

The early Republican gold and silver legends differ from the earlier colonial and imperial in two significant ways. The legends, which had been rendered in Latin, were now given in Spanish; and the fineness of the coins was openly stated upon them. The reverse legend of the early Republican gold and silver coins stated: the denomination, mint mark, date, assayer's or assayers' initials, and metallic fineness. The information is always in this order. Thus the silver coins of ½ *real* through 8 *reales* always bear a form of the legend

illustrated above — that is, "a coin of 8 *reales,* struck at México, in 1824, under the assayers J(osé García Anzaldo) and M(anuel Ruiz Tejada), with a fineness of 10 *dineros* and 20 *granos.*" The mint mark, date and initials will vary according to circumstances, the mark of value according to denomination.

The fineness "10 Dˢ 20 Gˢ" is an expression of a system of silver assay that dates from medieval times. Theoretical purity is counted as 12 *dineros,* each of which is divided into 24 *granos.* Thus this fineness can be represented in fractions as $\frac{10}{12} + \frac{20/24}{12}$ or in percentage as 90.27% fine.

The pre-decimal gold bore a similar form of reverse legend, for example: 8 E • M̊ • 1824 • J • M • 21 Qˢ. The last abbreviation represents *quilates* or carats; the fineness is 21 out of 24 carats, or 87.5%.

Two assayers' initials regularly appear on the silver and gold of the *real/ escudo* system, save that on a few occasions the mint of Durango used three initials. No attempt has been made to identify the assayers whose initials appear on the coins. The letters can stand for the two names of one person, or the baptismal or family names of two. In some cases their identity is known; in many others it can only be conjectured.

When the decimal standard was inaugurated the legends were adjusted to the new system. On the fractional silver, the scale peso, and the peso from

1898, fineness was stated in terms of thousandths fine, here 902.7. The decimal gold too was of the same alloy as that of the earlier system; "21 Q^S" was translated to "875" (thousandths fine). On the scale peso, fractional silver, and all gold only one assayer's initial was used (except for the Alamos 5¢, 10¢ and $10 of 1874-75, which bear two). Note, however, that the initials and fineness are missing from the 5¢ and 10¢ of Chihuahua, México, and San Luis Potosí of the types which preceded the regular 1869-1905 type. Neither are they found on any of the Maximilian gold or silver, nor on *any* copper or bronze. The only coins of this period with no mint mark are the copper-nickel 1¢, 2¢, and 5¢ of 1882-83.

With the reform of 1905, all mints except for México were closed. Since then all coins — even those struck outside the country — have borne some

Alamos mint 5 and 10 centavos (enlarged) showing two assayer's initials DL in place of the normal single initial.

form of the México mint mark save for the $1 silver of 1910-14. Assayer's initials were dropped and have not reappeared; they are found only on the $1 of 1908 and 1909 which were struck to the pre-reform type. Fineness too was not stated again on the gold, nor on the silver until the debasement to 720 thousandths in 1919. Since 1919 all silver coins at least 500 thousandths fine have borne an indication of fineness; any piece dated after 1919 and not showing the fineness — for example, the 50¢ of 1935, or the $1 of 1950 — contains less than 50% pure silver.

GLOSSARY OF TERMS

The Latin legends of the Mexican coinage of Agustín are consistent throughout both gold and silver: obv., AUGUSTINUS DEI PROVIDENTIA (= Agustín, by God's providence), probably intended to avoid the *Dei Gratia* of the immediately preceding colonial coinages; and rev., MEX•I•IMPERATOR•CONSTITUT• (= First constitutional Emperor of Mexico).

GLOSSARY OF TERMS

Spanish words and phrases found on the faces or edges of the Republican coins are as follows:

Agricultura Industria Comercio	Agriculture Industry Commerce
Año de Carranza	Year (Anniversary) of Carranza
Año de Hidalgo	Year (Anniversary) of Hidalgo
Casa de Moneda de México	The México Mint
Centenario de la Constitución de México	Centennial of the Constitution of Mexico
Cinco	Five
Cincuenta	Fifty
Constitución	Constitution
Cuartilla	Quarter *real*
Cuarto	Quarter *real*
Departamento de	Department (= state) of
Diez	Ten
Dos	Two
Dos y medio	Two and a half
Equidad en la Justicia	Equity in Justice
Estado de	State of
Estado Libre de	Free State of
Estado Libre Federato de	Free Federated State of
Estado Libre y Soberano de	Free and Sovereign State of
Estado Soberano de	Sovereign State of
Estados Unidos Mexicanos	United Mexican States
Gramos (Gr., G.)	Grams
Igualdad en la Ley	Equality under Law
Imperio Mexicano	Mexican Empire
Inauguración del Ferrocarril del Sureste	Inauguration of the Southeastern Railway
Independencia y Libertad	Independence and Liberty
Juegos de la XIX Olimpiada	Games of the 19th Olympiad
Ley (on book or scroll)	Law
Ley (on silver $5, $10, $25 and Onza)	Alloy; fineness (as *Ley 0.900,* "900 fine")
Libertad	Liberty
Libertad en el Orden	Liberty under Order
Libertad en la Ley	Liberty under Law
Libertad y Reforma	Liberty and Reform
Maximiliano Emperador	Maximilian Emperor
Medio Octavo	Half *Octavo* (Sixteenth *real)*
México Libre	Free Mexico
Octavo	Eighth *real*
Oro puro	Pure gold
Peso (on $5 silver and Onza)	Weight
Plata pura	Pure silver
Provincia	Province
Quartilla	Quarter *real*
República Mexicana	Mexican Republic
Sufragio Efectivo No Reelección	Effective Suffrage, No Re-election
Sufragio Libre	Free Suffrage
Un, Una	One
Veinte	Twenty
Veinticinco	Twenty-five

ON COLLECTING MEXICAN COINS

There are and have been many important collections of Mexican coins formed both in Europe and in the Americas. The material is so rich, and historically so interesting, that any student of the history of the Americas would naturally be drawn to it. However it has been generally true that certain phases of the coinage of Mexico have not been especially popular with serious collectors in the past. Until recently emphasis was placed on the colonial rather than the Republican period, on Republican gold rather than silver, on the silver 8 *reales* or pesos rather than fractions, and on the 19th rather than the 20th century. That is, the smaller the coin and the later its date, the less likely it was that anyone gave it serious attention.

One reason for this lay in the final closing of the branch mints in 1905. After that date no mint mark other than that of México is found on the coins; an important source of their earlier variety has ceased to exist. The reform of 1905 also brought about the first significant intrinsic alteration of the coinage since the founding of the Republic. Thereafter, repeated redefinitions of the coinage created an apparent confusion, especially in comparison with the more placid coinage of the United States.

Today the relative popularity of the various coinages is much different, primarily because many earlier issues have become less available and higher in price. Colonial coins and Republican gold by date and mint are now beyond the reach of the collector of average means; the same is becoming true of Republican 8 *reales*. As detailed information has become available, the interest of collectors has focused on modern coins from 1905 to the present, and to a slightly lesser extent on the minor issues of the 19th century. The completely revised market values herein stand as a testimonial to the fact that practically all series of Mexican coins have now come into their own.

INTRODUCTION TO THE CATALOG

This catalog covers the coins struck in all metals at the various Federal mints of the Mexican Republic, including the coppers struck in the names of the states. Also included are the coins of the two Mexican Empires under Agustín I and Maximilian, respectively. The catalog does not include any of the earlier Spanish colonial coinage, revolutionary issues of the 19th and 20th centuries, nor municipal and private coinages. The coins in each catalog section are arranged in chronological order under each denomination, and as in the other Whitman catalogs the smallest denominations are found first, rising to the gold. Descriptions and physical characteristics are given for every type. Varieties if any will appear under each denomination by date and mint. Minor variations and die conditions which appear as dots, bumps, missing letters, etc., especially on the more recent coinage, are not considered to be an important part of this series. These have not been included in this catalog.

Overdates and Over-initials

The practice of re-using old dies by overdating them was very common in 19th century Mexican coinage. Overdates will therefore be found throughout the listings, and cannot in most cases be considered as rare. There are even cases where the normal date coinage is scarcer than the overdate (example: 8 *reales* 1887 O^). Whenever there was a change of assayer, a strong possibility exists that over-initials will be found on some of the coins. On a few occasions dies were even re-used at a second mint. Proof of this can be seen in the examples of over-mint marks that have been listed and illustrated. All of these varieties are indicative only of common mint practices of the time, and must be taken in their proper perspective.

Overdates in the 20th century, although known, are much less common because modern mint techniques permit the easy replacement of dies under normal operating conditions. Less than a dozen overdates are known since the coinage reform of 1905.

Reports and Omissions of Coinage

Especially true of the 19th, but also valid for the 20th centuries, the fact that a mint does *not* report a certain issue is no guarantee that such does not exist (examples: 5 centavos 1931, S. L. P^{l} 1 centavo 1891, etc.). The opposite also holds true — the fact that an issue *is* reported does not guarantee its actual existence. There are coinages duly reported, specimens of which have never been found anywhere. The practice of recutting dates and assayers' initials, however, suggests a scrupulousness on the part of the mints' officials which has justified the inclusion in the catalog of issues contained in the mint reports but not yet actually known. These would be mostly small issues, difficult to obtain in any case. While it is conceivable that predated dies were used occasionally, the frequency of overdating would suggest that the use of incorrect dates was uncommon. (The one exception was the general use of predated Republican dies in mints under Imperial control, 1863-1867, when Imperial dies were not available.)

For the coinage struck prior to the 1905 reform the assayers' initials are given. An omitted initial indicates that the coin, whose existence is well attested, has not been seen by the cataloger and the initial is as yet uncertain. After the date, mint, and initials is given the number of pieces coined when these statistics are known.

The simple figure.......1,028 is the total number coined during the calendar year. These figures are complete for all issues of 1886 and after, save where the coin is omitted in the report.

An italic figure.........*1,028* is a partial figure for the calendar year. Only part of the report has been seen in these cases. The number may be a full total, but there is as yet no way of saying; it does represent at least a minimum for the year.

The figure omitted.......... indicates that the report has not been seen.

A dash...............——— means the coin is omitted in the complete report.

The mint statistics offer a general check on relative rarity, with some few exceptions (see remarks on the Guadalajara mint, page 13).

Market Values

It should be noted that the values are suggested only. Current market figures have been consulted in the case of the gold, the 8 *reales,* and all decimal coinage, and values have been determined through the cooperation of people in close contact with retail sales. Undoubtedly many of the prices for the earlier Republican coinage are still theoretical. Values for the commonest coins in ordinary condition were set from the standard handbooks and from experience. The rarer coins, and those in better condition, can be valued only by a careful calculation. As a rule the prices are much lower than would be the case for U.S. material of comparable rarity. Prices are meant only as a rough, relative indication of value; in actual sale the coins may bring more or less.

Values are given for several grades of condition. In each series these grades reflect the quality of coins actually available on the market. Thus, the state and Federal coppers are valued in grades from Fair to Extremely Fine, as Uncirculated is simply not applicable. Most other issues are valued from Good-Very Good to Uncirculated. The past few years have seen many 19th century minor coins appear in grades high enough to justify their being cataloged in Uncirculated. For the 8 *reales* and 19th century pesos, and for decimal gold, Uncirculated remains a collectible condition. But in many cases strictly uncirculated specimens are hard to find; the collector who buys for condition will often have to be satisfied with Extremely Fine. Although most 20th century types are more easily found Uncirculated, certain dates are quite rare in this condition.

Every attempt has been made to present the Mexican Republican coinage complete in this guide book. Some rare issues and varieties doubtless have been omitted, owing to their not having come to the attention of the authors. Since the coinage statistics are only sporadically available before 1886, each issue has had to be verified from an actual specimen before its inclusion in the catalog. Collectors are urged to report any new material not included here.

Note: All market values in this catalog are in U.S. dollars.

2 | THE FIRST EMPIRE— AGUSTIN I 1822-1823

Mexico's war for independence from Spain culminated with the fall of the Spanish colonial government and the immediate declaration of a Mexican Empire on September 28, 1821. A temporary regency was then established, headed by the former royalist officer Agustín Iturbide. Under the *Plan de Iguala* it had been intended to call one of the Spanish royal family, possibly even King Fernando VII himself, to the Mexican throne. However, by the time the Congress met in May of 1822 Iturbide had managed to sway public opinion so strongly in his favor that he was himself proclaimed Emperor of Mexico. He was confirmed by the Congress on May 19, 1822, and crowned as Agustín I in the cathedral of the capital on June 21. His reign was financially precarious and politically oppressive. On March 19, 1823, less than a year after he assumed the throne, Agustín's abdication was forced, the Congress nullified the Plan de Iguala and Mexico became an independent republic.

The regular issue Imperial coins of Iturbide were struck only at México. The branch mints continued to produce coinage of Spanish colonial type, using predated dies. In addition a series of local provisional silver was struck in Honduras at Comayagua and Tegucigalpa, and a regional copper issue at Durango for the province of Nueva Vizcaya.

NATIONAL COINAGE — MEXICO MINT

The México mint struck the minor silver denominations of ½ *real* and 2 *reales* in both 1822 and 1823; that of 1 *real* in a small issue dated 1822 only. No 4 *reales* were produced. All the minor silver coins bear a medium size portrait of the style introduced late in 1822 and so presumably were not among the earliest strikings of the mint under Agustín. Copper coins were twice authorized, but production never began.

SILVER ISSUES
½ Real 1822-1823

The ½ *real,* like other minor silver denominations, occurs only with the second portrait of Agustín; the obverse legend is spelled out in full. Likewise, the Imperial eagle is of the second type. As in the case of Spanish colonial portrait issues, the ½ *real* bears no denomination.

Diameter 16 mm; weight 1.692 grams; composition .9027 silver, .0973 copper; edge: ornamented with circle and rectangle pattern.

Date	Mint	Assayer	F	VF	EF	Unc.
1822	M̥	JM......................	$17.50	$37.50	$65.00	$325.00
1823	M̥	JM......................	13.50	25.00	60.00	325.00

1 Real 1822

The 1 *real* of Iturbide is identical in design to the ½ *real,* with the exception that the denomination "1 R" appears below the eagle. The wavy truncation of the bust is similar to variety 4C of the 8 *reales,* suggesting that coinage occurred very late in 1822.

Diameter 20 mm; weight 3.384 grams; composition .9027 silver, .0973 copper; edge: ornamented with circle and rectangle pattern.

1822	M̥	JM......................	85.00	130.00	275.00	700.00

2 Reales 1822-1823

The design of the 2 *reales* follows the style of the smaller pieces, with its denomination "2 R" appearing below.

Diameter 27 mm; weight 6.768 grams; composition .9027 silver, .0973 copper; edge: ornamented with circle and rectangle pattern.

1822	M̥	JM......................	30.00	60.00	250.00	1,000
1823	M̥	JM......................	20.00	35.00	200.00	1,000

8 Reales Type I 1822

The 8 *reales* of 1822 show a development of portrait, eagle, obverse legend form, and reverse legend position in the chronological order listed below. Agustín's portrait on the first type is quite youthful in appearance and noticeably smaller than on other coinage. The small head gave way to the large, since the former is found only in 1822 and only with the obverse legend abbreviated. Similarly the small eagle, with wings widely outstretched, is the earliest reverse type.

Diameter 39 mm; weight 27.073 grams; composition .9027 silver, .0973 copper; edge: ornamented with circle and rectangle pattern.

Date	Mint	Assayer	F	VF	EF	Unc.
1822	M̊	JM *varieties:*..............	$50.00	$100.00	$275.00	$1,000

Variety 1A Obverse 1: small head, AUGUST.
Reverse A: small eagle, legend begins at upper right.
Variety 1a/A Obverse 1a: bust as on obverse of 8 escudos gold on page 27,
otherwise as Obverse 1.

8 Reales Type II 1822-1823

The second type of Iturbide 8 *reales* is distinguished by an entirely different portrait and a larger, more natural eagle. The large head occurs with both abbreviated and full obverse legend. While this large portrait was in use, the reverse legend, which had begun at the upper right (following the practice of the colonial 8 *reales*), was shifted half way around the field so as to begin at the lower left, presumably to emphasize the imperial claim which on the earlier dies had to be read almost upside down. (Only with the abbreviated obverse legend does the eagle's crown of the reverse bear an evident cross.) Finally the medium size portrait closed out the year, and it alone was used in 1823.

Diameter 39 mm; weight 27.073 grams; composition .9027 silver, .0973 copper; edge: ornamented with circle and rectangle pattern.

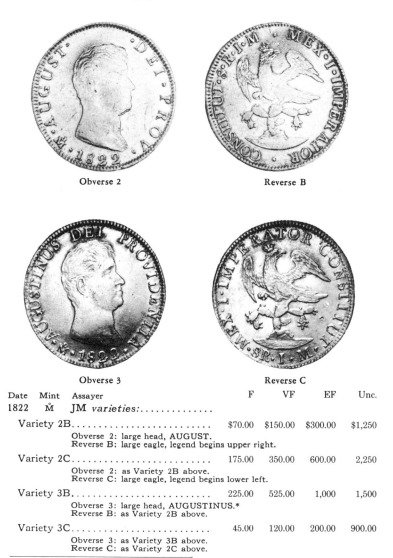

| Obverse 2 | Reverse B |
| Obverse 3 | Reverse C |

Date	Mint	Assayer	F	VF	EF	Unc.
1822	M̊	JM *varieties:*.............				
		Variety 2B........................	$70.00	$150.00	$300.00	$1,250
		Obverse 2: large head, AUGUST. Reverse B: large eagle, legend begins upper right.				
		Variety 2C........................	175.00	350.00	600.00	2,250
		Obverse 2: as Variety 2B above. Reverse C: large eagle, legend begins lower left.				
		Variety 3B........................	225.00	525.00	1,000	1,500
		Obverse 3: large head, AUGUSTINUS.* Reverse B: as Variety 2B above.				
		Variety 3C........................	45.00	120.00	200.00	900.00
		Obverse 3: as Variety 3B above. Reverse C: as Variety 2C above.				

*In variety 3B the portrait ends on a long, straight truncation.

Obverse 4   Reverse C

			F	VF	EF	Unc.
Variety 4C.........................			$50.00	$100.00	$200.00	$1,000

Obverse 4: medium head, AUGUSTINUS.
Reverse C: as Variety 2C above.

Variety 5C.........................				Rare		

Obverse 5: extremely long trunk on neck.
Reverse C: as Variety 2C above.

Date	Mint	Assayer				
1823	M̊	JM.......................	50.00	100.00	200.00	1,000

As 1822 Variety 4C except for date.

GOLD ISSUES
4 Escudos 1823

The 4 *escudos* was struck only in 1823, with an obverse identical to all other coins of Iturbide in that year. On the reverse is a small rendition of the second eagle design in an elaborate cartouche with arms.

Diameter 30 mm; weight 13.536 grams; composition .875 gold, .125 copper; edge: ornamented with circle and rectangle pattern.

Date	Mint	Assayer				
1823	M̊	JM.......................	900.00	1,600	2,200	4,500

8 Escudos Type I 1822

The gold 8 *escudos* of 1822, the only gold denomination of the year for Agustín, bears a version of the small head of the earliest 8 *reales,* and must have been struck soon after Iturbide's accession on May 19. The reverse figuration is that of the small eagle on the *nopal* (as used on the first 8 *reales)* with the addition of a pile of arms.

Diameter 37 mm; weight 27.073 grams; composition .875 gold, .125 copper; edge: ornamented with circle and rectangle pattern.

Date	Mint	Assayer	F	VF	EF	Unc.
1822	M̥	JM *varieties:*	$900.00	$1,600	$2,250	$4,500
		normal legend; error: AUGSTINUS.				

8 Escudos Type II 1823

This issue bears the obverse common to all 1823 coinage, and its reverse is
identical to the 4 *escudos.*

1823	M̥	JM	900.00	1,600	2,250	4,500

Gold "1 Peso" Fantasy Pieces

Recently a small gold piece has appeared on the market, purporting to be a
gold peso of Agustín. It comes several years after, and perhaps from the same
source as the similar modern fabrications in the name of Maximilian (see p. 120).
The style of the piece is neat but uncharacteristically heavy; it bears no indication of weight, fineness or denomination; and at ca. 0.50 grams it could
not be fit into the monetary system of the 1820's at any point. On the reverse
the dates 1822-1823 presumably mark the extent of Agustín's reign; the piece
therefore could not conceivably have been issued by him.

For completeness there should be mentioned another recent gold piece of
similar background; this one has a bust of Cuauhtémoc on one side and an
eagle on the other.

HONDURAS PROVISIONAL SILVER COINAGE

Mexico reached its farthest territorial extent during the reign of Agustín I. On his accession the limits of the country already stretched in the west to the northern border of California and in the east to the Sabine River at the edge of Louisiana. Now, with the annexation on January 5, 1822 of what had been the *Capitanía General de Guatemala*, the Mexican Empire reached south to the border of what is today Panama. A series of proclamation medals was issued, probably from the México mint, for Chiapas, Quezaltenango, Guatemala and León; but the only coinage struck in the area during the 18 months of Mexican domination originated in the province of Honduras.

The dies are crude and plainly of local manufacture. All the coins in question are dated 1823 and all are rare. The earliest is a portrait 2 *reales* of Agustín, inspired by the proclamation medals. It was most probably struck at Comayagua, the center of pro-Mexican sympathies in Honduras. The reverse die of the eagle is found later in the same year at Tegucigalpa, which had opposed the annexation, with an obverse type drawn from the Spanish colonial coinage. The omission of Agustín doubtless indicates that the piece was struck after his abdication but before the final break with Mexico. Finally the cross die is linked into a larger series struck at Tegucigalpa which forms a purely provincial coinage. This last group, not listed here, has no Mexican reference and was struck after the annexation of Central America to Mexico was voided on July 1, 1823.

2 Reales — Comayagua

The obverse of this piece bears the legend ENPER[ADOR] *(sic)* *(Emperor)* AGUSTIN / • 1823 • around a crude bust of the emperor facing left. Equally crude, the reverse shows the crowned Imperial eagle perched on a cactus plant with the legend M[ONEDA] P[ROVISIONAL] *(Provisional Coin)*, 2 R. Contrary to normal Latin American practice, the issue bears no indication of weight or fineness.

Diameter 21-22 mm; weight 5.1-5.6 grams; composition: silver alloy; edge: plain.

Date
1823   (Buttrey 1)*...2 known

2 Reales — Tegucigalpa

The second of the Honduras issues has an obverse bearing an early form of Spanish arms. A pointed equilateral cross divides four arcs, under which appear the traditional Spanish lions and castles. The legend is TEGVSIGALPA L[IBRE] *(Free)* A[ÑO] *(Year)* 1823. The reverse is the same used for the Comayagua coin.

---

*Reference numbers are from T. V. Buttrey's 1967 article published by the American Numismatic Society (see Bibliography page 252).

The third piece is a mule of the two reverses of the Mexican and independent periods. The obverse employs the Imperial eagle die which was used as the reverse on the first two issues, while the reverse has a more familiar form of Spanish arms crowned between pillars of Hercules. The legend reads 2 R. M[ONEDA] TEGVSIGALPA L[IBRE] / A[NO] 1823. As with the other issues, neither weight nor fineness is specified.

Diameter 23-27 mm; weight 5.6-6.6 grams; composition: silver alloy; edge: plain.

Date
1823   Cross obverse (B-2)...................................5 known
1823   Spanish arms (B-7)...................................1 known

NUEVA VIZCAYA

The province of Nueva Vizcaya covered a vast area including what are now the states of Durango and Chihuahua, as well as territory further to the north which passed under the control of the United States as a result of the Mexican War. Its capital was Durango. The province was broken up in 1824.

The mint at Durango had struck crude copper $\frac{1}{8}$ *real*s during the last decade of Spanish rule. With the separation from Spain the mint turned to producing $\frac{1}{4}$ and $\frac{1}{8}$ *real*s bearing the provincial coat of arms with mint mark and denomination on the obverse, and the identifying legend and date on the reverse. Of the two denominations the $\frac{1}{4}$ *real* is by far the scarcer. A peculiarity of the denomination mark of these issues is the appearance of the 1 in the fraction as a period.

⅛ Real   *¼ Real*

⅛ Real

Diameter 17 mm; weight ca. 2.5-3.5 grams; composition: copper; edge: plain or obliquely reeded.

Date	G	VG	F	VF
1821.................................	$15.00	$30.00	$45.00	$75.00
1822.................................	7.50	12.50	17.50	40.00
1823.................................	8.50	13.50	20.00	35.00

¼ Real

Diameter 20 mm; weight ca. 5.5 grams; composition: copper; edge: plain.

	G	VG	F	VF
1822.................................	200.00	300.00	400.00	600.00

THE MEXICAN REPUBLIC—
REAL/ESCUDO SYSTEM

STATE AND FEDERAL COPPER

Under Spanish rule coinage in copper had been the exception. An early issue of copper two and four *maravedises,* struck in the 1540's and 1550's, was badly received. So little public confidence was shown in the base metal that it was not until 1814 that the colonial government again turned to striking copper fractions, to support a depleted treasury. The ⅛, ¼ and ²⁄₄ *reales* were struck in large quantities and doubtless continued to circulate during the early years of the Republic. Nonetheless in 1824 the Congress prohibited the striking of copper by the Federal government, even while permitting it in the individual states.

The result was that the Republic was flooded with a great diversity of state issues. They were of little intrinsic value, varied greatly in size with respect to a given denomination, and were difficult to amortize. Although some may have been intended to facilitate trade, the possibility of funding state government expenditures at a fraction of their gold and silver value by the issuance of fiduciary coin was too great a temptation. The Federal government itself fell victim to the inducement, for in 1829 a Federal issue of copper was authorized. Small at first, it ultimately ran to over one hundred and fifty million pieces for a nation of only about seven million inhabitants. These circulated along with a growing mass of state copper, commercial tokens, and counterfeits. The result was universal discontent, both for the inconvenience in handling such a disparate coinage, and for the dangers involved in trading with a medium which was only fiduciary. Discounting was common; often prices simply rose on the tender of copper. Finally copper coinage was prohibited everywhere by a law of early 1837, and in March all the copper in circulation (but not the brass of Zacatecas) was devalued by half.

The cessation of copper coinage was only temporary, however, and it did not remedy the immediate difficulty of the amortization of the coin already in circulation. That was to be a problem for years. Ultimately the states resumed striking copper; by the late 1850's and early 1860's eight different copper coinages were being produced outside of the México mint. The utter confusion was not solved until the complete decimalization of the coinage required a single standard copper coin, the *centavo,* to be struck by the mints of the Republic.

CHIHUAHUA
Standing Indian Issues 1833-1856

The first of the two types of Chihuahua state copper bears on the obverse a standing Indian holding a bow and an arrow, with a quiver slung across his back. The reverse is inscribed with the denomination and the date, both within a wreath. Although this coinage covered a period of almost a quarter of a century, the dies were always badly cut and the coins poorly struck. Completely legible specimens are uncommon.

Four different obverse legends were used, reflecting the frequent changes in political sentiment between a liberal federal system and a conservative central government during these years.

⅛ Real

Diameter 20 mm; weight 3.54 grams; edge: plain.

ESTADO SOBERANO   ESTADO only

Legend: ESTADO SOBERANO DE CHIHUAHUA

Date	G	VG	F	VF
1833	$4.50	$7.00	$20.00	$40.00
1834	4.50	7.00	20.00	40.00
1835	4.50	7.00	20.00	40.00

Legend: ESTADO DE CHIHUAHUA

1855	3.50	5.00	18.00	40.00

¼ Real

Diameter 27 mm; weight 7.08 grams; edge: 1833-35 ornamented with herringbone pattern, 1835-56 plain.

ESTADO SOBERANO   Reverse   ESTADO LIBRE

Legend: ESTADO SOBERANO DE CHIHUAHUA

1833	8.00	12.00	20.00	40.00
1834	5.00	8.00	12.00	30.00
1835	5.00	8.00	12.00	30.00

Legend: ESTADO LIBRE DE CHIHUAHUA

*1846 *varieties*	4.00	6.00	12.00	30.00

normal fraction; without fractional bar.

*Dr. Pradeau takes these to be counterfeits manufactured in the United States in 1860 (Historia Numismática vol. II, pp. 263-265). They did circulate in Mexico.

DEPARTAMENTO

ESTADO

Legend: DEPARTAMENTO DE CHIHUAHUA

Date	G	VG	F	VF
1855 *varieties:*............................	$3.00	$5.00	$10.00	$30.00
normal legend; DE over ꓷE.				

Legend: ESTADO DE CHIHUAHUA

	G	VG	F	VF
1855...............................	3.00	5.00	10.00	30.00
1856...............................	3.00	5.00	10.00	30.00

Seated Liberty ¼ Real 1860-1866

A new series of Chihuahua coppers was introduced in 1860. Although of the ¼ *real* denomination, its design was identical with that of the ⅛ *real* which had been struck at México in the 1840's and 1850's and was to be struck again in 1861. The module of 28 millimeters was only slightly smaller than the México piece. On the obverse the state signature has been added to the left of the seated figure of Liberty: E.*(=Estado)* CHIHᴬ.

Diameter 28 mm; weight ca. 11.0-11.5 grams; edge: plain.

	G	VG	F	VF
1860...............................	2.00	4.00	8.00	15.00
1861...............................	2.00	4.00	8.00	15.00
1865...............................	2.00	4.00	8.00	15.00
1866...............................	2.00	4.00	8.00	15.00

DURANGO
Eagle/Rays ⅛ Real 1824-1828

No fewer than eleven types of state copper were struck at the Durango mint from 1824 to 1872. The first of these issues is also the earliest of all regularly struck state copper. The obverse bears the Republican eagle with snake, in an eccentric style, with the indication of value to the left, ⅛, and the mint mark D at the right. The reverse displays a band inscribed LIBERTAD, with rays above. The date is below. These pieces were frequently struck over 1821-1823 Nueva Vizcaya ⅛ real pieces. All known examples are collectable contemporary counterfeits.

Diameter 17-18 mm; weight ca. 2.5-4 grams; edge: obliquely reeded.

A specimen on which much of the original Nueva Vizcaya legend is evident. ⟶

Date	G	VG	F	VF
1824	$5.00	$10.00	$25.00	$75.00
1828	100.00	150.00	250.00	450.00

Indian and Tree ⅛ Real 1828

The second issue of copper at Durango was small and of a peculiar design. On the obverse an Indian carrying a bow and arrow faces what is apparently the flowering trunk of a tree. On the reverse a Liberty cap with rays is set above the legend which states the denomination, mint, and date: OCTᵒ DE R. DE Dᵒ (=*Octavo de Real de Durango*) 1828 — the entire type in imitation of the reverse of the silver 1 *real*. The issue seems to have been small.

Diameter 18-19 mm; weight ca. 3.3 grams; edge: obliquely reeded.

1828	6.00	15.00	25.00	75.00

Circle and Wreath Issues 1833-1845

In 1833, just after the introduction on silver and gold of the obverse eagle peculiar to Durango (see paragraph on page 13), a very small issue of ⅛ *reales* was struck bearing the same eagle. The workmanship is not quite as fine as that of the silver and gold dies, suggesting that the dies of this issue were cut locally in imitation of the imported work. The reverse merely bears the denomination and date within a linear circle and a wreath.

When the enormous 1829-37 México copper issues were being recalled in 1842, a few of the ⅛ *reales* were overstruck in Durango and returned to circulation. (The Fonrobert collection contained an atypical example, No. 6642, struck over a México ¼ *real* of the same series.) The coin bears no mint designation and until recently has been attributed to México, but it is unmistakably the product of Durango: the style is that of the rare 1833 issue, and in this case the obverse die was that used regularly for the silver 1 *real*.

Since the overstrike appears not to be mentioned in official documentation, its purpose can only be speculated upon. Perhaps so much of the older copper was submitted to the state treasury (a "departmental" treasury at the time) that a shortage of small change resulted, and the overstrike relieved the situation while permitting control of the amount in circulation. Or more likely, it may have been a device to avoid the amortization of some of the older copper by simply reissuing it in another guise.

A new copper denomination for the Durango mint was introduced in 1845 with the striking of a ¼ *real*. In type the coin continued the conception of the preceding two issues, save that the reverse wreath was redesigned to admit the mint name. The obverse is struck from a silver 2 *reales* die. The piece is very rare, and may be a pattern.

⅛ Real
Legend: ESTADO DE DURANGO

Diameter 20 mm; weight ca. 3.5 grams.

Date	G	VG	F	VF
1833	$150.00	$200.00	$300.00	$450.00

Legend: REPUBLICA MEXICANA

Diameter 19 mm (flans 19-23 mm); weight ca. 3.5 grams.

1842 *varieties:* . . . .   Rare
    42 over 33; normal date.

1842,
42 over 33

¼ Real

Diameter ca. 27 mm; weight ca. 7 grams.

Date		
1842	....	Rare
1845	....	Rare

Large Numeral ⅛ Real 1845-1854

During the years 1845-47 the Durango mint produced ⅛ *reales* of almost the same module as earlier issues. Again, obverse dies intended for the 1 *real* were used. The reverse design was new, the value with a large numeral 8⁰ (=*octavo*) surrounded by the legend DEPARTAMENTO DE DURANGO and the date. The piece was struck again beginning in 1851 with the reverse legend ESTADO DE DURANGO.

Diameter 19 mm; weight ca. 3.5-3.8 grams; edge: ornamented with arc and dot pattern.

Obverse DEPARTAMENTO ESTADO

Legend: DEPARTAMENTO DE DURANGO

	G	VG	F	VF
1845..................................	$6.00	$10.00	$15.00	$50.00
1846..................................		Rare		
1847..................................	3.00	5.00	8.00	20.00

Legend: ESTADO DE DURANGO

1851..................................	4.00	5.00	8.00	20.00
1852 *varieties*:.....................	4.00	5.00	8.00	20.00
2 over 1; normal date.				

Wreathless ¼ Real 1858

The year 1858 saw two different types of the ¼ *real* in copper. The first of these bore an obverse identical with the standard Federal silver obverse and may well have been struck from the 2 *reales* dies. The reverse merely states the mint name, date, and denomination. This is apparently a politically conservative issue, as it uses the national legend REPUBLICA MEXICANA on the obverse. The piece is rare.

Diameter 27 mm; weight ca. 7.5 grams; edge: ornamented with arc and dot pattern.

Date	G	VG	F	VF
1858...............................		Rare		

"Constitución" ¼ Real 1858

Also struck in 1858 was a ¼ *real* in copper reflecting liberal political sentiment. The obverse is of the same type as the last, but the legend ESTADO DE DURANGO reveals that the issuing authority leaned toward the idea of a federal rather than a central Republic. So does the reverse legend CONSTITUCION, which is set above the Liberty cap, denomination, date and two rather inadequate branches.

Diameter 27 mm; weight ca. 7.5 grams; edge: ornamented with arc and dot pattern.

	G	VG	F	VF
1858...............................	$3.00	$6.00	$12.00	$35.00

Circular Wreath ¼ Real 1860-1866

The ¼ *real* struck at Durango in 1860 and 1866 repeats the national emblem on the obverse, with the legend DEPARTAMENTO DE DURANGO. On the reverse the conservative slogan LIBERTAD EN EL ORDEN surrounds the denomination and date, all within a wreath.

Diameter 27 mm; weight ca. 7.0-7.5 grams; edge: ornamented with arc and dot pattern.

Date	G	VG	F	VF
1860	$2.00	$5.00	$15.00	$30.00
1866	2.00	5.00	15.00	30.00

"Independencia" ¼ Real 1866

This piece is the second issue of 1866. In this year, as in 1858, the two types of ¼ *real* in copper struck at Durango illustrate the two political divisions which came to blows again and again in Mexico during the first half century of independence. This second type bears the national eagle with the liberal legend ESTADO DE DURANGO on the obverse, and on the reverse the legend INDEPENDENCIA Y LIBERTAD with the denomination and date above two laurel branches.

Diameter 26-27 mm; weight ca. 7.0 grams; edge: ornamented with arc and dot pattern.

1866	3.00	5.00	12.00	30.00

"Sufragio Libre" ¼ Real 1872

The last of the Durango copper issues was struck in 1872 by a short-lived rebel movement. The denomination is improper for the period since the decimal system was legally in force. The larger decimal denominations had already been struck at Durango — the 50¢ and $1 silver, $10 and $20 gold — and it was from their representation of the facing eagle that the obverse type of this copper issue was derived. Above is the legend ESTADO DE DURANGO. On the reverse are the denomination, the date, and the legend SUFRAGIO LIBRE, all set within a laurel wreath.

Diameter 27 mm; weight ca. 7.5 grams; edge: ornamented with arc and dot pattern.

Date	G	VG	F	VF
1872	$3.00	$5.00	$15.00	$30.00

GUANAJUATO

Seated Liberty Coinage 1828-1830

The earlier of the two types of state copper struck at Guanajuato bears on the obverse a seated female figure bearing a cornucopia and olive branch. Above, ESTADO LIBRE DE GUANAJUATO; below, UN OCTAVO (⅛ *real*) or UNA CUARTILLA (¼ *real*). On the reverse the Liberty cap, surrounded by a ring of clouds and rays, surmounts the date.

⅛ Real

Diameter 21 mm; weight 3.5 grams; edge: ornamented with incuse dots.

	G	VG	F	VF
1829 *varieties:*	3.00	5.00	10.00	20.00
normal legend; error: GUANJUATO (illustrated).				
1830	8.00	12.00	20.00	40.00

¼ Real

Diameter 27 mm; weight 7.0 grams; edge: ornamented with incuse dots.

Date	G	VG	F	VF
1828 *varieties:*	$4.00	$7.00	$10.00	$35.00
normal legend; error: GUANJUATO.				
1829	4.00	7.00	10.00	35.00

Oval Arms Coinage 1856-1857

In 1856 and 1857 the ⅛ and ¼ *reales* were again struck at Guanajuato. The obverse design is the Republican eagle and snake, under an abbreviated form of *Estado libre de Guanaxuato* and the date. Below is the denomination. On the reverse the Liberty cap with rays stands over a vignette of two hands holding hammer and chisel. Below is the Latin legend OMNIA VINCIT LABOR ("Labor conquers all") and a wreath.

The 1856 pieces were struck in brass, those of 1857 in both brass and copper.

Large ⅛ *Real*   Small ⅛ *Real*

Large ⅛ Real

Diameter 29 mm; weight 7.2 grams; edge: plain.

1856	4.00	6.00	10.00	20.00

Small ⅛ Real

Diameter 25 mm; weight 7.1-7.2 grams; edge: plain.

1856		Rare		
1857 *varieties:*				
brass	4.00	6.00	10.00	20.00
copper	12.00	20.00	35.00	60.00

¼ Real

Diameter 32 mm; weight 14 grams; edge: plain.

Date	G	VG	F	VF
1856 *varieties:*............................				
brass............................	$4.00	$7.00	$10.00	$20.00
copper............................	6.00	9.00	15.00	35.00
1857 *varieties:*............................				
brass............................	4.00	7.00	10.00	20.00
copper............................	6.00	9.00	15.00	35.00

JALISCO

Seated Liberty Coinage 1828-1836

The two groups of state copper produced at the Guadalajara mint in the name of Jalisco bear the same designs, differing only in module. The earlier group, issued during the years 1828-36, consists of the *octavo* (⅛ *real*) and *quarto* (¼ *real*). Each bears on the reverse the seated figure of Liberty, holding the Liberty cap on a pole; on the obverse a flag surmounting a bow and quiver is surrounded by the legend ESTADO LIBRE DE JALISCO or (in 1836 only) DEPARTAMENTO DE JALISCO and the date.

⅛ Real

Diameter 21 mm; weight 4.80 grams; edge: obliquely reeded.

	G	VG	F	VF
1828................................	3.00	5.00	8.00	20.00
1831................................	75.00	100.00	150.00	200.00
1832 *varieties:*.......................	3.00	5.00	8.00	20.00
32 over 28; normal date.				
1833................................	3.00	5.00	8.00	20.00
1834................................	5.00	8.00	15.00	30.00

¼ Real

Diameter 28 mm; weight 9.35 grams; edge: obliquely reeded.

ESTADO LIBRE   Reverse   DEPARTAMENTO

Legend: ESTADO LIBRE DE JALISCO

Date	G	VG	F	VF
1828	$4.00	$6.00	$12.00	$25.00
1829 *varieties:*	3.00	5.00	8.00	25.00
9 over 8; normal date.				
1830 *varieties*	3.00	5.00	8.00	20.00
30 over 29; 3 over 2; normal date.				
1831		Very Scarce		
1832 *varieties:*	3.00	5.00	8.00	20.00
32 over 20; 32 over 28; normal date.				
1833 3 over 2	3.00	5.00	8.00	20.00
1834	3.00	5.00	8.00	20.00
1835 *varieties:*	3.00	5.00	8.00	20.00
5 over 3; normal date.				
1836		Rare		

Legend: DEPARTAMENTO DE JALISCO

	G	VG	F	VF
1836	6.00	10.00	17.50	35.00

Larger Size Coinage 1856-1862

In 1856 the same denominations were struck again, but on larger flans and with the addition of the ⅟₁₆ *real* or *medio octavo*. The ¼ *real* is now inscribed UNA CUARTILLA in place of the earlier UN QUARTO. The *Estado* legend appears on coins dated 1856-58 and 1861-62, while *Departamento* is found on others of 1858-60 and 1862. Dates later than these are found on private fabrications.

1/16 Real

Diameter 21 mm; weight ca. 4.75 grams; edge: obliquely reeded.

DEPARTAMENTO   ESTADO LIBRE

Legend: DEPARTAMENTO DE JALISCO

Date	G	VG	F	VF
1860	$3.00	$5.00	$10.00	$35.00

Legend: ESTADO LIBRE DE JALISCO

1861	3.00	5.00	10.00	35.00

⅛ Real

Diameter 28 mm; weight ca. 9.5 grams; edge: obliquely reeded.

ESTADO LIBRE   Reverse   DEPARTAMENTO

Legend: ESTADO LIBRE DE JALISCO

1856	4.00	7.00	10.00	20.00
1857	4.00	7.00	10.00	20.00
1858	4.00	7.00	10.00	20.00

Legend: DEPARTAMENTO DE JALISCO

1858	3.00	5.00	8.00	15.00
1859	3.00	5.00	8.00	15.00
1860 *varieties*:	3.00	5.00	8.00	15.00

60 over 59; normal date.

ESTADO LIBRE Legend Resumed

1861	4.00	7.00	10.00	20.00
1862 *varieties*	4.00	7.00	10.00	20.00

2 over 1; normal date.

DEPARTAMENTO Legend Resumed

1862	6.00	10.00	20.00	40.00

¼ Real

Diameter 32 mm; weight ca. 19 grams; edge: obliquely reeded.

ESTADO LIBRE   Reverse   DEPARTAMENTO

Legend: ESTADO LIBRE DE JALISCO

Date	G	VG	F	VF
1858	$3.00	$5.00	$8.00	$15.00

Legend: DEPARTAMENTO DE JALISCO

	G	VG	F	VF
1858	3.00	5.00	8.00	15.00
1859 *varieties:*	3.00	5.00	8.00	15.00
9 over 8; normal date.				
1860	3.00	5.00	8.00	15.00

ESTADO LIBRE Legend Resumed

	G	VG	F	VF
1861	3.00	5.00	9.00	17.50
1862	3.00	5.00	8.00	15.00

OCCIDENTE
Liberty Cap ⅛ Real 1828-1829

The earliest coinage at Alamos consisted of a small issue of ⅛ *reales* struck for the state of Occidente. The design shows the national eagle with Liberty cap and rays. The obverse legend, however, makes no mention of the Republic, but reads *Estado de Occidente*. The reverse legend, below the cap and rays, reads: C 1828 (or 1829) ⅛. The letter C is perhaps the mint mark, an abbreviation for the full name of the city, *Concepción de Alamos*. The coins are scarce, and fully legible examples very difficult to encounter.

Diameter 17-18 mm; weight ca. 2-3 grams; edge: obliquely reeded.

Date	G	VG	F	VF
1828 Reversed s in ESTADO.............	$10.00	$17.50	$35.00	$60.00
1829.................................	7.00	15.00	30.00	50.00

SAN LUIS POTOSI

Seated Indian Issues 1828-1862

The first type of state copper struck at San Luis Potosí was issued from 1828 to 1832 and again in 1859 and 1860. The obverse bears a seated Indian woman holding the Liberty cap on a scepter, and an Aztec club. Above her is the legend MEXICO LIBRE. The reverse design of an open law book and the denomination, all within wreath, is surrounded by the legend ESTADO LIBRE DE SAN LUIS POTOSI and the date.

The second copper issue is identical with the first save in two of the legends: on the obverse, REPUBLICA MEXICANA, and on the open book of the reverse, LIBERTAD EN LA LEY. The ¼ *real* was the only denomination of this issue.

⅛ Real

Diameter 21 mm; weight (1829-31) ca. 4.5-5.5 grams, (1859) ca. 4-4.5 grams; edge: obliquely reeded.

1829.................................	6.00	9.00	15.00	30.00
1830.................................	8.00	12.00	20.00	40.00
1831.................................	5.00	8.00	12.00	25.00
1859................................	5.00	8.00	12.00	25.00

¼ Real

Diameter 25-31 mm; weight (1828-32) ca. 9-10 grams, (1859-60) ca. 8-9 grams; edge obliquely reeded.

MEXICO LIBRE   Reverse   REPUBLICA MEXICANA

Legend: MEXICO LIBRE

Date	G	VG	F	VF
1828	$3.00	$4.00	$6.00	$10.00
1829	3.00	4.00	6.00	10.00
1830	3.00	4.00	6.00	10.00
1832	3.00	4.00	6.00	10.00
1859 *varieties:*	3.00	4.00	6.00	10.00
LIBRE in large letters; LIBRE in small letters.				
1860	3.00	4.00	6.00	10.00

Legend: REPUBLICA MEXICANA

Quantity Minted

		G	VG	F	VF
1862 *varieties:*	1,366,752	3.00	4.00	6.00	10.00
normal legend; error: LIBR on reverse.					

Cap in Wreath ¼ Real 1867

In spite of having already produced the 1 centavo in 1863, and contrary to the decimal legislation of the years immediately prior to the French intervention, the mint at San Luis Potosí once more struck a fractional *real* piece in the copper ¼ *real* of 1867. The obverse eagle is the regular representation, with the legend LIBERTAD Y REFORMA. On the reverse the Liberty cap and rays, with denomination, is surrounded by a wreath of oak and laurel, and then by the inscription ESTADO LIBRE Y SOBERANO DE S. L. POTOSI and the date.
An example of the piece is known overstruck on a centavo of 1863.

Diameter 27-28 mm; weight ca. 9-10 grams; edge: reeded, also comes with plain edge.

		G	VG	F	VF
1867 *varieties:*	3,176,704	3.00	4.00	7.00	15.00
initials AFG below date; no initials.					

SINALOA
Liberty Head ¼ Real 1847-1866

A single type and denomination of Sinaloa copper was struck at the Culiacán mint. The obverse bears a small head of Liberty (in imitation of the Federal silver ¼ *reales*), within a wreath of laurel, the whole surrounded by the legend ESTADO LIBRE Y SOBERANO DE SINALOA. On the reverse the denomination and date are enclosed by branches of oak and laurel. These pieces appear to have been struck to the module of the Federal reduced size ¼ *reales* coined during the years 1829-37.

Diameter 27 mm; weight ca. 7 grams; edge: reeded.

Date Quantity Minted	G	VG	F	VF
1847 brass..............................	$5.00	$10.00	$17.50	$35.00
copper...........................	3.00	5.00	8.00	15.00
1848...................................	3.00	5.00	8.00	15.00
1859...................................	2.00	3.00	4.00	7.00
1861...................................	2.00	3.00	4.00	7.00
1862...................................	2.00	3.00	4.00	7.00
1863...................................	2.00	3.50	4.50	8.50
1864 *varieties:*......................	2.00	3.00	4.00	7.00
4 over 3; normal date.				
1865	2.00	3.00	4.00	7.00
1866 *varieties* 7,400,953	2.00	3.00	4.00	7.00
6 over 5; normal date.				

SONORA
Arrow and Quivers ¼ Real 1832-1836

After the division of Occidente into the two states of Sinaloa and Sonora, a mint was opened at Hermosillo, the capital of Sonora, for the production of copper coinage for the new state. From 1832 to 1836 the ¼ *real* denomination was struck annually. (The varieties dated 1837 and 1838 are apparently false.) The obverse shows an arrow flanked by two quivers, with the legend EST. D. SONORA UNA CUART. On the reverse is seen the standard Federal design of Liberty cap with rays, surrounded by the date, assayer's initials and mint name. Specimens of this issue are poorly struck and their weights very irregular.

Diameter 21-22 mm; weight 2.3-5.5 grams; edge: obliquely reeded.

Date	G	VG	F	VF
1831		Rare		
1832	3.00	5.00	9.00	30.00
1833	2.50	4.00	7.00	25.00
1834	2.50	4.00	7.00	25.00
1835	2.50	4.00	7.00	25.00
1836	2.50	4.00	7.00	25.00

Seated Liberty Coinage 1859-1863

A second issue of copper in the name of the state of Sonora was struck from 1859 to 1863. The obverse is the Federal eagle with state legend, an abbreviation of *Estado libre y soberano de Sonora.* The reverse portrays a seated Liberty holding the Liberty cap upon a pole. Around is the legend of denomination and the date.

Since the mint at Hermosillo had long since been closed, the 1859 strikings were contracted out to the mint at Culiacán. Hermosillo opened again in 1861, but part of that year's output too was struck at Culiacán. There are no mint marks upon the coins; therefore the products of the two mints cannot be distinguished.

⅛ Real

Diameter 28 mm; weight 6.7 grams (one example); edge: reeded.

1859 . . . .   Rare

¼ Real

Diameter 32 mm; weight ca. 14.3 grams; edge: reeded.

Date	G	VG	F	VF
1859	$3.00	$5.00	$8.00	$15.00
1861 *varieties:*	3.00	5.00	8.00	15.00
61 over 59; normal date.				
1862	3.00	5.00	8.00	15.00
1863 3 over 2	5.00	10.00	20.00	35.00

ZACATECAS

Flying Eros Coinage 1824-1863

A single design was struck at Zacatecas over a period of almost forty years (the ¼ *real* of 1824 may be a trial piece). On the obverse a flying Eros carries a radiate Liberty cap on the point of his arrow. On the reverse a pyramid sustains the open book of the law and a wreath. Around is the legend, an abbreviation of *Estado libre federato de Zacatecas,* with the date and denomination QUARTILLA or OCTAVO. From 1836 through part of 1846 the obverse legend is DEPARTAMENTO DE ZACATECAS.

This issue was unusual in not generally suffering counterfeiting because of its brass alloy, .640 copper, .360 zinc.

⅛ Real

Diameter 21 mm; weight ca. 4 grams; edge: obliquely reeded.

Obverse	ESTᵒ LIBᴱ FEDᵒ	DEPARTAMENTO

Legend: ESTᵒ LIBᴱ FEDᵒ DE ZACATECAS

	G	VG	F	VF
1825	3.00	5.00	8.00	15.00
1827 *varieties:*	3.00	5.00	8.00	15.00
normal legend; error: OCTAVO.				
1829	4.00	6.00	10.00	20.00

Date	G	VG	F	VF
1830	$3.00	$5.00	$8.00	$15.00
1831	4.00	6.00	10.00	20.00
1832	3.00	5.00	8.00	15.00
1833	3.00	5.00	8.00	15.00
1835	4.00	6.00	10.00	20.00

Legend: DEPARTAMENTO DE ZACATECAS

1836	4.00	8.00	12.00	25.00
1845	6.00	10.00	16.00	30.00
1846	4.00	8.00	12.00	25.00

EST⁰ LIBᴱ Legend Resumed

1846	4.00	6.00	10.00	20.00
1851	4.00	6.00	10.00	20.00
1852	4.00	6.00	10.00	20.00
1858	3.00	5.00	8.00	15.00
1859	3.00	5.00	8.00	15.00
1862	3.00	5.00	8.00	15.00
1863 6 reversed	3.00	5.00	8.00	15.00

¼ Real

Diameter 28-29 mm; weight ca. 8 grams; edge: obliquely reeded.

Obverse   EST⁰ LIBᴱ FED⁰   DEPARTAMENTO

Legend: EST⁰ LIBᴱ FED⁰ DE ZACATECAS

	G	VG	F	VF
1824		Rare		
1825	3.00	5.00	8.00	15.00
1826	3.00	5.00	8.00	15.00
1827 2 over 1	3.00	5.00	8.00	15.00
1829	3.00	5.00	8.00	15.00
1830	3.00	5.00	8.00	15.00
1831	3.00	5.00	8.00	15.00
1832	3.00	5.00	8.00	15.00
1833	3.00	5.00	8.00	15.00
1834	3.00	5.00	8.00	15.00
1835	3.00	5.00	8.00	15.00

Legend: DEPARTAMENTO DE ZACATECAS

1836	5.00	8.00	12.00	20.00
1845		Rare		
1846	3.00	5.00	8.00	15.00

EST^O LIB^E Legend Resumed

Date	G	VG	F	VF
1846	$3.00	$5.00	$8.00	$15.00
1847	3.00	5.00	8.00	15.00
1852	3.00	5.00	8.00	15.00
1853	3.00	5.00	8.00	15.00
1855	5.00	10.00	17.50	45.00
1858	3.00	5.00	8.00	15.00
1859	3.00	5.00	8.00	15.00
1860	3.00	5.00	9.00	17.50
1862 *varieties:*	3.00	5.00	8.00	15.00
62 over 57; 62 over 59; normal date.				
1863 *varieties:*	3.00	5.00	8.00	15.00
3 over 2; normal date.				
1864 64 over 58	5.00	10.00	17.50	45.00

FEDERAL COPPER — MEXICO MINT
Fraction in Wreath Coinage 1829

Six of the states had already begun to strike their own copper when the mint at México was authorized by the Federal Congress to undertake a similar coinage. The obverse bears a rendition of the facing eagle; the reverse, simply the fraction ⅛ or ¼ with mint mark M̊, the letter A. (=Año), and the date within a wreath. The large size of the coins is the result of an attempt to give them intrinsically their value in exchange. Immediate complaints about their inconvenience in trade caused a smaller module of the same type to be introduced during the same year.

⅛ Real   *¼ Real*

⅛ Real
Diameter 27 mm; weight ca. 7 grams; edge: ornamented with small incuse rectangles.

	G	VG	F	VF
1829 M̊	50.00	75.00	100.00	200.00

¼ Real
Diameter 33 mm; weight ca. 14 grams; edge: ornamented with small incuse rectangles.

	VG	F	VF	EF
1829 M̊	8.00	15.00	45.00	100.00

Reduced Size Coinage 1829-1837

The smaller size issue of 1829-37, including an additional denomination of ⅟₁₆ *real,* was produced in a total of 150 to 200,000,000 pieces. Not only was trade thrown into confusion by this huge quantity but, since the coins were now of less intrinsic than exchange value, counterfeiting was practiced on a wide scale. Merchants declined to accept them at their face value, even those of legal issue, and considerable private hardship and public unrest resulted. The issue was not finally withdrawn from circulation for some years.

¹⁄₁₆ *Real*

¹⁄₈ *Real*

1/16 Real

Diameter 17 mm; weight ca. 1.75 grams; edge: ornamented with small incuse rectangles.

Date			VG	F	VF	EF
1831	M̥	....	$10.00	$15.00	$25.00	$65.00
1832	M̥	*varieties:*..................	10.00	15.00	25.00	65.00
		2 over 1; normal date.				
		brass	12.00	17.50	30.00	50.00
1833	M̥	copper......................	10.00	15.00	25.00	65.00
		brass........................	12.00	17.50	30.00	80.00

¹⁄₈ Real

Diameter 21 mm; weight ca. 3.5 grams; edge: ornamented with small incuse rectangles.

			G	VG	F	VF
1829	M̥	....	8.00	12.00	20.00	40.00
1830	M̥	....	2.00	3.00	5.00	10.00
1831	M̥	....	2.00	4.00	6.00	12.00
1832	M̥	....	2.00	4.00	6.00	12.00
1833	M̥	*varieties:*..................	2.00	3.00	5.00	10.00
		second 3 over 2; normal date.				
1834	M̥	....	2.00	3.00	5.00	10.00
1835	M̥	*varieties:*..................	2.00	3.00	5.00	10.00
		5 over 4; normal date.				

¹⁄₄ Real

Diameter 27 mm; weight ca. 7.0 grams; edge: ornamented with small incuse rectangles.

Date		VG	F	VF	EF
1829	M̊	$12.00	$20.00	$40.00	$100.00
1830	M̊	2.00	3.00	4.00	8.00
1831	M̊ copper	2.00	3.00	4.00	8.00
	brass with JM counterstamp	8.00	15.00	25.00	50.00
	brass without JM	—	—	—	—
1832	M̊	5.50	10.00	15.00	25.00
1833	M̊	2.00	3.00	4.00	8.00
1834	M̊	2.00	3.00	4.00	8.00
• 1835	M̊	2.00	3.00	4.00	8.00
1836	M̊	2.00	3.00	4.00	8.00
1837	M̊	5.00	10.00	15.00	30.00

Seated Liberty ⅛ Real 1841-1861

A new issue of ⅛ *real* pieces began in 1841, larger and heavier than any of this denomination previously struck at any Mexican mint. Undertaken along with amortization of the older, discredited copper, it restored some faith in the base metal coinage, at least that of the México mint. The obverse bears a figure of Liberty seated to the right, holding a spear and leaning upon the tablets of the law. The national legend does not appear, simply the word LIBERTAD in the right field. On the reverse the denomination is stated within a wreath of laurel and oak. The mint mark is found below the wreath on all dates except 1850, on which it appears just below the date. This type was imitated later by the Chihuahua ¼ *reales* of the 1860's, and by the earliest 1 centavo pieces struck at México and San Luis Potosí in 1863.

Diameter 29-30 mm; weight 14 grams; edge: 1841-42 lettered REPUBLICA MEXICANA, 1850-61 plain.

		G	VG	F	VF
1841	M̊	6.00	10.00	20.00	40.00
1842	M̊	3.00	5.00	9.00	20.00
1850	M°	15.00	20.00	30.00	60.00
1861	M̊	8.00	12.00	25.00	50.00

(Pieces dated 1860 are known only as counterfeits.)

SILVER AND GOLD COINAGE

The gold and silver coins of the new Republic were intrinsically identical with those of Spanish colonial days and the First Empire of Agustín, and circulated along with them. We must suppose that for a good many years after the foundation of the Republic the greater part of the currency was composed of the pre-Republican issues. However, the Republic did need coin types symbolic of the nation itself and of its new liberty, as against a foreign rule or an individual tyrant. Therefore the traditional Aztec image of the eagle clutching the snake, itself a symbol of victory, was redesigned to fit the circular field of a coin and to become the symbol of the Mexican Republic. In its two basic forms, "hooked neck" — i.e., seen curved from the side — and "facing," the eagle has remained to this day the obverse design of almost all Republican gold and silver and most of the Federal base metal issues.

Two differing designs were created for the respective reverses of the gold and silver. On the gold, the legend LIBERTAD EN LA LEY *(Liberty Under Law)* surrounds the representation of a hand holding the Liberty cap upon a pole and pointing at the open Constitution. This type, together with the eagle obverse, was employed for all gold coins of the *escudo* system, so that the various denominations differed only in module and in the denominational legend which each bore. Similarly for the silver, the reverse type of Liberty cap upon a burst of rays was the design for all denominations from ½ *real* to 8 *reales*. The only novelty in the silver series was to be the ¼ *real*, introduced in 1842, which bore the new design of Liberty head/value. In this the mint engravers followed the Spanish colonial usage; then too all the silver denominations bore the same design, save for the tiny ¼ *real.**

The obvious conservatism in Republican *real* and *escudo* types, struck at 14 different mints over a period of 50 years (and beyond, for the 8 *reales*), suggests a system of coinage far better organized and controlled than was in fact the case. Behind this static façade lay a great variety of situations: government mints and private, operating under differing contractual obligations, equipment both modern and decaying, various levels of engraving and assaying competence or honesty. For a few glimpses of this complicated and fascinating story, see the Introduction, pp. 5-7; for the details at length, Dr. A. F. Pradeau's *Historia Numismática de México de 1823 a 1950.*

SILVER ISSUES — ¼ REAL
Liberty Head Type 1842-1863

Owing to the desperate state of the small change, corrupted by enormous issues of state and Federal coppers of ⅟₁₆, ⅛ and ¼ *reales,* a law of February 18, 1842 defined a new silver ¼ *real* piece. It was declared mandatory for all mints of the Republic to strike the new coin to the extent of at least 1% of the total coinage. This injunction was honored in the breach of it.

The obverse shows a head of Liberty facing left. At her left is the mint mark, at the right the initials which ought to be of the local assayer but which are usually (and inexplicably) LR, the initials of Luciano Rovira, engraver of the México mint. Initials do not occur on issues of this denomination from San Luis Potosí. The reverse bears merely the fraction ¼ surrounded by the legend and date.

This denomination was suspended after 1863 on the changeover to the decimal system.

Diameter 12 mm; weight .846 grams; composition .9027 silver, .0973 copper; edge: plain.

---

*For Republican innovations in edge design, see José Luis Franco, "Notas sobre el cordón de la moneda mexicana", in *Boletín de la Sociedad numismática de México* vol. 2, no. 20 (July-Sept. 1958), pp. 164-169.

Date	Mint	Assayer		VG	F	VF	EF
1842	D^O	LR		12.00	20.00	30.00	80.00
	G^A	JG		2.50	5.50	8.00	15.00
	G^O	PM		4.00	6.00	10.00	18.50
		LR		2.00	4.00	8.00	15.00
	M^O	LR		2.00	4.00	5.00	12.00
	S.L.P^I			2.00	4.00	6.00	10.00
	Z	LR	*varieties:*	2.00	4.50	7.50	13.50
			2 over 1; normal date.				
1843	C^A	RG		60.00	100.00	200.00	325.00
	D^O	LR		20.00	25.00	35.00	100.00
	G^A	JG		6.00	9.00	12.50	22.50
		MC		4.00	6.50	9.00	16.50
	G^O	LR	*varieties:*	2.50	5.00	8.00	15.00
			3 over 2; normal date.				
	M^O	LR		2.00	4.00	6.00	12.00
	S.L.P^I		*varieties:*	1.50	3.00	5.00	10.00
			3 over 2; normal date.				
1844	G^A	MC		4.00	6.50	9.00	16.50
		LR		2.50	5.00	7.50	13.50
	GC	LR		50.00	70.00	100.00	175.00
	G^O	LR		2.00	3.50	6.00	10.00
	M^O	LR		4.00	6.50	9.00	16.50
	S.L.P^I			1.50	3.00	5.00	10.00
1845	G^A	LR		2.50	4.50	7.50	13.50
	G^O	LR		8.00	12.00	20.00	40.00
	M^O	LR		4.00	6.50	9.00	16.50
	S.L.P^I		*varieties:*	1.50	3.00	5.00	10.00
			5 over 4; 5 over 3; normal date.				
			5 over 3; normal date.				
1846	G^A	LR		5.00	8.00	10.00	18.50
	G^O	LR		4.00	6.50	9.00	16.50
	M^O	LR		4.00	5.00	8.00	15.00
1847	G^A	LR		4.00	6.50	9.00	16.50
	G^O	LR		1.50	3.00	5.00	8.00
	S.L.P^I		*varieties:*	2.00	3.50	6.00	10.00
			7 over 5; normal date.				
1848	G^A	LR	*varieties:*		Rare		
1848	G^O	LR	*varieties:*	2.00	3.50	6.00	10.00
			8 over 7; normal date.				
1849	G^O	LR	*varieties:*	1.50	3.00	5.50	9.00
			9 over 7; normal date.				

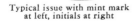

Typical issue with mint mark
at left, initials at right

San Luis Potosí issue with
mint mark only (S.L.P^I)

Date	Mint	Assayer	VG	F	VF	EF
1850	G^A	LR	$300.00	—	—	—
	G^O	LR	2.00	$3.50	$5.50	$10.00
	M^O	LR	5.00	10.00	15.00	27.50
1851	G^A	LR	6.00	10.00	16.50	30.00
	G^O	LR	2.00	3.50	5.50	10.00
	S.L.P^I		5.50	9.00	12.50	22.50
1852	G^A	LR	6.00	10.00	15.00	27.50
	G^O	LR	1.50	3.00	5.00	10.00
1853	G^O	LR	2.00	3.50	6.00	10.00
1854	G^A	LR	5.00	10.00	12.50	30.00
	S.L.P^I		5.50	9.00	13.50	25.00
1855	C	LR (Culiacán)	40.00	65.00	125.00	225.00
	G^A	LR	5.00	8.00	10.00	30.00
	G^O	LR	5.50	9.00	12.00	20.00
1856	G^O	LR	6.00	9.00	12.50	22.50
	S.L.P^I		7.00	8.00	11.50	20.00
1857	G^A	LR	6.50	10.00	15.00	27.50
	S.L.P^I		5.50	9.00	13.50	25.00
1858	M^O	LR	6.00	10.00	12.50	22.50
1859	M^O	LR	4.00	6.50	9.00	16.50
1860	M^O	LR	4.00	6.50	9.00	16.50
1861	M^O	LR	1.50	4.50	7.00	13.50
1862	G^A	LR	5.50	10.00	15.00	30.00
	G^O	LR	1.75	4.00	7.00	15.00
	M^O	LR	4.00	6.50	9.00	16.50
	S.L.P^I	62 over 57	5.00	10.00	15.00	30.00
1863	G^O	LR	1.50	4.00	7.00	13.50
	M^O	LR	4.00	6.50	9.00	16.50

½ REAL
Hooked Neck Eagle 1824

The earliest coins of the Republic bore on the obverse the national emblem in the first of two versions which have been used on almost every Federal coin. The eagle sits perched upon a cactus which rises from the waters of Lake Texcoco, holding a snake in his beak and claw. The eagle is seen from its left. To the left below is a branch of oak, to the right a branch of laurel. The legend REPUBLICA MEXICANA forms a semicircle above. The reverse bears a Liberty cap, inscribed *Libertad* across the peak in incuse cursive letters, upon a burst of rays. The legend below states the denomination, mint, date, assayers' initials, and fineness.

Only one issue of the hooked neck ½ *real* is known.

Diameter 16 mm; weight 1.692 grams; composition .9027 silver, .0973 copper; edge: ornamented.

		F	VF	EF	Unc.
1824 M̊	JM	40.00	60.00	125.00	400.00

Silver ½ Real

Facing Eagle Type 1825-1870

In 1824 a new variety of obverse was introduced to circulation. The heraldic details were unaltered but with the eagle seen from the front, its head raised high. The reverse remained as before save that the Liberty cap was slightly redesigned and the inscription LIBERTAD moved to its brim where it was cut in incuse block letters.

According to an order of December 27, 1862, the coinage of ½ *reales* was to be suspended inasmuch as the denomination could not be accommodated to the decimal system, given its equivalent value of 6¼¢. Production thereafter fell sharply but was not actually terminated until 1870.

Diameter 16 mm; weight 1.692 grams; composition .9027 silver, .0973 copper; edge: ornamented.

Date	Mint	Assayer	F	VF	EF	Unc.
1825	G^A	FS	$30.00	$40.00	$75.00	$150.00
	M̥	JM	8.00	12.00	25.00	60.00
1826	G^A	FS	11.00	15.00	30.00	60.00
	G	MJ	125.00	250.00	350.00	—
	M̥	JM	4.50	8.50	20.00	50.00
	Z	AZ	3.50	8.50	17.50	50.00
		AO	5.00	10.00	20.00	50.00
1827	G	MJ 7 over 6	6.00	12.00	30.00	50.00
	M̥	JM *varieties:*	5.00	8.50	20.00	50.00
		7 over 6; normal date.				
	Z	AO	3.50	8.50	17.50	40.00
1828	G^A	FS 8 over 7	12.50	20.00	40.00	80.00
	G	MJ 8 over 7	6.50	16.50	40.00	70.00
		MR	4.50	12.00	30.00	55.00
	M̥	JM *varieties:*	12.50	17.50	30.00	65.00
		8 over 7; normal date.				
	Z	AO 8 over 7	4.50	10.00	21.50	50.00
1829	E^{O}M^O	LF	175.00	275.00	400.00	1,250
	G^A	FS	6.00	12.00	30.00	60.00
	G	MJ *varieties:*	3.00	7.50	20.00	35.00
		normal legend; reversed N in MEXICANA.				
	M̥	JM	6.00	9.00	20.00	45.00
	Z	AO	5.00	10.00	17.50	45.00
1830	G^A	FS 30 over 29	25.00	35.00	60.00	100.00
	G	MJ	3.00	7.50	20.00	35.00
	M̥	JM	5.00	9.00	20.00	45.00
	Z	OV	3.25	9.00	17.50	45.00
1831	G^A	LP	125.00	150.00	300.00	—
	G	MJ *varieties:*	6.00	12.00	30.00	45.00
		31 over 29; normal date.				
	M̥	JM	5.00	9.00	20.00	45.00
	P^I	JS	7.00	12.00	20.00	45.00
	Z	OV	3.25	8.00	17.50	40.00
		OM	3.00	8.00	17.50	40.00

Silver ½ Real

Silver ½ Real **REPUBLIC**

Date	Mint	Assayer	F	VF	EF	Unc.
1832	Dᴼ	RM	$20.00	$35.00	$50.00	$90.00
	Gᴬ	FS	9.00	12.00	25.00	40.00
	G	MJ *varieties:*	3.50	7.50	20.00	35.00
		2 over 1; normal date.				
	M̊	JM	8.50	12.00	27.50	50.00
	Z	OM	3.00	8.00	17.50	40.00
1833	Dᴼ	RL	12.00	17.50	30.00	60.00
		RM *varieties:*	12.00	17.50	30.00	70.00
		3/1, M/L; normal date.				
	G	MJ *varieties:*	3.00	7.50	20.00	40.00
		round top 3; flat top 3.				
	M̊	MJ	12.00	16.00	28.00	45.00
	Z	OM	3.00	7.00	17.50	40.00
1834	Dᴼ	RM	12.00	17.50	30.00	50.00
	Gᴬ	FS	9.00	12.00	25.00	60.00
	G	PJ	3.00	7.50	20.00	35.00
	M̊	ML	4.00	8.00	20.00	45.00
	Z	OM	3.00	8.00	17.50	40.00
1835	Gᴬ	FS 5/4/3, FS/LP	12.50	17.50	25.00	50.00
	G	PJ	3.00	7.50	20.00	35.00
	M̊	ML	4.50	8.00	20.00	45.00
	Z	OM *varieties:*	3.00	7.00	17.50	40.00
		5 over 4; normal date.				
1836	G	PJ	3.00	7.50	20.00	45.00
	M̊	ML *varieties:*	8.00	10.00	22.50	45.00
		6/5, L/F; normal date, L/F.				
	Z	OM	3.00	7.00	17.50	40.00
1837	Dᴼ	RM 7 over 6	13.50	20.00	33.50	55.00
	Gᴬ	JG 7 over 6	10.00	15.00	30.00	60.00
	G	PJ	3.00	7.50	20.00	45.00
	Z	OM	3.00	7.00	17.50	40.00
1838	Gᴬ	JG 8 over 7	15.00	17.50	30.00	55.00
	G	PJ 8 over 7	4.50	7.50	20.00	45.00
	M̊	ML	4.00	8.00	20.00	45.00
	Z	OM	3.00	7.00	17.50	40.00
1839	Gᴬ	JG 9/8, JG/FS	37.50	75.00	150.00	250.00
		MC	9.00	15.00	25.00	50.00

1839 Guanajuato
REPUBLIGA error

			F	VF	EF	Unc.
	G	PJ *varieties:*	3.00	7.50	20.00	40.00
		normal legend; error: REPUBLIGA.				
	H̊			Unique		
	M̊	ML *varieties:*	3.00	7.50	20.00	45.00
		9 over 8; normal date.				
	Z	OM	3.00	7.00	17.50	40.00
1840	Gᴬ	MC	12.00	20.00	30.00	55.00

       Silver ½ Real

Date	Mint	Assayer	F	VF	EF	Unc.
	G̊	PJ *varieties:*	$3.00	$7.00	$20.00	$35.00
		straight J; curved J.				
	M̊	ML	3.00	7.50	20.00	45.00
	Z	OM	3.50	7.00	17.50	40.00
1841	D^O	RM 41 over 33	15.00	25.00	40.00	65.00
	G^A	MC	10.00	20.00	35.00	65.00
	G̊	PJ *varieties:*	3.00	7.00	20.00	35.00
		4 over 3; normal date.				
	M̊	ML	3.00	7.50	20.00	45.00
	P^I	JS 41 over 36	25.00	35.00	45.00	75.00
	Z	OM	15.00	20.00	30.00	60.00
1842	D	RM *varieties:*	9.00	15.00	25.00	55.00
		4 over 3; normal date.				
	G^A	JG	5.00	10.00	25.00	45.00
	G̊	PJ *varieties:*	3.50	8.00	22.50	45.00
		2 over 1; normal date.				
		PM *varieties:*	3.50	8.00	22.50	45.00
		2 over 1; normal date; M over J.				
	M̊	ML	3.00	7.50	20.00	45.00
		MM	3.00	7.50	20.00	45.00
	P^I	JS	30.00	40.00	55.00	100.00
		PS 2/1, P/J	32.50	45.00	60.00	110.00
	Z	OM 2 over 1	4.00	7.00	17.50	45.00
1843	D	RM 4 over 3	15.00	25.00	45.00	75.00
	G^A	JG *varieties:*	10.00	20.00	35.00	70.00
		3 over 2; normal date.				
		MC *varieties:*	10.00	20.00	35.00	65.00
		MC over JG; normal initials.				
	G̊	PM *varieties:*	3.50	7.00	20.00	35.00
		convex wings; concave wings; ½/8, 4/3.				
	M̊	MM	3.00	7.50	20.00	45.00
	P^I	PS *varieties:*	15.00	20.00	30.00	60.00
		3 over 2; normal date.				
		AM	11.00	15.00	20.00	50.00
	Z	OM	40.00	75.00	100.00	200.00
1844	C^A	RG	75.00	125.00	175.00	275.00
	G^A	MC	3.00	7.50	25.00	45.00
	GC	MP	25.00	50.00	75.00	125.00
	G̊	PM *varieties:*	3.00	6.00	20.00	35.00
		4 over 3; normal date.				
	M̊	MF	3.00	7.50	20.00	45.00
	P^I	AM	10.00	15.00	30.00	60.00
	Z	OM	5.00	8.00	17.50	40.00
1845	C^A	RG	75.00	125.00	150.00	250.00
	D^O	RM *varieties:*	10.00	20.00	30.00	60.00
		4 over 3; 45 over 31; 45 over 34.				
	G^A	MC	5.00	10.00	25.00	55.00
		JG	5.00	10.00	25.00	55.00
	GC	MP	30.00	45.00	75.00	125.00
	G̊	PM *varieties:*	3.00	6.00	20.00	35.00
		5 over 4; normal date.				
	M̊	MF *varieties:*	3.00	7.50	20.00	45.00
		5 over 4; normal date.				

Date	Mint	Assayer	F	VF	EF	Unc.
	Pⁱ	AM	$250.00	$350.00	$450.00	—
	Z	OM	3.75	7.00	17.50	45.00
1846	C	CE	30.00	50.00	75.00	150.00
	Dᴼ	RM	30.00	50.00	80.00	125.00
	Gᴬ	MC	3.75	7.50	25.00	55.00
		JG	3.75	7.50	25.00	50.00
	GC	MP	25.00	50.00	90.00	150.00
	G̊	PM *varieties:*	3.00	6.00	20.00	35.00
		48 over 35; 6 over 4; 6 over 5; normal date.				
	M̊	MF	3.00	5.00	20.00	45.00
	Pⁱ	AM 6 over 5	40.00	75.00	100.00	150.00
	Z	OM	3.00	6.00	17.50	35.00
1847	Gᴬ	JG	3.00	6.50	25.00	50.00
	GC	MP	25.00	45.00	75.00	125.00
	G̊	PM *varieties:*	3.00	5.00	20.00	35.00
		7 over 6; normal date.				
	M̊	RC	3.00	5.00	20.00	45.00
	Pⁱ	AM 7 over 6	15.00	25.00	35.00	55.00
	Z	OM	3.00	6.00	17.50	35.00
1848	C	CE 8 over 7	15.00	25.00	45.00	85.00
	Dᴼ	RM *varieties:*	37.50	65.00	100.00	160.00
		8 over 5; 8 over 6.				
	Gᴬ	JG 8 over 7	6.00	10.00	25.00	50.00
	GC	MP	25.00	35.00	60.00	100.00
	G̊	PM	3.00	6.00	20.00	35.00
		PF, F over M	3.50	7.00	20.00	35.00
	M̊	GC 8/7, G/R	3.50	5.50	22.50	50.00
	Pⁱ	AM	15.00	25.00	35.00	55.00
	Z	OM	3.00	6.00	17.50	35.00
1849	C	CE 9 over 8	10.00	15.00	25.00	50.00
	Dᴼ	JMR	25.00	35.00	55.00	100.00
	Gᴬ	JG	5.00	10.00	25.00	55.00
	GC	MP	25.00	35.00	75.00	125.00
	G̊	PF *varieties:*	3.50	7.00	20.00	35.00
		4 over 3; normal date; error: MEXCANA.				
	M̊	GC	3.00	4.00	20.00	55.00
	Pⁱ	MC	12.50	21.50	35.00	55.00
	Z	OM	3.00	5.00	17.50	35.00
1850	Dᴼ	JMR	22.50	40.00	60.00	100.00
		RM	100.00	240.00	400.00	650.00
	Gᴬ	JG	3.75	7.50	25.00	55.00
	GC	MP	30.00	37.50	75.00	135.00
	G̊	PF	3.00	6.00	20.00	35.00
	M̊	GC	3.00	5.00	20.00	45.00
	Pⁱ	MC	10.00	15.00	25.00	50.00
	Z	OM	4.00	7.00	17.50	35.00
1851	Dᴼ	JMR	20.00	35.00	60.00	90.00
	Gᴬ	JG 1 over 0	3.75	7.50	25.00	55.00
	GC	MP	25.00	35.00	60.00	100.00
	G̊	PF	4.00	6.00	20.00	35.00
	M̊	GC	3.00	4.00	20.00	45.00
	Pⁱ	MC	8.50	14.00	23.00	45.00

Date	Mint	Assayer	F	VF	EF	Unc.
	Z	OM	$3.00	$5.00	$17.50	$35.00
1852	C	CE	8.00	12.50	25.00	50.00
	D^O	JMR	30.00	50.00	100.00	150.00
	G^A	JG	6.00	10.00	25.00	60.00
	G	PF *varieties:*	3.00	5.00	20.00	35.00
		2 over 1; normal date.				
	M̊	GC	3.00	4.00	20.00	45.00
	P^I	MC	5.00	8.50	17.50	40.00
	Z	OM	3.00	5.00	17.50	35.00
1853	C	CE 3 over 1	10.00	17.50	35.00	60.00
	D^O	CP	7.50	12.50	25.00	50.00
	G^A	JG	3.00	6.00	25.00	40.00
	G	PF	3.00	5.00	20.00	35.00
	M̊	GC	3.00	4.00	15.00	45.00
	P^I	MC	7.00	12.00	20.00	45.00
	Z	OM	6.00	8.50	17.50	35.00
1854	C	CE	20.00	35.00	55.00	100.00
	D^O	CP	25.00	35.00	50.00	85.00
	G^A	JG	8.00	12.00	25.00	55.00
	G	PF	3.00	5.00	20.00	35.00
	M̊	GC	3.00	4.50	15.00	45.00
	P^I	MC	6.00	10.00	17.50	40.00
	Z	OM *varieties:*	4.00	6.00	17.50	35.00
		4 over 3; normal date.				
1855	D^O	CP	25.00	40.00	60.00	100.00
	G^A	JG *varieties:*	8.00	12.00	25.00	55.00
		2nd 5 over 4; normal date.				
	G	PF	3.00	5.00	20.00	35.00
	M̊	GC	3.00	4.00	15.00	45.00
		GF-F over C	3.00	4.00	15.00	45.00
	P^I	MC	15.00	20.00	30.00	50.00
	Z	OM	4.00	7.00	17.50	35.00
1856	C	CE	12.00	20.00	35.00	65.00
	D^O	CP 6 over 5	17.50	25.00	45.00	70.00
	G^A	JG	5.00	7.00	25.00	50.00
	G	PF *varieties:*	3.00	5.00	20.00	35.00
		6 over 4; 6 over 5; normal date.				
	M̊	GF 6 over 5	3.50	4.50	16.50	50.00
	P	MC	5.00	8.50	17.50	40.00
	Z	OM	4.00	7.00	17.50	35.00
1857	C	CE *varieties:*	15.00	25.00	45.00	85.00
		7 over 6; normal date.				
	D^O	CP	17.50	25.00	45.00	70.00
	G^A	JG	6.00	10.00	25.00	50.00
	G	PF *varieties:*	3.00	5.00	20.00	35.00
		7 over 6; normal date.				
	M̊	GF	3.00	4.00	15.00	45.00
	P^I	MC	8.50	12.00	20.00	45.00
		PS	10.00	15.00	25.00	50.00
	Z^s	MO	3.00	5.00	17.50	35.00
1858	C	CE 1 instead of ½	12.00	20.00	35.00	65.00
	D^O	CP 8 over 7	17.50	25.00	45.00	70.00

Date	Mint	Assayer	F	VF	EF	Unc.
	Gᴬ	JG *varieties:* 8 over 7; normal date.	$7.50	$12.00	$25.00	$55.00
	G	PF *varieties:* 8 over 7; normal date.	4.00	7.00	20.00	40.00
	M̊	FH *varieties:* 8 over 9 (*sic*); normal date.	3.00	4.00	15.00	45.00
	Pᴵ	MC	11.00	20.00	30.00	60.00
		PS	11.00	20.00	30.00	60.00
	Zˢ	MO	3.00	5.00	17.50	35.00
1859	Dᴼ	CP	17.50	25.00	40.00	70.00
	Gᴬ	JG 9 over 7	7.50	12.00	25.00	55.00
	G	PF	3.00	6.00	20.00	35.00
	M̊	FH	3.00	4.00	15.00	45.00
	Pᴵ	MC	11.50	16.00	25.00	55.00
	Zˢ	MO	6.00	8.50	17.50	35.00
		VL	6.00	8.50	17.50	40.00
1860	C	PV	7.00	10.00	25.00	45.00
	Dᴼ	CP 60 over 59	17.50	25.00	45.00	70.00
	Gᴬ	JG 60 over 59	7.50	12.00	25.00	55.00

1860 México
6 over 5, FH over GC

Date	Mint	Assayer	F	VF	EF	Unc.
	G	PF *varieties:* 60 over 59; small fraction; large fraction.	3.50	6.50	22.50	45.00
	M̊	FH *varieties:* FH/GC, 6/5; normal date and initials.	3.00	4.00	15.00	45.00
		TH	4.00	6.00	15.00	45.00
	Pᴵ	PS 60 over 59	12.00	16.00	25.00	55.00
	Zˢ	MO	3.00	5.00	17.50	40.00
		VL *varieties:* 60 over 59, V of VL is inverted A; normal die.	3.00	5.00	17.50	40.00
1861	C	PV	9.00	15.00	30.00	50.00
	Dᴼ	CP	100.00	140.00	220.00	325.00
	Gᴬ	JG	3.00	6.00	25.00	40.00
	G	PF *varieties:* small fraction; large fraction.	3.00	6.00	20.00	35.00
	M̊	CH	3.00	4.00	15.00	45.00
	Pᴵ	RO	10.00	15.00	25.00	50.00
	Zˢ	VL	3.00	5.00	17.50	40.00

Date	Mint	Assayer	F	VF	EF	Unc.
1862	A	PG	—	—	Rare	—
	Dᴼ	CP	25.00	35.00	55.00	85.00

Silver ½ Real

Date	Mint	Assayer	F	VF	EF	Unc.
	Gᴬ	JG 2 over 1	$10.00	$15.00	$30.00	$65.00
	G	YF	3.00	6.00	20.00	35.00
		YE *varieties:*	3.00	6.00	20.00	35.00
		2 over 1; normal date.				
	Ħ	FM	65.00	100.00	135.00	240.00
	Ṁ	CH *varieties:*	3.00	4.00	15.00	45.00
		6 over 5; normal date.				
	Pᴵ	RO	8.00	11.00	15.00	40.00
	Zˢ	VL	6.00	9.00	17.50	40.00
1863	C	CE 1 instead of ½	15.00	25.00	45.00	80.00
	Ṁ	CH	3.00	4.00	15.00	45.00
		TH/GC, 63/55	4.00	6.00	16.50	50.00
	Pᴵ	RO 3 over 2	13.00	22.00	35.00	60.00
	Zˢ	VL	6.00	10.00	17.50	40.00
1864	Dᴼ	LT	20.00	30.00	45.00	75.00
1867	C	CE	15.00	20.00	40.00	70.00
	G	YF	3.00	6.00	20.00	35.00
	Ħ	PR 6/inverted 6, 7/1, PR/FM	100.00	160.00	225.00	375.00
1868	G	YF	3.00	6.00	20.00	35.00
1869	C	CE 1 instead of ½	12.00	20.00	35.00	60.00
	Dᴼ	CP	40.00	75.00	125.00	200.00
	Zˢ	YH	3.00	5.00	17.50	40.00
1870	G	YF	—	—	—	—

1 REAL
Hooked Neck Eagle 1824

As in the case of the ½ *real,* this denomination first bore the obverse design of the hooked neck eagle. The reverse is also similar to that of the smaller coin, with thick rays and incuse *Libertad.* The type was struck only at Durango in 1824, and is very scarce.

Diameter 20 mm; weight 3.384 grams; composition .9027 silver, .0973 copper; edge: ornamented.

		F	VF	EF	Unc.
1824 Dᴼ	RL	2,500	3,000	3,800	5,000

Facing Eagle Type 1825-1869

As part of the general redesigning which took place during 1824 and 1825, the 1 *real* was altered to show the familiar style known as the "Facing Eagle."

The silver *real,* like the ½ and ¼ *real,* ought not to have been struck after 1862, owing to its incompatability with the decimal system. However, the *real* was still struck at the México mint in 1863, and in a few of the branch mints until as late as 1869.

Diameter 20 mm; weight 3.384 grams; composition .9027 silver, .0973 copper; edge: ornamented.

Date	Mint	Assayer		F	VF	EF	Unc.
1825	M̥	JM		$7.00	$9.00	$18.00	$70.00
1826	Gᴬ	FS		14.00	17.50	30.00	80.00
	G	JJ 6 over 5		3.00	4.00	11.00	60.00
		MJ		2.25	3.00	10.00	55.00
	M̥	JM		2.25	3.00	10.00	55.00
	Zˢ	AZ		2.25	3.00	10.00	55.00
		AO		3.25	5.00	15.00	60.00
1827	G	MJ		3.75	5.00	12.00	60.00
		JM		7.75	10.00	18.50	65.00
	M̥	JM		2.25	3.00	10.00	60.00
	Zˢ	AO		3.25	5.00	10.00	55.00
1828	EᴼMᴼ	LF		200.00	300.00	450.00	1,500
	Gᴬ	FS 8 over 7		18.00	25.00	40.00	85.00
	G	MJ *varieties:*		2.25	3.00	10.00	55.00
		G, straight J, sm. 8; G, full J, lg. 8; G, full J, lg. 8.					
	G	MR *varieties:*		2.25	3.00	10.00	55.00
		8 over 7; normal date.					
	M̥	JM		4.00	6.00	15.00	75.00
	Zˢ	AO *varieties:*		2.25	4.00	10.00	55.00
		normal A; A is inverted V.					
1829	Gᴬ	FS		12.50	18.00	30.00	75.00

Small eagle   Large eagle

				F	VF	EF	Unc.
	G	MJ *varieties:*		2.25	3.00	10.00	50.00
		9 over 8, sm. eagle; normal date, sm. eagle; large eaglc.					
	Zˢ	AO		2.25	3.00	10.00	50.00
1830	Gᴬ	FS		12.00	18.00	30.00	75.00
	G	MJ *varieties:*		2.25	3.00	10.00	50.00
		large initials; medium initials; small initials; reversed N in MEXICANA.					
	M̥	JM *varieties:*		2.25	3.00	10.00	55.00
		30 over 29; normal date.					
	Zˢ	OV		3.00	4.50	10.00	50.00
	Z	OV		4.00	5.00	10.00	50.00
1831	Gᴬ	LP *varieties:*		15.00	23.50	30.00	75.00
		LP over FS; normal initials.					

Date	Mint	Assayer	F	VF	EF	Unc.
	ᵷ	MJ *varieties:*................	$2.25	$3.00	$10.00	$55.00
		1/0, reversed N in MEXICANA; normal date and N.				
	M̥	JM........................	100.00	200.00	300.00	—
	Pᴵ	JS.........................	5.00	7.00	18.00	65.00
	Zˢ	OV........................	2.25	3.00	10.00	55.00
		OM........................	3.25	5.00	10.00	50.00
1832	Dᴼ	RM *varieties:*...............	4.00	6.00	15.00	70.00
		2/1, normal M; normal date, M/L.				
	Gᴬ	FS.........................	200.00	250.00	325.00	—
	ᵷ	MJ........................	2.25	3.00	10.00	55.00
	M̥	JM........................	3.25	4.50	10.00	50.00
	Zˢ	OM........................	2.25	3.00	10.00	50.00
1833	Gᴬ	FS.........................	100.00	125.00	200.00	—
	ᵷ	MJ *varieties:*...............	2.25	3.00	10.00	50.00
		round top 3; flat top 3.				
	M̥	MJ 3 over 2...............	3.75	5.00	11.00	55.00
	Zˢ	OM *varieties:*..............	2.25	3.00	10.00	50.00
		3 over 2; normal date.				
1834	Cᴬ	AM................. Does not exist in 1 Real; only in 2 Real				
	Dᴼ	RM *varieties:*..............	10.00	12.50	25.00	75.00
		4/2, M/L; 4/3, M/L; normal date.				
	G	FS (Guadalajara)				
		4 over 3.................	11.50	17.50	35.00	85.00
	ᵷ	PJ.........................	2.25	3.00	10.00	50.00
	Zˢ	OM *varieties:*..............	2.25	3.00	10.00	50.00
		4 over 3; normal date.				
1835	Gᴬ	FS.........................	—	—	—	—
	ᵷ	PJ.........................	5.50	6.50	10.00	50.00
	Zˢ	OM *varieties:*..............	2.25	3.00	10.00	50.00
		5 over 4; normal date.				
1836	Dᴼ	RM *varieties:*..............	3.25	4.50	12.00	60.00
		6 over 4; normal date.				
	ᵷ	PJ.........................	2.00	4.00	10.00	50.00
	Zˢ	OM *varieties:*..............	2.25	3.00	10.00	50.00
		6 over 5; normal date.				
1837	Dᴼ	RM........................	12.50	15.00	30.00	70.00
	Gᴬ	JG/FS, 7 over 6.............	12.50	15.00	30.00	75.00
	ᵷ	PJ.........................	2.25	3.00	10.00	50.00
	Pᴵ	JS.........................	750.00	850.00	1,000	—
	Zˢ	OM........................	2.25	3.00	10.00	50.00
1838	Gᴬ	JG/FS, 8 over 7.............	12.50	15.00	30.00	75.00
	ᵷ	PJ 8 over 7.................	2.75	3.50	12.50	60.00
	Pᴵ	JS.........................	20.00	30.00	40.00	85.00
	Zˢ	OM........................	2.25	3.00	10.00	55.00
1839	Gᴬ	JG.........................	250.00	300.00	400.00	—
	ᵷ	PJ.........................	2.25	3.00	10.00	55.00
	Zˢ	OM........................	2.25	3.00	10.00	55.00
1840	Gᴬ	JG.........................	12.00	15.00	30.00	70.00
		MC........................	7.50	10.00	18.00	60.00
	ᵷ	PJ *varieties:*...............	2.25	3.00	10.00	55.00
		40 over 39; normal date.				
	Pᴵ	JS *varieties:*...............	6.00	8.00	20.00	65.00
		40 over 39; normal date.				

Date	Mint	Assayer	F	VF	EF	Unc.
	Z^S	OM........................	$2.25	$3.00	$10.00	$50.00
1841	D^O	RM........................	7.00	9.00	20.00	70.00
	G^A	MC........................	15.00	20.00	30.00	75.00
	G	PJ *varieties:*..............	2.00	3.00	10.00	50.00
		4 over 3; normal date.				
	P^I	JS........................	8.50	10.00	18.00	65.00
	Z^S	OM........................	17.50	25.00	50.00	—
1842	D	RM *varieties:*.............	7.00	9.00	18.00	65.00
		4 over 3; normal date.				
	G^A	JG *varieties:*.............	6.00	8.00	15.00	65.00
		2/0, JG/MC; normal date and initials.				
	G	PJ........................	4.00	5.00	10.00	55.00
		PM........................	3.00	4.00	10.00	55.00
	P^I	JS........................	10.00	15.00	30.00	70.00
		PS........................	4.50	5.75	18.00	60.00
	Z^S	OM *varieties:*.............	2.00	3.00	10.00	55.00
		2 over 1; normal date.				
1843	D^O	RM........................	4.50	5.75	15.00	65.00
	G^A	JG........................	150.00	175.00	250.00	—
		MC........................	4.00	5.00	15.00	65.00
	G	PM *varieties:*.............	2.25	4.00	10.00	55.00
		convex wings; concave wings.				
	P^I	PS........................	11.00	15.00	20.00	75.00
		AM........................	40.00	60.00	80.00	—
	Z^S	OM........................	2.00	3.00	10.00	50.00
1844	C^A	RG........................	400.00	—	—	—
	D^O	RM first 4 over 3............	13.50	18.50	25.00	85.00
	G^A	MC........................	6.00	8.50	20.00	70.00
	GC	MP........................	45.00	65.00	85.00	150.00
	G	PM........................	2.00	4.00	10.00	50.00
	P^I	AM........................	40.00	60.00	80.00	—
	Z^S	OM........................	2.00	3.00	10.00	55.00
1845	C^A	RG........................	500.00	1,000	1,500	2,000
	D^O	RM........................	3.25	5.50	15.00	70.00
	G^A	MC........................	10.00	12.50	20.00	70.00
		JG........................	4.00	6.00	15.00	65.00
	GC	MP........................	40.00	50.00	75.00	135.00
	G	PM *varieties:*.............	1.50	3.00	10.00	50.00
		5 over 4; normal date.				
	P^I	AM........................	7.00	9.00	18.00	65.00
	Z^S	OM........................	2.00	3.00	10.00	50.00
1846	C	CE........................	12.50	15.00	30.00	80.00
	D^O	RM........................	7.00	9.00	20.00	70.00
	G^A	JG........................	12.50	15.00	30.00	75.00
	GC	MP........................	30.00	50.00	75.00	135.00
	G	PM........................	2.00	3.00	10.00	50.00
	P^I	AM 6 over 5.................	8.00	10.00	20.00	70.00
	Z^S	OM *varieties:*.............	2.00	3.00	10.00	50.00
		old font and obverse; new font and obverse.				
1847	D^O	RM........................	10.00	15.00	20.00	60.00
	G^A	JG *varieties:*.............	10.00	15.00	20.00	60.00
		7 over 6; normal date.				
	GC	MP........................	40.00	55.00	75.00	135.00

Date	Mint	Assayer		F	VF	EF	Unc.
	G̵	PM *varieties:*..................		$2.00	$3.00	$10.00	$50.00
		7 over 6; normal date.					
	PI	AM *varieties:*...............		7.00	9.00	18.00	65.00
		7 over 6; normal date.					
	ZS	OM.........................		2.00	3.00	10.00	50.00
1848	C	CE.........................		11.50	15.00	25.00	75.00
	DO	RM *varieties:*...............		7.50	10.00	18.00	65.00
		48 over 31; 48 over 33; 8 over 5; normal date.					
	GA	JG.........................		350.00	450.00	650.00	—
	GC	MP.........................		35.00	50.00	70.00	125.00
	G̵	PM.........................		3.25	4.50	10.00	50.00
	PI	AM 8 over 7.................		8.00	10.00	20.00	70.00
	ZS	OM.........................		2.00	3.00	10.00	50.00
1849	DO	CM 9 over 8.................		8.50	11.00	20.00	70.00
	GA	JG.........................		7.00	9.00	18.00	65.00
	GC	MP *varieties:*...............		30.00	45.00	75.00	135.00
		9 over 7; 9 over 8; normal date.					
	G̵	PF.........................		2.00	3.00	10.00	50.00
	PI	PS.........................		7.00	9.00	18.00	70.00
		SP.........................		15.00	25.00	40.00	85.00
	ZS	OM.........................		2.00	3.00	10.00	50.00
1850	C	CE.........................		7.00	9.00	20.00	70.00
	DO	JMR.........................		15.00	24.00	35.00	80.00
	GA	JG.........................		175.00	250.00	325.00	—
	GC	MP.........................		30.00	45.00	75.00	135.00
	G̵	PF.........................		3.25	4.50	10.00	50.00
	M̊	C C.........................		3.25	4.50	10.00	55.00
	PI	MC.........................		4.00	5.00	10.00	50.00
	ZS	OM.........................		3.25	4.50	10.00	50.00
1851	C	CE 1 over 0.................		11.50	25.00	35.00	75.00
	DO	JMR.........................		15.00	20.00	30.00	75.00
	GA	JG.........................		10.00	12.50	18.00	65.00
	GC	MP.........................		30.00	50.00	75.00	135.00
	G̵	PF.........................		3.25	4.50	10.00	50.00
	PI	MC *varieties:*...............		6.00	8.00	12.00	65.00
		1 over 0; normal date.					
	ZS	OM.........................		2.00	3.00	10.00	50.00
1852	C	CE 2 over 1.................		7.00	9.00	20.00	70.00
	DO	JMR.........................		15.00	20.00	35.00	80.00
	GA	JG.........................		10.00	12.50	20.00	65.00
	M̊	GC.........................		250.00	400.00	500.00	—
	PI	MC *varieties:*...............		7.00	9.00	15.00	70.00
		2 over 1 over 0; normal date.					
	ZS	OM.........................		2.00	3.00	10.00	50.00
1853	C	CE 3 over 2.................		7.50	10.00	22.50	75.00
	DO	CP.........................		12.50	16.00	25.00	75.00
	GA	JG 3 over 2.................		11.00	13.50	22.50	70.00
	G̵	PF.........................		2.00	3.00	10.00	50.00
	PI	MC *varieties:*...............		9.50	12.50	16.00	65.00
		3 over 1; normal date.					
	ZS	OM.........................		2.00	3.00	10.00	50.00
1854	C	CE.........................		7.50	10.00	18.00	70.00
	DO	CP *varieties:*...............		7.50	10.00	18.00	70.00
		4 over 1; normal date.					

Date	Mint	Assayer	F	VF	EF	Unc.
	G^A	JG	$11.00	$15.00	$25.00	$70.00
	G	PF *varieties:*	2.00	3.00	10.00	50.00
		4 over 3; large eagle; small eagle.				
	M̊	GC	7.50	10.00	15.00	55.00
	P^I	MC 4 over 3	13.00	17.50	25.00	70.00
	Z^S	OM *varieties:*	3.50	4.50	12.00	55.00
		4 over 2; 4 over 3; normal date.				
1855	C^A	RG	100.00	150.00	200.00	275.00
	D^O	CP	9.00	12.00	20.00	75.00
	G^A	JG	18.00	22.50	30.00	80.00
	G	PF *varieties:*	2.00	3.00	10.00	50.00
		5 over 3; 5 over 4; normal date.				
	M̊	GF	2.00	3.00	10.00	50.00
	P^I	MC *varieties:*	12.50	17.50	25.00	65.00
		5 over 4; normal date.				
	Z^S	OM *varieties:*	2.00	3.00	10.00	50.00
		5 over 4; normal date.				
	Z^S	MO	2.00	3.50	10.00	50.00
1856	C	CE	40.00	65.00	100.00	175.00
	D^O	CP	12.50	17.50	25.00	75.00
	G^A	JG	7.00	9.00	15.00	60.00
	G	PF *varieties:*	2.00	3.00	10.00	50.00
		6 over 5; normal date.				
	M̊	GF	2.00	3.50	10.00	50.00
	P^I	MC	14.00	20.00	30.00	75.00
	Z^S	MO	2.00	3.00	10.00	50.00
1857	C	CE *varieties:*	8.50	11.00	16.50	70.00
		7 over 4; 7 over 6.				
	D^O	CP	11.50	15.00	20.00	75.00
	G^A	JG 7 over 6	12.50	17.50	25.00	75.00
	G	PF *varieties:*	2.00	3.00	10.00	55.00
		7 over 6; normal date.				
	M̊	GF	3.00	4.00	10.00	55.00
	P^I	PS	20.00	30.00	40.00	90.00
		MC	25.00	40.00	55.00	125.00
	Z^S	MO	2.00	3.00	10.00	50.00
1858	C	CE	4.00	5.50	12.00	60.00
	D^O	CP	12.50	16.50	25.00	75.00
	G^A	JG 8 over 7	15.00	22.50	27.50	80.00
	G	PF	2.00	3.00	10.00	55.00
	M̊	FH	2.00	3.00	10.00	55.00
	P^I	MC	12.50	16.50	25.00	75.00
	Z^S	MO	2.25	3.00	10.00	55.00
1859	C	CE	—	—	—	—
	D^O	CP	7.50	10.00	15.00	70.00
	G^A	JG 9 over 8	12.50	16.50	25.00	75.00
	G	PF	2.00	3.00	10.00	60.00
	M̊	FH	2.00	3.00	10.00	60.00
	P^I	PS	10.00	12.50	18.00	75.00
	Z^S	MO	1.50	3.00	10.00	60.00
1860	C	PV	5.00	7.00	15.00	70.00
	D^O	CP 60 over 59	8.50	11.00	16.50	80.00
	G^A	JG 60 over 59	25.00	45.00	75.00	200.00

Date	Mint	Assayer	F	VF	EF	Unc.
	Ꞡ	PF *varieties:*...............	$2.00	$3.00	$10.00	$60.00
		6 over 5; normal date.				
	P^I	PS 60 over 59...............	10.00	12.50	18.00	75.00
	Z^S	VL.......................	2.00	3.00	10.00	60.00
1861	C	PV.......................	4.00	5.00	12.00	65.00
	D^O	CP.......................	14.00	20.00	35.00	75.00

1861 G^A, 1 over 0   1867 H^O, sm. 7 over 1

	G^A	JG *varieties:*...............	14.00	20.00	35.00	75.00
		1 over 0; normal date.				
	Ꞡ	PF`.......................	2.00	3.00	10.00	60.00
	M̥	CI.......................	2.00	3.00	10.00	55.00
	P^I	PS.......................	7.50	10.00	20.00	70.00
		RO.......................	12.50	15.00	30.00	80.00
	Z^S	VL.......................	2.00	3.00	12.00	60.00
1862	D^O	CP 2 over 1...............	250.00	300.00	375.00	—
	G^A	JG.......................	7.00	9.00	15.00	75.00
	Ꞡ	YE.......................	2.00	3.00	10.00	60.00
		YF.......................	2.00	3.00	12.00	65.00
	M̥	CH.......................	2.00	3.00	12.00	65.00
	P^I	RO *varieties:*...............	7.00	9.00	15.00	70.00
		2 over 1; normal date.				
	Z^S	VL.......................	2.00	3.00	12.00	65.00
1863	M̥	CH 3 over 2...............	2.25	3.50	13.50	70.00
1864	D^O	LT.......................	15.00	20.00	30.00	85.00
1867	Ꞡ	YF.......................	2.00	3.00	12.00	60.00
	Ḣ	PR *varieties:*...............	55.00	65.00	100.00	150.00
		small 7 over 1; large 7 over small 7.				
1868	Ꞡ	YF 8 over 7...............	2.25	3.50	13.50	65.00
	Ḣ	PR.......................	55.00	65.00	100.00	150.00
	Z^S	JS.......................	25.00	45.00	90.00	150.00
1869	C	CE.......................	3.50	4.50	10.00	60.00
	Z^S	YH.......................	2.00	3.00	22.50	60.00

2 REALES

Hooked Neck Eagle 1824

Like the lower denominations, the 2 *reales* employed the attractive eagle in profile, which for some reason was replaced after only a brief period. This type was struck in 1824 only, at the mints of Durango and México.

Diameter 27 mm; weight 6.768 grams; composition .9027 silver, .0973 copper; edge: ornamented.

Date	Mint	Assayer	F	VF	EF	Unc.
1824	D^O	RL........................	$60.00	$125.00	$300.00	$750.00
	M̊	JM........................	20.00	45.00	75.00	150.00

Facing Eagle Type 1825-1872

Coinage of the 2 *reales* showing the well-known facing eagle design began in 1825. Since the 2 *reales* could easily be understood as equivalent to 25¢ and so was in effect a decimal denomination, it was more frequently struck after 1862 than the smaller silver. The Alamos mint ended the series with a small issue in 1872.

Diameter 27 mm; weight 6.768 grams; composition .9027 silver, .0973 copper; edge: ornamented.

Date	Mint	Assayer	F	VF	EF	Unc.
1825	G^A	FS........................	15.00	18.00	28.00	95.00
	Ğ	JJ........................	6.50	11.50	18.00	125.00
	M̊	JM........................	6.00	8.00	13.00	100.00
	Z^S	AZ........................	7.50	11.50	18.50	90.00
1826	D^O	RL........................	17.50	25.00	35.00	95.00
	G^A	FS........................	7.00	9.00	18.00	90.00
	Ğ	JJ *varieties:*...............	6.00	8.00	12.00	125.00
		6 over 5; normal date.				
		MJ........................	6.00	8.00	12.00	85.00
	M̊	JM........................	6.00	8.00	14.00	110.00
	Z^S	ΛV (A is inverted V)..........	6.00	9.00	18.00	90.00
		ΛZ........................	6.00	8.00	12.00	80.00
		AO........................	7.50	11.50	18.00	90.00
1827	Ğ	MJ *varieties:*...............	6.00	8.00	12.00	85.00
		7 over 6; normal date.				
	M̊	JM........................	6.00	8.00	12.00	100.00
	Z^S	ΛO........................	6.00	8.00	12.00	85.00

Date Mint	Assayer	F	VF	EF	Unc.
1828 E^{O}M^O	LF	$275.00	$500.00	$850.00	$2,500
G^A	FS 8 over 7	17.50	25.00	35.00	100.00
G	MR 8 over 7	7.50	11.50	20.00	90.00
	MJ	6.00	8.00	12.00	85.00
	JM	6.00	8.00	14.00	90.00
M̥	JM	6.00	8.00	12.00	100.00
Z^S	AO *varieties:*	6.00	8.00	12.00	85.00
	8 over 7; ΛO (inverted V); normal date and initials.				
1829 G^A	FS	10.00	15.00	25.00	95.00
G	MJ	6.00	8.00	12.00	85.00
M̥	JM *varieties:*	6.00	8.00	12.00	100.00
	9 over 8; normal date.				
P^I	JS	9.00	14.00	25.00	95.00
Z^S	AO	6.00	8.00	12.00	85.00
	OV	6.00	8.00	12.00	85.00
1830 M̥	JM	6.00	8.00	12.00	100.00
P^I	JS 3 over 2	10.00	15.00	27.50	110.00
Z^S	OV	6.00	8.00	12.50	80.00
1831 G	MJ	6.00	8.00	14.00	85.00
M̥	JM	6.00	8.50	14.00	100.00
Z^S	OV	6.00	8.00	12.00	80.00
	OM *varieties:*	6.00	8.00	12.00	80.00
	M over V; normal initials.				
1832 C^A	MR	45.00	60.00	75.00	150.00
D^O	RM *varieties:*	17.50	25.00	35.00	100.00
	style of pre-1832; style of post-1832.				
G^A	FS	6.50	10.00	18.00	90.00
G	MJ	6.00	8.00	12.00	80.00
M̥	JM	6.00	8.50	14.00	100.00
Z^S	OM	6.00	8.00	14.00	85.00
1833 C^A	MR	25.00	75.00	100.00	500.00
G^A	FS/LP, 3 over 2	12.00	15.00	25.00	100.00
G	MJ	6.00	8.00	12.00	80.00
M̥	MJ/JM, 3/2	10.00	15.00	22.00	110.00
Z^S	OM *varieties:*	6.00	8.00	12.00	80.00
	33 over 27; 3 over 2; normal date.				
1834 C^A	MR	35.00	75.00	100.00	500.00
	AM	40.00	75.00	100.00	500.00
D^O	RM *varieties:*	17.50	25.00	35.00	100.00
	4 over 2; 4 over 3.				
G^A	FS	10.00	15.00	25.00	95.00
G	PJ	6.00	8.00	12.00	80.00
M̥	ML	6.00	8.00	12.00	95.00
Z^S	OM	6.00	8.00	12.00	80.00
1835 C^A	AM	30.00	75.00	100.00	500.00
D^O	RM 5/4, M/L	10.00	16.00	25.00	95.00
G^A	FS	2,100	—	—	—
G	PJ	6.00	8.00	12.00	80.00
Z^S	OM	6.00	8.00	12.00	80.00
1836 C^A	AM	20.00	30.00	45.00	120.00
G	PJ	6.00	8.00	12.00	80.00
M̥	ML	6.00	8.00	15.00	95.00
	MF	6.00	8.00	12.00	90.00
Z^S	OM	6.00	8.00	12.00	80.00

Date	Mint	Assayer	F	VF	EF	Unc.
1837	G^A	JG	$10.00	$14.00	$25.00	$90.00
	G͡	PJ *varieties:*	6.00	8.00	12.00	80.00
		7 over 6; normal date.				
	M̊	ML	7.50	14.00	22.00	100.00
	P^I	JS	10.00	15.00	22.00	90.00
	Z^S	OM	6.00	8.00	12.00	80.00
1838	G^A	JG	10.00	15.00	22.00	95.00
	G͡	PJ *varieties:*	6.00	8.00	12.00	80.00
		8 over 7; normal date.				
	Z^S	OM	6.00	8.00	12.00	80.00
1839	G͡	PJ	6.00	8.00	12.00	80.00
	Z^S	OM	6.00	8.00	12.00	80.00
1840	G^A	MC 4 over 3	11.00	16.50	25.00	100.00
	G͡	PJ	6.00	8.00	12.00	80.00
	M̊	ML	6.00	8.00	16.00	90.00
	Z^S	OM	6.00	8.00	12.00	80.00
1841	D^O	RM	9.00	15.00	20.00	95.00
	G^A	MC	11.50	15.00	20.00	95.00
	G͡	PJ	6.00	8.00	12.00	80.00
	M̊	ML	6.00	8.00	10.00	90.00
	P^I	JS	6.00	9.00	14.00	90.00
	Z^S	OM *varieties:*	6.00	8.00	12.00	85.00
		1 over 0; normal date.				
1842	D^O	RM 4 over 3	11.50	15.00	25.00	100.00
	G^A	JG *varieties:*	6.50	10.00	15.00	90.00
		JG/MC, 4/3; normal die.				
	G͡	PJ	6.00	8.00	12.00	80.00
		PM *varieties:*	6.00	8.00	12.00	80.00
		M over J; normal initials.				
	M̊	ML	6.00	8.00	12.00	90.00
	P^I	JS *varieties:*	6.00	8.00	14.00	85.00
		2 over 1; normal date.				
		PS	17.50	25.00	35.00	95.00
	Z^S	OM	6.00	8.00	12.00	80.00
1843	D^O	RM-M over L	6.50	10.00	15.00	90.00
	G^A	JG	9.00	15.00	22.50	95.00
		MC over JG	8.00	11.50	17.00	90.00
	G͡	PM *varieties:*	6.00	8.00	9.00	80.00
		3/2, concave wings, thin rays, small letters;				
		normal date, convex wings, thick rays, large letters.				
	P^I	PS	10.00	16.00	22.00	85.00
		AM	6.00	9.00	20.00	85.00
	Z^S	OM	6.00	8.00	12.00	80.00
1844	C^A	RG	—	—	Unique	—
	D^O	RM	17.50	25.00	35.00	100.00
	G^A	MC	6.50	11.50	18.00	90.00
	GC	MP	35.00	55.00	75.00	150.00
	G͡	PM	6.00	8.00	12.00	80.00
	P^I	AM	6.00	8.00	14.00	85.00
	Z^S	OM	6.00	8.00	12.00	80.00
1845	C^A	RG	25.00	35.00	45.00	120.00
	D^O	RM 45/34, M/L	10.50	16.00	25.00	95.00
	G^A	MC/JG, 5 over 4, 5 over 3	7.50	11.00	22.50	100.00
		JG	6.50	10.00	20.00	95.00

Date	Mint	Assayer	F	VF	EF	Unc.
	GC	MP..........................	$35.00	$45.00	$65.00	$135.00
	G̊	PM *varieties:*...............	6.00	8.00	12.00	80.00
		5 over 4; normal date.				
	Pᴵ	AM..........................	6.00	9.00	15.00	90.00
	Zˢ	OM *varieties:*...............	6.00	8.00	12.00	80.00
		small letters, leaves; large letters, leaves.				
1846	C	CE 8 over 1..................	17.50	25.00	40.00	125.00
	Dᴼ	RM 4 over 3.................	10.50	16.00	25.00	95.00
	Gᴬ	JG...........................	6.50	10.00	18.00	90.00
	GC	MP..........................	35.00	55.00	75.00	150.00
	G̊	PM..........................	6.00	8.00	12.00	80.00
	Pᴵ	AM..........................	6.50	10.00	18.00	90.00
	Zˢ	OM.,........................	6.00	8.00	12.00	80.00
1847	C	CE..........................	10.00	18.00	35.00	100.00
	Gᴬ	JG 7 over 6..................	7.00	11.00	20.00	100.00
	GC	MP..........................	35.00	47.50	65.00	150.00
	G̊	PM..........................	6.00	8.00	12.00	80.00
	M̊	RC..........................	6.00	8.00	12.00	90.00
	Zˢ	OM..........................	6.00	8.00	12.00	80.00
1848	C	CE..........................	12.50	20.00	25.00	90.00
	Dᴼ	RM *varieties:*...............	10.50	16.00	25.00	95.00
		48 over 36; 48 over 37; 8 over 7; normal date.				
	Gᴬ	JG 8 over 7..................	10.00	13.00	20.00	100.00
	GC	MP..........................	30.00	45.00	65.00	125.00
	G̊	PM *vari·ties:*...............	7.50	11.00	15.00	80.00
		8 over 7; normal date.				
	G̊	PF..........................	30.00	37.50	47.50	100.00
	M̊	GC..........................	6.00	8.00	12.00	90.00
	Zˢ	OM..........................	6.00	8.00	12.00	80.00
1849	Dᴼ	CM..........................	6.00	9.00	18.00	85.00
	Gᴬ	JG...........................	10.00	13.00	25.00	95.00
	GC	MP..........................	42.50	55.00	80.00	160.00
	G̊	PF *varieties:*...............	6.00	8.00	12.00	90.00
		9/8, F/M; normal date and initials.				
	M̊	GC..........................	6.00	8.00	12.00	90.00
	Pᴵ	MC..........................	7.50	11.50	18.00	90.00
	Zˢ	OM..........................	6.00	8.00	12.00	80.00
1850	C	CE..........................	30.00	37.50	47.50	110.00
	Gᴬ	JG 5 over 4..................	10.00	13.00	25.00	100.00
	GC	MP..........................	42.50	60.00	80.00	160.00
	G̊	PF *varieties:*...............	6.00	8.00	12.00	80.00
		5 over 4; normal date.				
	M̊	GC..........................	6.00	8.00	12.00	90.00
	Pᴵ	MC..........................	7.50	11.50	18.00	90.00
	Zˢ	OM..........................	6.00	8.00	12.00	80.00
1851	C	CE..........................	11.50	15.00	25.00	95.00
	Dᴼ	JMR over RL.................	12.00	16.00	25.00	95.00
	GC	MP *varieties:*...............	42.50	55.00	80.00	160.00
		1 over 0; normal date.				
	Gᴬ	JG...........................	—	—	—	—
	G̊	PF..........................	6.00	8.00	12.00	80.00
	M̊	GC..........................	6.00	8.00	12.00	90.00
	Zˢ	OM..........................	6.00	8.00	12.00	80.00

Date	Mint	Assayer	F	VF	EF	Unc.
1852	C	CE 2 over 1	$11.50	$15.00	$25.00	$100.00
	D^O	JMR	10.00	18.00	26.00	80.00
	G^A	JG	10.00	15.00	22.00	75.00
	G̶	PF *varieties:*	6.00	8.00	12.00	65.00
		2 over 1; normal date.				
	M̊	GC	6.00	8.00	12.00	90.00
	Z^S	OM	6.00	8.00	12.00	65.00
1853	C	CE 3 over 2	11.50	15.00	25.00	100.00
	G^A	JG 3 over 1	11.50	17.50	25.00	85.00
	G̶	PF	6.00	8.00	12.00	65.00
	M̊	GC	6.00	8.00	18.00	90.00
	Z^S	OM	6.00	8.00	10.00	60.00
1854	C	CE	15.00	22.50	35.00	95.00
	D^O	CP, P over R	30.00	37.50	50.00	100.00
	G^A	JG	42.50	50.00	65.00	100.00
	G̶	PF *varieties:*	6.00	8.00	12.00	60.00
		old font and obverse; new font and obverse.				
	M̊	GC 5 over 4; 54 over 44	6.50	9.00	20.00	100.00
	Z^S	OM *varieties:*	6.00	8.00	12.00	60.00
		4 over 3; normal date.				
1855	C^A	RG	30.00	37.50	50.00	100.00
	D^O	CP	50.00	60.00	75.00	120.00
	G^A	JG	18.00	22.50	30.00	90.00
	G̶	PF *varieties:*	6.00	8.00	12.00	60.00
		normal mint mark; mintmark star in G.				
	M̊	GC	6.00	8.50	12.00	95.00
		GF *varieties:*	6.00	8.00	12.00	95.00
		F over C; normal initial.				
	Z^S	OM *varieties:*	6.00	8.00	12.00	65.00
		5 over 4; normal date.				
		MO	6.00	8.00	12.00	65.00
1856	C	CE	17.50	25.00	35.00	85.00
	D^O	CP	50.00	60.00	85.00	130.00
	G^A	JG	10.00	15.00	20.00	80.00
	G̶	PF 6/5	10.00	13.00	17.50	75.00
	M̊	GF 6/5, F/C	6.50	9.00	13.50	100.00
	P^I	MC	40.00	50.00	65.00	110.00
	Z^S	MO *varieties:*	6.00	8.00	12.00	60.00
		6 over 5; normal date.				
1857	C	CE	10.00	15.00	22.50	75.00
	G^A	JG	10.00	16.00	25.00	80.00
	G̶	PF *varieties:*	6.00	8.00	12.00	60.00
		7 over 6; normal date.				
	M̊	GF	6.00	8.00	13.00	95.00
	P^I	MC	—	—	—	—
	Z^S	MO	6.00	8.00	12.00	60.00
1858	D^O	CP	12.50	20.00	26.00	75.00
	G̶	PF *varieties:*	6.00	8.00	12.00	60.00
		8 over 7; normal date.				
	M̊	FH *varieties:*	6.00	8.00	12.00	90.00
		FH over GF; normal initials.				
	P^I	MC	12.50	20.00	30.00	85.00
	Z^S	MO	6.00	8.00	12.00	60.00

Date	Mint	Assayer	F	VF	EF	Unc.
1859	D^O	CP 9 over 8.................	$12.50	$20.00	$32.50	$95.00
	G^A	JG *varieties:*..............	10.00	16.00	25.00	80.00
		9 over 8; normal date.				
	G	PF *varieties:*..............	6.00	8.00	14.00	65.00
		9 over 7; normal date.				
	M̥	FH.......................	6.00	8.00	12.00	90.00
	P^I	MC.......................	50.00	70.00	100.00	150.00
	Z^S	MO.......................	6.00	8.00	12.00	65.00
1860	C	PV.......................	10.00	15.00	22.50	80.00
	G	PF *varieties:*..............	6.00	8.00	14.00	65.00
		60 over 59; 6 over 5; normal date.				
	M̥	FH.......................	6.00	8.00	15.00	95.00
		TH.......................	6.00	8.00	14.00	95.00
	Z^S	MO *varieties:*.............	6.00	8.00	14.00	65.00
		60 over 59; normal date.				
	Z^S	VL.......................	6.00	8.00	13.00	60.00
1861	C	PV.......................	18.00	22.50	30.00	95.00
	D^O	CP.......................	12.50	20.00	30.00	95.00
	G	PF *varieties:*..............	6.00	8.00	12.00	65.00
		61 over 57; 6 over 5; 1 over 0; normal date.				
	H̥	FM.......................	200.00	300.00	400.00	500.00
	M̥	TH.......................	6.00	8.00	15.00	100.00
		CH.......................	6.00	8.00	15.00	100.00
	P^I	PS.......................	10.00	15.00	25.00	95.00
	Z^S	VL.......................	6.00	8.00	15.00	65.00
1862	G^A	JG 2 over 1................	11.50	17.50	27.50	95.00

1862 Hermosillo,
6 over 5, H^O FM over C. CE

1863 C^E ML

			F	VF	EF	Unc.
	G	YE *varieties:*..............	6.00	8.00	14.00	75.00
		2 over 1; 62 over 57; YE over PF; normal date and initials.				
		YF.......................	6.00	8.00	14.00	75.00
	H^O	FM-6/5, H^{O}FM				
		over C. CE..............	225.00	325.00	450.00	550.00
	M̥	CH.......................	6.00	8.00	14.00	95.00
	P^I	RO.......................	10.00	16.00	30.00	95.00
	Z^S	VL.......................	6.00	8.00	15.00	80.00
1863	C^E	ML.......................	125.00	185.00	300.00	650.00
	G	YF *varieties:*..............	6.00	8.00	15.00	85.00
		63 over 52; normal date.				
	M̥	CH.......................	6.00	8.00	15.00	95.00
		TH.......................	6.00	8.00	15.00	95.00
	P^I	RO.......................	18.00	22.50	35.00	95.00

Date	Mint	Assayer	F	VF	EF	Unc.
	Z^S	MO......................	$6.00	$8.00	$15.00	$85.00
		VL.......................	6.00	8.00	15.00	80.00
1864	Z^S	MO......................	6.00	8.00	15.00	80.00
		VL.......................	6.00	8.00	14.00	80.00
1865	Z^S	MO......................	6.00	8.00	16.00	80.00
1867	G	YF 6 over 5..............	6.00	8.00	15.00	85.00
	H̊	PR/FM, 7/1..............	120.00	175.00	250.00	300.00
	M̊	CH......................	6.00	8.00	13.50	90.00
	Z^S	JS.......................	6.00	8.00	14.00	80.00
♪1868	G	YF 68 over 57...........	10.00	13.50	25.00	85.00
	M̊	CH......................	7.00	12.00	18.00	95.00
		PH......................	6.00	8.00	15.00	95.00
	P^I	PS.......................	6.00	9.00	16.00	80.00
	·Z^S	JS.......................	6.00	8.00	15.00	80.00
		·YH.....................	6.00	8.00	14.00	75.00
1869	C	CE......................	10.00	16.00	30.00	95.00
	P^I	PS *varieties:*...........	8.50	13.00	20.00	85.00
		9 over 8; normal date.				
	Z^S	YH......................	6.00	8.00	14.50	80.00
1870	Z^S	YH......................	6.00	8.00	15.00	80.00
1872	A	AM reeded edge				
		15,417 minted...........	45.00	65.00	100.00	175.00

4 REALES
Facing Eagle Type 1827-1870

The obverse of this design shows the usual upright or facing eagle with cactus and serpent, and the reverse bears the inscribed Liberty cap with rays.

This was the least favored of the *real* silver denominations. Production was slow to begin; by the time of the earliest issue the obverse hooked neck eagle had already been superceded so that no 4 *reales* of the earliest Republican design were struck. Although the denomination came to be minted in some quantity at Guanajuato and Zacatecas, and in shorter series at Guadalajara and San Luis Potosí, the other mints produced this denomination very irregularly. As a group the 4 *reales* are the least common of the *real* denominations.

Diameter 32 mm; weight 13.536 grams; composition .9027 silver, .0973 copper; edge: ornamented.

1827	M̊	JM......................	50.00	80.00	125.00	400.00

Date Mint	Assayer	F	VF	EF	Unc.
1831 Z^S	OM........................	$15.00	$30.00	$75.00	$175.00
1832 Z^S	OM *varieties:*...............	12.50	25.00	50.00	150.00
	2 over 1; normal date.				
1833 Z^S	OM *varieties:*...............	15.00	30.00	60.00	150.00
	33 over 27; 3 over 2; normal date.				
1834 Z^S	OM........................	15.00	30.00	60.00	150.00
1835 G	PJ.........................	12.50	25.00	50.00	150.00
Z^S	OM........................	12.50	25.00	50.00	150.00
1836 G	PJ *varieties:*...............	12.00	20.00	50.00	150.00
	6 over 5; normal date.				
Z^S	OM........................	12.50	25.00	50.00	150.00
1837 G	PJ.........................	12.00	20.00	50.00	150.00
P^I	JS.........................	20.00	30.00	70.00	175.00
Z^S	OM *varieties:*...............	15.00	30.00	60.00	175.00
	7 over 5; 7 over 6; normal date.				
1838 G	PJ *varieties:*...............	12.00	30.00	75.00	175.00
	8 over 7; normal date.				
P^I	JS.........................	30.00	45.00	80.00	175.00
Z^S	OM 8 over 7...............	17.50	35.00	70.00	200.00
1839 G	PJ.........................	12.00	20.00	50.00	150.00
Z^S	OM........................	15.00	30.00	60.00	150.00
1840 G	PJ 4 over 3................	21.50	35.00	90.00	225.00
Z^S	OM........................	15.00	25.00	50.00	150.00
1841 G	PJ 4 over 3................	21.50	35.00	90.00	225.00
Z^S	OM........................	12.50	20.00	45.00	150.00
1842 G^A	JG *varieties:*...............	35.00	50.00	80.00	175.00
	2 over 1; normal date.				
G	PJ.........................	22.50	40.00	100.00	250.00
	PM........................	12.00	22.50	60.00	150.00
P^I	PS.........................	15.00	30.00	70.00	175.00
Z^S	OM *varieties:*...............	12.50	25.00	50.00	150.00
	large letters; small letters.				
1843 G^A	MC........................	15.00	25.00	60.00	160.00

Convex wings   Concave wings

G	PM *varieties:*...............	12.00	20.00	50.00	175.00
	3/2, convex wings, thick rays;				
	normal date, concave wings, thin rays.				

Date	Mint	Assayer	F	VF	EF	Unc.
	P^I	PS *varieties:*.................	$16.00	$35.00	$75.00	$175.00
		3 over 2 (3 cut from 8 punch);				
		3 over 2, normal digits; normal date.				
		AM........................	15.00	30.00	70.00	175.00
	Z^S	OM........................	12.50	25.00	50.00	150.00
1844	G^A	MC 4 over 3................	15.00	27.50	60.00	190.00
	GC	MP........................	400.00	550.00	750.00	1,000
	G̶	PM *varieties:*.............	12.00	20.00	50.00	150.00
		4 over 3; normal date.				
	P^I	AM........................	12.00	25.00	60.00	175.00
	Z^S	OM........................	12.50	25.00	50.00	150.00
1845	G^A	MC........................	12.00	18.50	50.00	150.00
		JG........................	12.00	27.50	50.00	150.00
	GC	MP........................	3,000	4,000	5,000	8,000
	G̶	PM *varieties:*.............	12.00	20.00	50.00	150.00
		5 over 4; normal date.				
	P^I	AM *varieties:*.............	12.00	25.00	50.00	175.00
		5 over 4; normal date.				
	Z^S	OM........................	12.50	25.00	50.00	150.00
1846	C	CE........................	60.00	85.00	150.00	500.00
	G^A	JG........................	12.50	25.00	60.00	160.00
	GC	MP........................	400.00	550.00	750.00	1,000
	G̶	PM *varieties:*.............	12.00	20.00	50.00	150.00
		6 over 5; normal date.				
	P^I	AM........................	15.00	30.00	60.00	175.00
	Z^S	OM........................	12.50	25.00	50.00	150.00
1847	G^A	JG........................	12.00	22.50	60.00	160.00
	GC	MP........................	400.00	550.00	750.00	1,000
	G̶	PM *varieties:*.............	11.50	20.00	50.00	150.00
		7 over 6; normal date.				
	P^I	AM........................	15.00	30.00	60.00	175.00
	Z^S	OM........................	12.50	25.00	50.00	150.00
1848	G^A	JG 8 over 7................	15.00	27.50	75.00	200.00
	G̶	PM *varieties:*.............	12.00	22.50	55.00	160.00
		8 over 7; normal date.				
	P^I	AM........................	12.50	25.00	65.00	175.00
	Z^S	OM........................	12.50	25.00	50.00	150.00
1849	G^A	JG........................	25.00	40.00	75.00	160.00
	GC	MP........................	400.00	550.00	750.00	1,000
	G̶	PF........................	14.00	22.50	55.00	150.00
	P^I	MC *varieties:*.............	12.00	25.00	60.00	175.00
		MC over AM; normal initials.				
		PS........................	12.00	25.00	60.00	175.00
	Z^S	OM........................	12.50	25.00	50.00	150.00
1850	C	CE........................	30.00	50.00	100.00	400.00
	G^A	JG........................	65.00	90.00	125.00	200.00
	GC	MP........................	400.00	550.00	700.00	900.00
	G̶	PF........................	12.00	20.00	45.00	150.00
	M̊	GC........................	15.00	25.00	50.00	350.00
	P^I	MC........................	20.00	30.00	60.00	175.00
	Z^S	OM........................	12.50	20.00	45.00	150.00
1851	G̶	PF........................	12.00	20.00	50.00	150.00
	P^I	MC........................	15.00	25.00	60.00	175.00

Date	Mint	Assayer	F	VF	EF	Unc.
	Z^S	OM......................	$12.50	$25.00	$50.00	$150.00
1852	C	CE.......................	30.00	70.00	125.00	400.00
	G^A	JG.......................	25.00	35.00	60.00	160.00
	G̵	PF.......................	12.00	20.00	50.00	150.00
	M̊	GC......................	25.00	40.00	90.00	350.00
	P^I	MC......................	15.00	30.00	60.00	175.00
	Z^S	OM......................	12.50	20.00	45.00	150.00
1853	G̵	PF.......................	14.00	22.50	55.00	150.00
	P^I	MC......................	15.00	25.00	70.00	175.00
	Z^S	OM......................	12.50	25.00	50.00	150.00
1854	G^A	JG.......................	15.00	22.50	50.00	150.00
	G̵	PF *varieties:*............	14.00	22.50	55.00	175.00
		large eagle; small eagle.				
	M̊	GC......................	15.00	25.00	45.00	350.00
	P^I	MC......................	22.50	40.00	80.00	175.00

1854 Z^S, 4 over 3   1855 México, F over C

	Z^S	OM *varieties:*............	15.00	30.00	65.00	175.00
		4 over 3; normal date.				
1855	G^A	JG.......................	15.00	22.50	50.00	150.00
	G̵	PF *varieties:*............	12.00	17.50	45.00	150.00
		5 over 4; normal date.				
	M̊	GF-F over C..............	40.00	60.00	150.00	500.00
	P^I	MC......................	15.00	25.00	50.00	175.00
	Z^S	OM *varieties:*............	12.50	20.00	45.00	150.00
		5 over 4; normal date.				
1856	G^A	JG.......................	25.00	50.00	80.00	175.00
	G̵	PF.......................	12.00	20.00	50.00	150.00
	M̊	GF, F over C	15.00	25.00	50.00	350.00
	P^I	MC......................	20.00	30.00	60.00	175.00
	Z^S	OM......................	12.50	25.00	50.00	150.00
		MO......................	12.50	25.00	50.00	150.00
1857	C	CE.......................	80.00	110.00	200.00	500.00
	G^A	JG 7 over 6..............	25.00	50.00	80.00	175.00
	G̵	PF.......................	12.00	20.00	50.00	150.00
	P^I	MC......................	30.00	45.00	90.00	175.00
		PS.......................	30.00	45.00	90.00	175.00
	Z^S	MO *varieties:*............	12.50	25.00	50.00	150.00
		7 over 5; normal date.				
1858	C	CE.......................	50.00	85.00	150.00	500.00
	G^A	JG.......................	15.00	25.00	60.00	160.00
	G̵	PF.......................	12.00	20.00	50.00	150.00

Date	Mint	Assayer	F	VF	EF	Unc.
	Z^S	MO........................	$12.50	$25.00	$50.00	$150.00
1859	G^A	JG 9 over 8................	17.50	25.00	60.00	160.00
	G	PF........................	12.00	17.50	45.00	150.00
	M̥	FH........................	12.00	20.00	50.00	350.00
	P^I	MC........................	20.00	35.00	60.00	175.00
	Z^S	MO........................	12.50	20.00	45.00	150.00
1860	C	PV........................	25.00	55.00	100.00	375.00
	G^A	JG........................	35.00	50.00	80.00	160.00
	G	PF *varieties*:..............	12.00	20.00	50.00	150.00
		60 over 59; normal date.				
	P^I	PS........................	30.00	50.00	75.00	175.00
	Z^S	MO *varieties*:..............	12.50	25.00	50.00	150.00
		60 over 59; normal date.				
		VL........................	12.50	20.00	45.00	150.00
1861	G	PF 6 over 5................	15.00	21.50	55.00	180.00
	H̥	FM........................	200.00	250.00	325.00	600.00
	M̥	CH........................	12.00	20.00	50.00	200.00

			F	VF	EF	Unc.
	O	FR *varieties*:..............	200.00	250.00	350.00	550.00
		ornamented edge; herringbone edge; obliquely reeded edge.				
	P^I	PS........................	15.00	30.00	60.00	175.00
		RO over PS................	15.00	30.00	60.00	175.00
	Z^S	VL *varieties*:..............	12.50	25.00	50.00	150.00
		1 over 0; normal date.				
1862	G	YE *varieties*:..............	12.00	20.00	50.00	150.00
		YE over PF; 2 over 1; normal date and initials.				
		YF *varieties*:..............	12.00	20.00	55.00	150.00
		2 over 1; normal date.				
	M̥	CH........................	15.00	25.00	60.00	200.00
	P^I	RO........................	12.50	25.00	50.00	175.00
	Z^S	VL *varieties*:..............	12.50	25.00	50.00	150.00
		2 over 1; normal date.				
1863	C^E	ML........................	150.00	300.00	850.00	3,200
	G^A	JG *varieties*:..............	150.00	350.00	1,250	5,000
		3 over 2; normal date.				
	G	YF *varieties*:..............	12.00	20.00	50.00	150.00
		6 over 5; Y over P; normal date and initials.				
	M̥	CH *varieties*:..............	15.00	25.00	60.00	200.00
		3 over 2; normal date.				

Date	Mint	Assayer	F	VF	EF	Unc.
	P^I	RO..........................	$12.50	$25.00	$50.00	$175.00
	Z^S	VL..........................	12.50	25.00	50.00	150.00
		MO.........................	12.50	25.00	50.00	150.00
1864	P^I	RO..........................	15.00	30.00	60.00	175.00
	Z^S	VL..........................	12.50	25.00	50.00	150.00
1867	G	YF 6 over 5, Y over P........	12.00	20.00	50.00	150.00
	Ȟ	PR/FM, 7/1.................	135.00	165.00	225.00	400.00
	M̌	CH.........................	15.00	25.00	60.00	200.00
1868	G	YF 6 over 5, Y over P........	12.00	20.00	50.00	150.00
	M̌	CH over PH................	12.00	20.00	50.00	200.00
		PH.........................	12.00	20.00	50.00	200.00
	P^I	PS..........................	12.50	25.00	50.00	175.00
	Z^S	JS..........................	12.50	20.00	45.00	150.00
		YH.........................	12.50	25.00	50.00	150.00
1869	G	YF.........................	14.00	22.50	55.00	150.00
	P^I	PS *varieties:*..............	12.50	25.00	50.00	175.00
		9 over 8; normal date.				
	Z^S	YH.........................	12.50	25.00	50.00	150.00
1870	G	FR..........................	12.00	17.50	40.00	150.00
	Z^S	YH.........................	12.50	20.00	45.00	150.00

8 REALES
Hooked Neck Eagle 1823-1825

On the proclamation of the Republic in 1823 the México mint issued two denominations, 8 *reales* in silver and 8 *escudos* in gold, both bearing the hooked neck eagle obverse. Although superceded at México by the facing eagle in the course of 1824, the hooked neck eagle type in silver continued to the end of that year at Durango and into 1825 at Guanajuato. The reverse is of a characteristic style found with all the hooked neck obverses, notable for thick rays, a rather tall cap, and the inscription *Libertad* in script.

Planchets of this series tend to be slightly smaller in size than the legally defined 39 millimeters.

Diameter 39 mm; weight 27.073 grams; composition .9027 silver, .0973 copper; edge: ornamented.

1824
Mexico
REPULICA
error

Date	Mint	Assayer	F	VF	EF	Unc.
1823	M̥	JM.........................	$150.00	$250.00	$650.00	$2,000
1824	D°	RL.........................	125.00	250.00	750.00	2,500
	G	JM.........................	150.00	350.00	900.00	3,000
	M̥	JM *varieties:*..............	125.00	225.00	425.00	1,500
		normal legend; error: REPULICA.				
1825	G	JJ *varieties:*...............	500.00	750.00	1,400	4,500
		5 over 4; normal date.				

Facing Eagle Type 1824-1897

The most familiar types of the 19th century coinage of Mexico are those of the 8 *reales* or *peso fuerte* ("heavy peso") with facing eagle obverse and redesigned reverse. From 1824 onward this type was to characterize the 8 *reales* for decade after decade. The brief interval of the Maximilian peso and the unsuccessful balance scale peso aside, the design (with some stylistic variation) survived on this denomination until 1897, and on the peso which succeeded it until 1909.

The 8 *reales* is by far the commonest of the *real* denominations. Since silver was struck mostly for export it was the most convenient denomination and would have overwhelmed the minor silver pieces entirely had not the mint leases specifically prohibited the operators from coining 8 *reales* alone.

Diameter 39 mm; weight 27.073 grams; composition .9027 silver, .0973 copper; edge: ornamented.

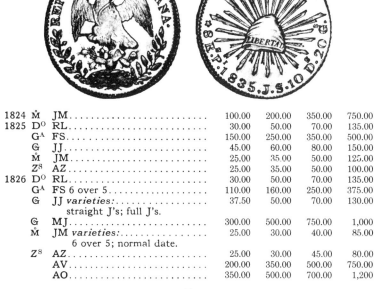

1824	M̥	JM.........................	100.00	200.00	350.00	750.00
1825	D°	RL.........................	30.00	50.00	70.00	135.00
	Gᴬ	FS.........................	150.00	250.00	350.00	500.00
	G	JJ.........................	45.00	60.00	80.00	150.00
	M̥	JM.........................	25.00	35.00	50.00	125.00
	Zˢ	AZ.........................	25.00	35.00	50.00	100.00
1826	D°	RL.........................	30.00	50.00	70.00	135.00
	Gᴬ	FS 6 over 5.................	110.00	160.00	250.00	375.00
	G	JJ *varieties:*..............	37.50	50.00	70.00	130.00
		straight J's; full J's.				
	G	MJ.........................	300.00	500.00	750.00	1,000
	M̥	JM *varieties:*..............	25.00	30.00	40.00	85.00
		6 over 5; normal date.				
	Zˢ	AZ.........................	25.00	30.00	45.00	80.00
		AV.........................	200.00	350.00	500.00	750.00
		AO.........................	350.00	500.00	700.00	1,200

Date	Mint	Assayer	F	VF	EF	Unc.
1827	D^O	RL *varieties:*	$30.00	$50.00	$70.00	$135.00
		7 over 6; normal date.				
	G^A	FS *varieties:*	100.00	150.00	225.00	350.00
		2 over 8; normal date.				
	G	MJ *varieties:*	50.00	75.00	100.00	150.00
		M over J; normal initials.				
		MR	55.00	75.00	100.00	150.00
	M̊	JM	25.00	30.00	40.00	75.00
	P^I	JS	500.00	750.00	1,250	2,000
	Z^S	AO *varieties:*	25.00	30.00	40.00	80.00
		O over Z; normal initials.				
1828	D^O	RL *varieties:*	30.00	50.00	70.00	135.00
		8 over 7; normal date.				
	E^{O}M^O	LF	500.00	900.00	1,600	3,000
	G^A	FS	100.00	150.00	225.00	350.00
	G	MJ	25.00	30.00	40.00	75.00
		MR	175.00	300.00	400.00	500.00
	M̊	JM	30.00	50.00	75.00	150.00
	P^I	JS *varieties:*	65.00	85.00	110.00	175.00
		8 over 7; normal date.				
	Z^S	AO	25.00	30.00	40.00	75.00
1829	D^O	RL	30.00	50.00	70.00	135.00
	E^{O}M^O	LF	750.00	1,000	1,500	3,000
	G^A	FS *varieties:*	150.00	250.00	350.00	500.00
		9 over 8; normal date.				
	G	MJ	25.00	30.00	45.00	85.00
	M̊	JM	25.00	30.00	40.00	90.00
	P^I	JS	55.00	75.00	125.00	175.00
	Z^S	AO	25.00	30.00	45.00	85.00
		OV	60.00	100.00	150.00	250.00
1830	D^O	RM	30.00	50.00	70.00	135.00
	E^{O}M^O	LF *varieties:*	1,000	1,500	2,000	3,750
		3 over 2; normal date.				
	G^A	FS *varieties:*	75.00	100.00	150.00	225.00
		30 over 29; normal date.				
		LP over FS	700.00	1,000	1,400	2,000
	G	MJ *varieties:*	17.50	25.00	40.00	75.00
		oblong beading, narrow J; regular beading, wide J.				
	M̊	JM *varieties:*	35.00	50.00	75.00	125.00
		3 over 2; normal date.				
	P^I	JS	35.00	50.00	90.00	140.00
	Z^S	OV	20.00	30.00	40.00	100.00
1831	C^A	MR	900.00	1,400	1,800	2,500
	D^O	RM	20.00	30.00	45.00	90.00
	G^A	LP	250.00	400.00	600.00	900.00
		FS *varieties:*	125.00	200.00	300.00	450.00
		FS over LP; normal initials.				
	G	MJ *varieties:*	17.50	25.00	40.00	75.00
		colon after date; 2 stars after date.				
	M̊	JM	30.00	50.00	100.00	200.00
	P^I	JS *varieties:*	25.00	35.00	65.00	110.00
		1 over 0; normal date.				
	Z^S	OV	20.00	40.00	75.00	125.00
		OM	17.50	25.00	35.00	75.00

Date	Mint	Assayer	F	VF	EF	Unc.
1832	C^A	MR........................	$125.00	$200.00	$300.00	$450.00
	D^O	RM *varieties:*...............	20.00	30.00	45.00	90.00
		Mexican dies; European dies, M over L.				
	G^A	FS *varieties:*................	40.00	70.00	100.00	150.00
		2 over 1, FS over LP; 2 over 1; normal date and initials.				
	G	MJ *varieties:*................	17.50	25.00	40.00	75.00
		1 of date over inverted 1; normal date.				
	M̊	JM *varieties:*................	25.00	30.00	40.00	75.00
		2 over 1; normal date.				
	P^I	JS *varieties:*................	25.00	35.00	65.00	110.00
		3 over 2; normal date.				
	Z^S	OM *varieties:*...............	17.50	25.00	35.00	75.00
		2 over 1; normal date.				
1833	C^A	MR........................	125.00	250.00	350.00	500.00
	D^O	RM *varieties:*...............	15.00	25.00	40.00	75.00
		3 over 2, M over L; normal date and initials.				
	G^A	FS *varieties:*................	40.00	70.00	100.00	150.00
		3/2/1, FS over LP; normal date and initials.				
	G	MJ.........................	17.50	25.00	40.00	75.00
		JM.........................	500.00	800.00	1,200	1,600
	M̊	MJ.........................	27.50	40.00	75.00	150.00
		ML.........................	600.00	1,000	1,500	2,250
	P^I	JS *varieties:*................	25.00	30.00	40.00	75.00
		3 over 2; normal date.				
	Z^S	OM *varieties:*...............	17.50	25.00	35.00	75.00
		M over O; 3 over 2; normal date and initials.				
1834	C^A	MR........................	500.00	800.00	1,000	1,400
		AM........................	500.00	800.00	1,000	1,400
	D^O	RM *varieties:*...............	15.00	20.00	40.00	75.00
		4 over 3 over 2, M over L; normal date.				
	G^A	FS *varieties:*................	30.00	45.00	60.00	100.00
		4 over 2; 4 over 3; normal date.				
	G	PJ.........................	17.50	25.00	40.00	75.00
	M̊	ML *varieties:*................	25.00	30.00	40.00	75.00
		4 over 3; normal date.				
	P^I	JS *varieties:*................	25.00	35.00	50.00	90.00
		4 over 3; normal date.				
	Z^S	OM........................	17.50	25.00	35.00	75.00
1835	C^A	AM........................	150.00	250.00	350.00	450.00
	D^O	RM *varieties:*...............	20.00	30.00	45.00	80.00
		5 over 4, M over L; normal date and initials.				
	G^A	FS.........................	40.00	60.00	65.00	100.00
	G	PJ.........................	17.50	25.00	40.00	75.00
	H^O	PP*.........................		Reported, not confirmed		
	M̊	ML.........................	25.00	30.00	40.00	75.00
	P^I	JS *varieties:*................	25.00	35.00	50.00	90.00
		denomination 8R; denomination $8R^S$.				
	Z^S	OM........................	17.50	25.00	35.00	75.00

---

*J. L. Riddell, *Monograph of the Silver Dollar* (New Orleans, 1845; reprint México, 1969), no. 182. On the Hermosillo pesos of 1835 and 1836 see Dr. A. F. Pradeau, "The Mexican Mint of Hermosillo," in *The Numismatist,* vol. 66 no. 8 (August 1953) pp. 804-806; and "The Mexican Mint of Hermosillo: additional data," in *The Numismatist,* vol. 66 no. 11 (November 1953) pp. 1155-1156.

Date	Mint	Assayer	F	VF	EF	Unc.
1836	C^A	AM.........................	$100.00	$150.00	$200.00	$275.00
	D^O	RM *varieties:*...............	20.00	30.00	45.00	80.00
		6 over 1; 6 over 4; normal date; initial M on snake.				
	G^A	FS........................	600.00	900.00	1,200	1,600
		JG *varieties:*...............	50.00	70.00	90.00	150.00
		6 over 1, JG over FS; JG over FS; normal initials.				
	G̥	PJ........................	17.50	25.00	40.00	75.00
	H^O	PP........................		Unique		
	M̥	ML *varieties:*...............	60.00	120.00	175.00	300.00
		L over F; normal initials.				
		MF *varieties:*...............	35.00	60.00	90.00	150.00
		F over L; normal initials.				
	P^I	JS........................	25.00	35.00	50.00	90.00
	Z^S	OM *varieties:*...............	17.50	25.00	35.00	75.00
		6 over 5; normal date.				
1837	C^A	AM........................	500.00	800.00	1,000	1,400
	D^O	RM *varieties:*...............	20.00	30.00	45.00	80.00
		7 over 1; normal date.				
	G^A	JG *varieties:*...............	30.00	45.00	60.00	100.00
		7 over 6, JG over FS; normal date.				
	G̥	PJ........................	17.50	25.00	40.00	75.00
	M̥	ML *varieties:*...............	30.00	45.00	65.00	125.00
		7 over 6; normal date.				
		MM *varieties:*...............	40.00	75.00	100.00	150.00
		7/6, 2nd M/L; 7/6, normal initials; normal date and initials.				
	P^I	JS........................	27.50	50.00	75.00	120.00
	Z^S	OM........................	17.50	25.00	35.00	75.00
1838	C^A	AM........................	100.00	150.00	200.00	275.00
	D^O	RM *varieties:*...............	20.00	30.00	45.00	80.00
		8 over 1; 8 over 7; normal date.				
	G^A	JG *varieties:*...............	65.00	100.00	125.00	200.00
		8 over 7; normal date.				
	G̥	PJ........................	17.50	25.00	40.00	75.00
	M̥	MM........................	40.00	60.00	80.00	150.00
		ML *varieties:*...............	25.00	35.00	50.00	85.00
		L over M; normal initials.				
	P^I	JS........................	25.00	35.00	45.00	85.00
	Z^S	OM *varieties:*...............	17.50	25.00	35.00	75.00
		8 over 7; normal date.				
1839	C^A	RG........................	400.00	600.00	800.00	1,000
	D^O	RM 9 over 1, M over L........	22.50	35.00	50.00	90.00
	G^A	MC *varieties:*...............	47.50	65.00	85.00	150.00
		MC over JG; normal initials.				
		JG........................	25.00	35.00	55.00	90.00
	G̥	PJ *varieties:*...............	17.50	25.00	40.00	75.00
		P over J (error); normal initials.				
	H̥	PR*........................		Unique		
	M̥	ML........................	15.00	35.00	35.00	75.00
	P^I	JS........................	25.00	40.00	60.00	100.00
	Z^S	OM........................	17.50	25.00	35.00	75.00
1840	C^A	RG *varieties:*...............	400.00	600.00	800.00	1,000
		1 dot after date; 3 dots after date.				

---

*T. V. Buttrey, "The Hermosillo Peso of 1839," in *American Numismatic Society Museum Notes* 17 (1971), pp. 255-261.

Date	Mint	Assayer	F	VF	EF	Unc.
	D^O	RM *varieties:* .... ₎	$22.50	$35.00	$50.00	$90.00
		40 over 38 over 31; 40 over 39.				
	G^A	MC *varieties:*	47.50	65.00	85.00	140.00
		4 over 3; normal date.				
	G̶	PJ *varieties:*	17.50	25.00	40.00	75.00
		4 over 3; normal date.				
	M̥	ML	15.00	25.00	35.00	75.00
	P^I	JS	17.50	30.00	40.00	75.00
	Z^S	OM	17.50	25.00	35.00	75.00
1841	C^A	RG	60.00	80.00	100.00	140.00
	D^O	RM 4 over 3	55.00	100.00	145.00	225.00
	G^A	MC	50.00	70.00	90.00	150.00
	G̶	PJ *varieties:*	17.50	25.00	40.00	75.00
		4 over 3; normal date.				
	M̥	ML	15.00	25.00	35.00	75.00
	P^I	JS *varieties:*	25.00	35.00	45.00	85.00
		normal mint mark; error: mint mark ^{I}P.				
	Z^S	OM	17.50	25.00	35.00	75.00
1842	C^A	RG	30.00	45.00	65.00	120.00
	D^O	RM *varieties:*	25.00	30.00	50.00	100.00
		4 over 3; 42 over 31; 42/31, B on base below cactus;				
		eagle of 1832-41; pre-1832 eagle resumed.				
	G^A	JG *varieties:*	27.50	40.00	55.00	90.00
		J over M; normal initials.				
	G̶	PJ	20.00	35.00	50.00	100.00
		PM *varieties:*	17.50	25.00	40.00	75.00
		normal date; 42 over 31; M over J; normal initials.				
	M̥	ML	15.00	25.00	35.00	75.00
		MM	15.00	25.00	35.00	75.00
	P^I	JS *varieties:*	40.00	60.00	80.00	125.00
		2 over 1; normal date.				
		PS *varieties:*	30.00	50.00	70.00	125.00
		2 over 1, P over J; normal date, P over J;				
		normal date and initials.				
	Z^S	OM	17.50	25.00	35.00	75.00
1843	C^A	RG	30.00	45.00	65.00	120.00
	D^O	RM 4 over 3	60.00	100.00	150.00	225.00
	G^A	JG	400.00	600.00	800.00	1,250
		MC *varieties:*	70.00	120.00	175.00	275.00
		3 over 2, MC over JG; normal date, MC over JG;				
		normal date and initials.				
	G̶	PM *varieties:*	17.50	25.00	40.00	75.00
		dot after date; triangle of dots after date.				
	M̥	MM	15.00	25.00	35.00	75.00
	P^I	PS *varieties:*	50.00	75.00	125.00	200.00
		3 over 2, round top 3; normal date, flat top 3.				
		AM *varieties:*	25.00	30.00	45.00	90.00
		round top 3; flat top 3.				
	Z^S	OM	17.50	25.00	35.00	75.00
1844	C^A	RG 2nd 4 over 1	32.50	50.00	65.00	130.00
	D^O	RM *varieties:*	55.00	75.00	125.00	175.00
		first 4 over 3; 44 over 35; normal date.				

Date	Mint	Assayer	F	VF	EF	Unc.
	G^A	MC........................	$60.00	$100.00	$125.00	$175.00
	GC	MP *varieties:*...............	350.00	500.00	750.00	1,200
		normal legend; error: reversed s in D^S and in G^S.				
	G̊	PM........................	17.50	25.00	40.00	75.00
	M̊	MF........................	15.00	25.00	35.00	75.00
	P^I	AM........................	25.00	30.00	45.00	90.00
	Z^S	OM........................	17.50	25.00	35.00	75.00
1845	C^A	RG........................	25.00	45.00	65.00	120.00
	D^O	RM *varieties:*...............	17.50	25.00	40.00	90.00
		45 over 31; 45 over 34; 4 over 3; normal date.				
	G^A	MC........................	60.00	80.00	100.00	165.00
		JG........................	650.00	1,000	1,250	1,750
	GC	MP........................	150.00	250.00	350.00	500.00
	G̊	PM........................	17.50	25.00	40.00	75.00
	M̊	MF *varieties:*...............	15.00	25.00	35.00	75.00
		5 over 4; normal date.				
	P^I	AM *varieties:*...............	25.00	40.00	60.00	100.00
		5 over 4; normal date.				
	Z^S	OM........................	17.50	25.00	35.00	75.00
1846	C^A	RG........................	60.00	80.00	100.00	175.00
	C	CE........................	100.00	200.00	300.00	500.00
	D^O	RM *varieties:*...............	17.50	25.00	40.00	85.00
		46 over 31; 4 over 3; normal date.				
	G^A	JG........................	65.00	100.00	130.00	175.00
	GC	MP *varieties:*...............	150.00	250.00	350.00	500.00
		square tail on eagle; rounded tail on eagle.				
	G̊	PM *varieties:*...............	17.50	25.00	40.00	75.00
		6 over 5; normal date.				
	M̊	MF *varieties:*...............	15.00	25.00	35.00	75.00
		6 over 5; normal date.				
	P^I	AM *varieties:*...............	25.00	30.00	45.00	90.00
		6 over 5; normal date.				
	Z^S	OM........................	17.50	25.00	35.00	75.00
1847	C^A	RG........................	60.00	100.00	125.00	150.00
	C	CE........................	150.00	250.00	350.00	600.00
	D^O	RM........................	25.00	30.00	50.00	100.00
	G^A	JG........................	100.00	150.00	200.00	300.00
	GC	MP........................	150.00	250.00	350.00	500.00
	G̊	PM........................	17.50	25.00	40.00	75.00
	M̊	MF 7 over 6........................	700.00	1,000	1,250	1,750
		RC *varieties:*...............	15.00	25.00	35.00	70.00
		RC over MF; normal initials.				
	P^I	AM........................	25.00	30.00	45.00	80.00
	Z^S	OM........................	17.50	25.00	35.00	75.00
1848	C^A	RG........................	50.00	70.00	90.00	150.00
	C	CE........................	125.00	200.00	250.00	400.00
	*D^O	RM *varieties:*...............	110.00	225.00	325.00	500.00
		8 over 7; normal date.				

*Many Durango dies of 1848-1849 include initials on obverse, Y near eagle's upraised claw, B and G near lower ends of wreath near water line; and on reverse, Y in rays near 7 o'clock, with or without B and G in upper rays between 11-2 o'clock. They abbreviate the name of the mint director, Bernardo Georgy.

Date	Mint	Assayer	F	VF	EF	Unc.
		CM *varieties:*	$25.00	$30.00	$40.00	$80.00
		8 over 7, C over R; normal date, CM over RM.				
	G^{A}	JG *varieties:*	50.00	75.00	100.00	150.00
		8 over 7; normal date.				
	GC	MP	150.00	250.00	400.00	600.00
	Ⓖ	PM *varieties:*	17.50	25.00	40.00	75.00
		8 over 7; normal date.				
	Ⓖ	PF	17.50	25.00	40.00	75.00
	M̊	GC	15.00	25.00	35.00	75.00
	P^{I}	AM *varieties:*	25.00	30.00	45.00	90.00
		8 over 7; normal date.				
	Z^{S}	OM *varieties:*	17.50	25.00	35.00	75.00
		8 over 7; normal date.				
1849	C^{A}	RG	60.00	100.00	150.00	250.00
	C	CE	65.00	100.00	150.00	250.00
	*D^{O}	CM 4 over 3	27.50	40.00	75.00	125.00
		JMR *varieties:*	200.00	300.00	400.00	600.00
		J.M.R. over CM, oval O; .JMR. normal initials, oval O; round O.				
	G^{A}	JG	90.00	115.00	150.00	250.00
	GC	MP	150.00	250.00	400.00	600.00
	Ⓖ	PF	17.50	25.00	40.00	75.00
	M̊	GC *varieties:*	15.00	25.00	35.00	75.00
		9 over 8; normal date.				
	P^{I}	AM	300.00	500.00	800.00	1,250
		PS *varieties:*	500.00	800.00	1,200	2,000
		9 over 8, PS over AM; normal date, PS over AM.				
		MC *varieties:*	60.00	100.00	200.00	350.00
		MC over PS; normal initials.				
	Z^{S}	OM	17.50	25.00	35.00	75.00
1850	C^{A}	RG *varieties:*	20.00	30.00	45.00	90.00
		5 over 4; normal date.				
	C	CE	65.00	100.00	150.00	250.00
	D^{O}	J.M.R.	120.00	175.00	225.00	350.00
	G^{A}	JG	40.00	100.00	150.00	250.00
	GC	MP	150.00	250.00	400.00	600.00
	Ⓖ	PF	17.50	25.00	40.00	75.00
	M̊	GC *varieties:*	15.00	25.00	35.00	75.00
		5 over 4; 50 over 49; normal date.				
	P^{I}	MC	50.00	80.00	150.00	250.00
	Z^{S}	OM	17.50	25.00	35.00	75.00
1851	C^{A}	RG *varieties:*	50.00	75.00	100.00	200.00
		5 over 4; normal date.				
	C	CE	125.00	200.00	300.00	450.00
	D^{O}	JMR *varieties:*	85.00	140.00	190.00	325.00
		1 over 0; normal date.				
	G^{A}	JG	200.00	300.00	450.00	700.00
	GC	MP	500.00	700.00	900.00	1,250
	Ⓖ	PF *varieties:*	17.50	25.00	40.00	75.00
		1 over 0; normal date.				
	M̊	GC	15.00	25.00	35.00	75.00
	P^{I}	MC	125.00	200.00	300.00	500.00
	Z^{S}	OM	17.50	25.00	35.00	75.00

Date	Mint	Assayer	F	VF	EF	Unc.
1852	C^A	RG 5 over 4..................	$70.00	$100.00	$125.00	$250.00
	C	CE 2 over 1..................	75.00	100.00	150.00	225.00
	D^O	JMR........................	200.00	300.00	400.00	600.00
		CP over JMR...............	700.00	1,000	1,500	2,250
	G^A	JG..........................	100.00	150.00	200.00	300.00
	GC	MP.........................	650.00	1,000	1,500	2,000
	G̃	PF *varieties:*..................	17.50	25.00	40.00	75.00
		2 over 1; normal date.				
	M̊	GC..........................	15.00	25.00	35.00	75.00
	P^I	MC..........................	75.00	125.00	200.00	350.00
	Z^S	OM..........................	17.50	25.00	35.00	75.00
1853	C^A	RG 5 over 4..................	100.00	150.00	200.00	350.00
	C	CE *varieties:*..................	150.00	200.00	300.00	400.00
		3 over 0; thick rays; error: MEXIGANA.				
	D^O	CP over JMR...............	150.00	250.00	350.00	500.00
	G^A	JG *varieties:*..................	90.00	115.00	150.00	250.00
		3 over 2; normal date.				
	G̃	PF *varieties:*..................	17.50	25.00	40.00	75.00
		3 over 2; normal date.				
	M̊	GC..........................	15.00	25.00	35.00	75.00
	P^I	MC..........................	100.00	150.00	225.00	400.00
	Z^S	OM..........................	25.00	35.00	60.00	100.00
1854	C^A	RG *varieties:*..................	40.00	55.00	75.00	120.00
		5 over 4; normal date.				
	C	CE *varieties:*..................	75.00	125.00	200.00	300.00
		large Sonora type eagle, large cap; normal eagle, normal cap.				
	D^O	CP..........................	25.00	35.00	65.00	110.00
	G^A	JG *varieties:*..................	50.00	70.00	90.00	150.00
		4 over 3; normal date.				
	G̃	PF..........................	17.50	25.00	40.00	75.00
	M̊	GC..........................	15.00	25.00	35.00	75.00
	P^I	MC..........................	100.00	150.00	250.00	350.00
	Z^S	OM..........................	17.50	25.00	35.00	75.00
1855	C^A	RG *varieties:*..................	50.00	75.00	100.00	200.00
		first 5 over 4; normal date.				
	C	CE *varieties:*..................	30.00	45.00	60.00	120.00
		second 5 over 6; normal date.				
	D^O	CP..........................	75.00	125.00	200.00	300.00
	G^A	JG second 5 over 4............	50.00	70.00	95.00	155.00
	G̃	PF *varieties:*..................	17.50	25.00	40.00	75.00
		large letters; small letters.				
	M̊	GC..........................	25.00	35.00	65.00	120.00
		GF *varieties:*..................	12.00	15.00	20.00	55.00
		F over C; normal initials.				
	P^I	MC..........................	150.00	200.00	300.00	400.00
	Z^S	OM..........................	25.00	30.00	50.00	90.00
		MO..........................	30.00	50.00	75.00	125.00
1856	C^A	RG 56 over 45................	90.00	120.00	150.00	225.00
		JC 6 over 5..................	600.00	1,000	1,250	1,750
	C	CE..........................	25.00	30.00	50.00	100.00
	D^O	CP..........................	100.00	125.00	200.00	300.00
	G^A	JG *varieties:*..................	60.00	80.00	100.00	160.00
		6 over 4; normal date.				

Date	Mint	Assayer	F	VF	EF	Unc.
	G̊	PF *varieties:*	$17.50	$25.00	$40.00	$75.00
		6 over 5; normal date.				
	M̊	GF *varieties:*	12.00	15.00	20.00	55.00
		6 over 4; 6 over 5; normal date.				
	Pᴵ	MC	100.00	150.00	225.00	400.00
	Zˢ	MO *varieties:*	17.50	25.00	35.00	75.00
		6 over 5; normal date.				
1857	Cᴬ	JC *varieties:*	20.00	30.00	50.00	120.00
		JC over RG; normal initials.				
	C	CE	17.50	25.00	40.00	75.00
	Dᴼ	CP	36.00	50.00	75.00	150.00
	Gᴬ	JG	25.00	32.50	45.00	85.00
	G̊	PF *varieties:*	17.50	25.00	40.00	75.00
		7 over 5; 7 over 6; normal date.				
	M̊	GF	12.00	15.00	20.00	55.00
	Pᴵ	MC	250.00	400.00	600.00	900.00
		PS *varieties:*	150.00	250.00	350.00	500.00
		PS over MC; normal initials.				
	Zˢ	MO *varieties:*	17.50	25.00	35.00	75.00
		7 over 5; normal date.				
1858	Cᴬ	JC	25.00	30.00	45.00	90.00
		BA	600.00	1,000	1,250	1,750
	C	CE	17.50	30.00	45.00	85.00
	Dᴼ	CP *varieties:*	25.00	30.00	50.00	100.00
		8 over 7; norm al date.				
	Gᴬ	JG	100.00	150.00	200.00	300.00
	G̊	PF	17.50	25.00	40.00	75.00
	M̊	FH	12.00	15.00	20.00	55.00
	O	AE	1,000	1,500	2,000	3,000
	O̵	AE	1,250	2,000	3,000	4,000
	Pᴵ	MC over PS	250.00	400.00	600.00	900.00
		PS	800.00	1,200	1,600	2,250
	Zˢ	MO *varieties:*	17.50	25.00	35.00	75.00
		8 over 7; normal date.				
1859	Cᴬ	JC	20.00	30.00	45.00	90.00
	C	CE	17.50	25.00	40.00	75.00
	Dᴼ	CP	25.00	30.00	50.00	100.00
	Gᴬ	JG *varieties:*	17.50	25.00	40.00	75.00
		9 over 7; 9 over 8; normal date.				
	G̊	PF *varieties:*	17.50	25.00	40.00	75.00
		9 over 7; 9 over 8; normal date.				
	M̊	FH	12.00	15.00	20.00	55.00
	O̵	AE	400.00	650.00	1,000	1,750
	Pᴵ	MC over PS, 9 over 8	1,250	1,800	2,650	3,150
		PS *varieties:*	1,200	1,750	2,500	3,000
		S over C; normal initials.				
	Zˢ	MO *varieties:*	17.50	25.00	35.00	75.00
		9 over 8; normal date.				
	Zˢ	VL *varieties:*	17.50	25.00	40.00	75.00
		VL over MO; normal initials.				
1860	Cᴬ	JC	20.00	30.00	60.00	175.00

Date	Mint	Assayer		F	VF	EF	Unc.
	C	CE.........................		$20.00	$30.00	$45.00	$80.00
		PV *varieties:*...............		45.00	60.00	80.00	150.00
		P over C, 0 over 9; normal date and initials.					
	D^O	CP *varieties:*...............		25.00	30.00	50.00	100.00
		60 over 59; normal date.					
	G^A	JG *varieties:*.................		300.00	500.00	700.00	1,000
		normal obverse; dot in loop of eagle's tail.*					
	G̊	PF *varieties:*................		12.00	15.00	20.00	50.00
		60 over 59; 6 over 5; normal date.					
	M̊	FH *varieties:*...............		12.00	15.00	20.00	55.00
		60 over 59; normal date.					
		TH.........................		12.00	15.00	20.00	55.00
	Ⓞ	AE.........................		200.00	400.00	700.00	1,250
	P^I	PS.........................		400.00	600.00	800.00	1,200
		MC.........................		600.00	1,000	1,500	2,000
	Z^S	MO *varieties:*...............		12.00	15.00	20.00	60.00
		60 over 59; normal date.					
		VL *varieties:*...............		12.00	15.00	20.00	60.00
		VL over MO; normal initials.					
1861	C^A	JC.........................		20.00	30.00	45.00	90.00

1861 Culiacán,
1 over 0

	C	PV over CE.................		90.00	150.00	225.00	325.00
		CE *varieties:*...............		17.50	30.00	45.00	80.00
		1 over 0; normal date.					
	D^O	CP.........................		25.00	30.00	50.00	100.00
	G^A	JG.........................		2,000	3,000	3,500	4,500
	G̊	PF *varieties:*...............		12.00	15.00	20.00	50.00
		6 over 5; 1 over 0; normal date.					
	H^O	FM reeded edge..............		800.00	1,200	1,800	2,500
	M̊	TH.........................		12.00	15.00	20.00	55.00
		CH.........................		12.00	15.00	20.00	55.00
	O	FR.........................		200.00	350.00	500.00	750.00
	Ⓞ	FR.........................		200.00	350.00	500.00	750.00
	P^I	PS.........................		20.00	25.00	35.00	90.00
		RO.........................		25.00	30.00	45.00	85.00
	Z^S	VL *varieties:*...............		12.00	15.00	20.00	60.00
		1 over 0, VL over MO; normal date and initials.					
1862	C^A	JC.........................		20.00	30.00	45.00	90.00
	C	CE.........................		17.50	25.00	40.00	75.00
	D^O	CP *varieties:*...............		25.00	40.00	60.00	100.00
		2 over 1; normal date.					
	G^A	JG.........................		1,200	2,000	2,500	3,500

*A secret mark, identifying an issue of base alloy. See Carlos Guzmán y Guzmán, "La moneda espuria de G^A del año de 1860," in *Boletín de la Sociedad numismática de México* vol. 3, no. 24 (July-Sept. 1959), pp. 56-59.

Date	Mint	Assayer	F	VF	EF	Unc.
	Ǥ	YE *varieties:*	$12.00	$15.00	$20.00	$50.00
		YE over PF; normal initials.				
		YF *varieties:*	12.00	15.00	20.00	50.00
		Y over P; normal initials.				
	H^O	FM *varieties:*	300.00	500.00	750.00	1,250
		normal edge; reeded edge.				
	Ṁ	CH	12.00	15.00	20.00	55.00
	O	FR	45.00	75.00	125.00	225.00
	⊚	FR	60.00	80.00	100.00	175.00
	P^I	RO *varieties:*	17.50	25.00	35.00	75.00
		2 over 1; normal date; oval O in RO; round O, 6 is inverted 9.				
	Z^S	VL *varieties:*	12.00	15.00	20.00	60.00
		2 over 1; normal date.				
1863	C^E	ML *varieties:*	375.00	625.00	1,000	2,250
		C^{E}ML over P^{I}MC; normal mint mark and initials.				
	C^A	JC	25.00	35.00	60.00	120.00
	C	CE	17.50	25.00	40.00	85.00
	D^O	CP *varieties:*	25.00	50.00	60.00	150.00
		3 over 2; normal date.				
	G^A	JG *varieties:*	40.00	45.00	75.00	125.00
		63 over 59; 3 over 2; 3 over 4; normal date.				
		FV	300.00	400.00	550.00	800.00
	Ǥ	YF *varieties:*	12.00	15.00	20.00	50.00
		6 over 5; normal date.				
	H^O	FM	300.00	500.00	700.00	1,000
	Ṁ	CH *varieties:*	12.00	15.00	20.00	55.00
		C over T; normal initials.				
		TH	12.00	15.00	20.00	55.00
	O	FR	27.50	40.00	60.00	100.00
		AE	27.50	40.00	60.00	100.00
	⊚	AE	100.00	150.00	250.00	400.00
	$\overset{A}{O}$	AE	1,000	1,750	2,500	3,500
	P^I	RO *varieties:*	20.00	25.00	35.00	100.00
		6 over inverted 6; 3 over 2; normal date.				
		FC	1,000	2,000	3,000	4,000
	Z^S	VL	12.00	15.00	20.00	60.00
		MO	12.00	15.00	20.00	60.00
1864	A	PG	500.00	700.00	900.00	1,500
	C^A	JC	35.00	50.00	65.00	125.00
	C	CE	17.50	25.00	40.00	80.00
	D^O	CP	50.00	75.00	100.00	150.00
		LT	25.00	40.00	60.00	120.00
	Ħ	FM	400.00	600.00	900.00	1,200
		PR	600.00	900.00	1,200	1,800
	O	FR	27.50	40.00	60.00	100.00
	P^I	RO	1,000	2,000	3,000	4,000
	Z^S	VL *varieties:*	12.00	15.00	20.00	60.00
		4 over 3; normal date.				
	Z^S	MO	12.00	15.00	20.00	60.00
1865	A	PG	400.00	600.00	800.00	1,200
	C^A	JC	150.00	200.00	350.00	500.00
		FP	750.00	1,250	1,500	2,000
	C	CE	200.00	350.00	500.00	750.00

Date	Mint	Assayer	F	VF	EF	Unc.
	D^O	LT..........................	$750.00	$1,000	$1,500	$2,000
	H̥	FM.........................	300.00	500.00	750.00	1,000
	Z^S	MO *varieties*:................	150.00	300.00	450.00	650.00
		5 over 4; normal date.				
1866	A	PG...........................	1,000	1,500	2,000	3,000
		DL...........................	1,000	1,250	1,750	2,500
	C^A	JC...........................	600.00	1,000	1,200	1,750
		FP...........................	1,000	1,500	2,500	3,250
		JG...........................	800.00	1,250	1,650	2,250
	C	CE...........................	750.00	1,200	2,500	3,500
	D^O	CM...........................	1,200	2,000	2,500	3,500
	H̥	FM...........................	750.00	1,250	2,000	2,750
		MP...........................	1,250	1,700	2,500	3,500
	(Z^S VL is a contemporary counterfeit.)			Contemporary counterfeit		
1867	A	DL...........................	700.00	1,000	1,500	2,000
	C^A	JG...........................	125.00	200.00	250.00	350.00
	C	CE...........................	150.00	200.00	350.00	500.00
	D^O	CP *varieties*:...............	25.00	30.00	45.00	90.00
		P over M; CP over LT.				
		CM...........................	25.00	30.00	40.00	80.00
	G^A	JM...........................	300.00	500.00	700.00	1,000
	G̶	YF *varieties*:...............	12.00	15.00	20.00	50.00
		6 over 5; normal date.				
	H̥	PR...........................	100.00	150.00	200.00	300.00
	M̥	CH...........................	12.00	15.00	20.00	55.00
	O	AE...........................	40.00	75.00	125.00	175.00
	P^I	CA...........................	500.00	800.00	1,200	2,000
		LR...........................	400.00	700.00	1,200	2,000
		PS...........................	60.00	100.00	150.00	300.00
	Z^S	JS...........................	800.00	1,200	1,800	2,500
1868	A	DL...........................	60.00	100.00	125.00	200.00
	C^A	JG...........................	100.00	150.00	200.00	300.00
		MM...........................	65.00	100.00	125.00	175.00
	C	CE *varieties*:...............	17.50	25.00	40.00	80.00
		8 over 7; normal date.				
	D^O	CP...........................	25.00	30.00	45.00	80.00
	G^A	JM *varieties*:...............	37.50	55.00	70.00	130.00
		8 over 7; normal date.				
	G̶	YF *varieties*:...............	12.00	15.00	20.00	50.00
		6 over 5; normal date.				
	H̥	PR...........................	25.00	30.00	45.00	85.00
	M̥	CH...........................	12.00	15.00	20.00	55.00
		PH...........................	12.00	15.00	20.00	55.00
	O	AE...........................	40.00	55.00	75.00	100.00
	P^I	PS *varieties*:...............	20.00	30.00	45.00	100.00
		8 over 7; normal date.				
	Z^S	JS...........................	12.00	15.00	20.00	50.00
		YH...........................	12.00	15.00	20.00	50.00

For the 1 Peso series of 1869-1873, see Chapter 5.

1869	A	DL...........................	60.00	100.00	125.00	200.00
	C^A	MM...........................	17.50	25.00	40.00	85.00
	C	CE...........................	25.00	35.00	50.00	85.00

Date	Mint	Assayer	Quantity Minted	F	VF	EF	Unc.
	D^O	CP		$25.00	$30.00	$40.00	$80.00
	G^A	JM		50.00	70.00	90.00	150.00
		IC		100.00	150.00	200.00	350.00
	H̊	PR		55.00	75.00	100.00	165.00
	M̊	CH		12.00	15.00	20.00	55.00
	O	AE		40.00	75.00	100.00	150.00
	P^I	PS *varieties:*		17.50	25.00	40.00	80.00
		9 over 8; normal date.					
	Z^S	YH		12.00	15.00	20.00	50.00
1870	A	DL		40.00	65.00	100.00	200.00
	C^A	MM		17.50	22.00	40.00	80.00
	C	CE		30.00	45.00	65.00	120.00
	D^O	CP *varieties:*		25.00	35.00	60.00	100.00
		70 over 69; 0 over 9; normal date.					
	G^A	IC 7 over 6		55.00	80.00	100.00	165.00
	G	YF		600.00	1,200	1,600	2,250
		FR *varieties:*		12.00	15.00	20.00	50.00
		7 over 6; normal date, FR over YF; normal date and initials.					
	H̊	PR		50.00	75.00	125.00	200.00
	O^A	AE		—	—	Rare	—
	P^I	PS		850.00	1,250	1,800	2,500
	Z^S	YH		—	—	Rare	—
1871	A	DL		20.00	30.00	45.00	125.00
	C^A	MM *varieties:*		17.50	30.00	40.00	85.00
		first M over inverted M; 1 over 0; normal date.					
	H̊	PR *varieties:*		30.00	50.00	75.00	150.00
		1 over 0; normal date.					
	P^I	JS		—	—	Rare	—
1872	A	AM		30.00	50.00	75.00	200.00
	H̊	PR *varieties:*		30.00	50.00	75.00	150.00
		2 over 1; normal date.					
1873	A	AM	508,730	20.00	30.00	50.00	200.00
	C^A	MM *varieties:*		20.00	25.00	35.00	75.00
		7 over retrograde 7; normal date.					
	C	MP		25.00	35.00	55.00	90.00
	D^O	CP		125.00	200.00	300.00	450.00
		CM		40.00	60.00	100.00	170.00
	G^A	IC		25.00	35.00	55.00	100.00
	G^O	FR		12.00	15.00	20.00	50.00
	H̊	PR	350,977	35.00	50.00	100.00	135.00
	M̊	MH *varieties:*		12.00	15.00	20.00	55.00
		M over H; normal initials.					
	O^A	AE		250.00	350.00	500.00	1,000
	P^I	MH		12.00	15.00	20.00	75.00
	Z^S	YH		12.00	15.00	20.00	50.00
1874	A	DL		15.00	20.00	30.00	125.00
	C^A	MM		12.00	15.00	20.00	50.00
	C	MP (Culiacán)		17.50	25.00	40.00	75.00
	C^N	MP (Culiacán)		125.00	200.00	300.00	450.00
	D^O	CM *varieties:*		12.00	15.00	20.00	60.00
		4 over 3; normal date.					
		JH		500.00	750.00	1,000	1,250
	G^A	IC		12.00	15.00	20.00	60.00
		MC		25.00	35.00	55.00	85.00

Silver 8 Reales

1874 Guanajuato,
4 over 3

Date	Mint	Assayer	Quantity Minted	F	VF	EF	Unc.
	G^O	FR *varieties:*		$12.00	$15.00	$20.00	$50.00
		4 over 3; normal date.					
	H̊	PR		20.00	30.00	45.00	100.00
	M̊	MH *varieties:*		12.00	15.00	20.00	55.00
		74 over 69; normal date.					
	M̊	BH *varieties:*		12.00	15.00	20.00	55.00
		BH over MM; B over M; normal initials.					
	O^A	AE 141,641		20.00	30.00	40.00	100.00
	P^I	MH *varieties:*		12.00	15.00	20.00	75.00
		4 over 3; normal date.					
	Z^S	YH		12.00	15.00	20.00	50.00
		JA *varieties:*		12.00	15.00	20.00	50.00
		J over Y; normal initials.					
1875	A	DL (Alamos)		15.00	20.00	30.00	125.00
	A^S	DL (Alamos)		15.00	20.00	30.00	125.00
	C^A	MM		12.00	15.00	20.00	50.00
	C^N	MP		12.00	15.00	20.00	50.00
	D^O	CM		12.00	15.00	20.00	60.00
		JH		125.00	200.00	300.00	400.00
	G^A	IC		17.50	25.00	40.00	75.00
		MC		12.00	15.00	20.00	60.00
	G^O	FR *varieties:*		12.00	15.00	20.00	50.00
		5 over 6; normal date.					
	H̊	PR		20.00	30.00	45.00	100.00
	M̊	BH		12.00	15.00	20.00	55.00
	O^A	AE *varieties:* 130,790		20.00	30.00	40.00	100.00
		5 over 4; normal date.					
	P^I	MH		12.00	15.00	20.00	75.00
	Z^S	JA		12.00	15.00	20.00	50.00
1876	A^S	DL		15.00	20.00	30.00	125.00
	C^A	MM		12.00	15.00	20.00	50.00
	C^N	GP		12.00	15.00	20.00	50.00
		CG		12.00	15.00	20.00	50.00
	D^O	CM		12.00	15.00	20.00	60.00
	G^A	IC		17.50	25.00	40.00	75.00
		MC .... } 559,460		125.00	175.00	250.00	350.00
	G^O	FR		12.00	15.00	20.00	50.00
	H̊	AF		20.00	30.00	45.00	100.00
	M̊	BH *varieties:*		12.00	15.00	20.00	55.00
		6 over 4; 6 over 5; normal date.					
	O^A	AE 139,878		20.00	30.00	40.00	100.00
	P^I	MH *varieties:*		12.00	15.00	20.00	75.00
		6 over 5; normal date.					
	Z^S	JA		12.00	15.00	20.00	50.00
		JS		12.00	15.00	20.00	50.00
1877	A^S	DL 515,425		15.00	20.00	30.00	125.00

Date	Mint	Assayer	Quantity Minted	F	VF	EF	Unc.
	C^A	EA	} 471,584	$12.00	$15.00	$20.00	$50.00
		GR		27.50	40.00	60.00	100.00
		JM		12.00	15.00	20.00	50.00
		AV		150.00	250.00	350.00	600.00
	C^N	CG varieties:	338,700	12.00	15.00	20.00	50.00

normal mint mark; error: mint mark G^N.

Date	Mint	Assayer	Quantity Minted	F	VF	EF	Unc.
		JA	incl. above	25.00	40.00	60.00	110.00
	D^O	CM	} 431,245	800.00	1,200	1,600	2,500
		CP		12.00	15.00	20.00	60.00
		JMP		700.00	1,000	1,300	1,750
	G^A	IC	} 928,048	12.00	15.00	20.00	50.00
		JA		12.00	15.00	20.00	50.00
	G^O	FR	2,477,000	12.00	15.00	20.00	50.00
	H̊	AF	} 409,832	20.00	30.00	45.00	100.00
		GR		55.00	70.00	100.00	165.00
		JA		25.00	35.00	45.00	90.00
	Ṁ	MH varieties:	898,000	12.00	15.00	20.00	55.00

M over B; normal initials.

Date	Mint	Assayer	Quantity Minted	F	VF	EF	Unc.
	O^A	AE	138,854	20.00	30.00	40.00	100.00
	P^I	MH	1,017,940	12.00	15.00	20.00	75.00
	Z^S	JS	2,700,000	12.00	15.00	20.00	50.00
1878	A^S	DL	512,886	15.00	20.00	30.00	125.00
	C^A	AV	438,922	12.00	15.00	20.00	50.00
	C^N	CG	483,235	20.00	25.00	35.00	90.00
		JD varieties:	incl. above	12.00	15.00	20.00	50.00

D over retrograde D; normal initials.

Date	Mint	Assayer	Quantity Minted	F	VF	EF	Unc.
	D^O	PE	} 409,347	20.00	35.00	50.00	100.00
		TB		12.00	15.00	20.00	60.00
	G^A	JA	764,455	12.00	15.00	20.00	50.00
	G^O	FR varieties:	2,273,000	12.00	15.00	20.00	50.00

8 over 7; normal date.

Date	Mint	Assayer	Quantity Minted	F	VF	EF	Unc.
		SM varieties:	incl. above	12.00	15.00	20.00	50.00

8 over 7; normal date; S over F

Date	Mint	Assayer	Quantity Minted	F	VF	EF	Unc.
	H̊	JA	450,777	17.50	25.00	40.00	75.00
	Ṁ	MH	2,154,000	12.00	15.00	20.00	50.00
	O^A	AE	124,675	20.00	30.00	40.00	100.00
	P^I	MH	1,045,875	12.00	15.00	20.00	75.00
	Z^S	JS	2,310,000	12.00	15.00	20.00	50.00
1879	A^S	DL		20.00	30.00	60.00	150.00
		ML		20.00	30.00	60.00	150.00
	C^A	AV		12.00	15.00	20.00	50.00
	C^N	JD		12.00	15.00	20.00	50.00
	D^O	TB		12.00	15.00	20.00	60.00
	G^A	JA		12.00	15.00	20.00	50.00
	G^O	SM varieties:		12.00	15.00	20.00	50.00

9 over 7; 9 over 8; normal date; SM over FR with 9 over 8 and normal date.

Date	Mint	Assayer	Quantity Minted	F	VF	EF	Unc.
	H̊	JA		17.50	25.00	40.00	75.00

1879 Mexico,
9 over 8

Date	Mint	Assayer	Quantity Minted	F	VF	EF	Unc.
	M̊	MH *varieties:*		$12.00	$15.00	$20.00	$50.00
		9 over 8; normal date.					
	Oᴬ	AE	153,000	20.00	30.00	40.00	100.00
	Pᴵ	MH *varieties:*		12.00	15.00	20.00	75.00
		9 over 8; normal date.					
		BE		30.00	50.00	75.00	150.00
		MR		40.00	60.00	100.00	200.00
	Zˢ	JS *varieties:*		12.00	15.00	20.00	50.00
		9 over 8; normal date.					
1880	Aˢ	ML		12.00	15.00	20.00	100.00
	Cᴬ	AV		200.00	300.00	400.00	600.00
		PM		400.00	700.00	900.00	1,200
		MG *varieties:*		12.00	15.00	20.00	50.00
		normal initials; tall initials.					
		MM		15.00	20.00	25.00	75.00
	Cᴺ	JD second 8 over 7		15.00	18.50	25.00	60.00
	Dᴼ	TB *varieties:*		13.50	16.50	22.50	65.00
		TB over JP, 8 over 7; second 8 over 7; normal date.					
		JP *varieties:*		12.00	15.00	20.00	60.00
		second 8 over 7; normal date.					
	Gᴬ	JA		12.00	15.00	20.00	50.00
		FS *varieties:*		12.00	15.00	20.00	50.00
		second 8 over 7; normal date.					
	Gᴼ	SB *varieties:*		12.00	15.00	20.00	50.00
		second 8 over 7; normal date, B over M.					
	H̊	JA		17.50	25.00	40.00	75.00
	M̊	MH *varieties:*		12.00	15.00	20.00	50.00
		80 over 79; normal date.					
	Oᴬ	AE	143,060	20.00	30.00	40.00	100.00
	Pᴵ	MR		300.00	500.00	750.00	1,200
		MH		12.00	15.00	20.00	75.00
	Zˢ	JS		12.00	15.00	20.00	50.00
1881	Aˢ	ML	966,327	12.00	15.00	20.00	100.00
	Cᴬ	MG	1,084,661	12.00	15.00	20.00	50.00
	C	JD (Culiacán)	1,032,071	12.00	15.00	20.00	50.00
	Cᴺ	JD *varieties:* incl. above		50.00	75.00	100.00	150.00
		1 over 0; normal date.					
	Dᴼ	JP	927,903	12.00	15.00	20.00	60.00
	Gᴬ	FS	1,300,214	12.00	15.00	20.00	50.00
	Gᴼ	SB *varieties:*	3,974,000	12.00	15.00	20.00	50.00
		second 8 over 7; 1 over 0; normal date.					
	H̊	JA	585,767	17.50	25.00	40.00	75.00
	M̊	MH	5,712,000	12.00	15.00	20.00	50.00
	Oᴬ	AE	133,545	20.00	30.00	40.00	100.00
	Pᴵ	MH	2,099,700	12.00	15.00	20.00	75.00
	Zˢ	JS	5,591,500	12.00	15.00	20.00	50.00
1882	Aˢ	ML	*480,164*	12.00	15.00	20.00	100.00
	Cᴬ	MG	*779,049*	12.00	15.00	20.00	50.00
		MM *varieties:* incl. above		12.00	15.00	20.00	50.00
		normal initials; second M over M̄.					

1882 Chihuahua,
second M over Ɯ

Date	Mint	Assayer	Quantity Minted	F	VF	EF	Unc.
	C^N	JD	⎫396,709	$12.00	$15.00	$20.00	$50.00
		AM	⎭	12.00	15.00	20.00	50.00
	D^O	JP	414,266	12.00	15.00	20.00	60.00
		MC *varieties:* incl. above		27.50	40.00	70.00	110.00
		MC over JP; normal initials.					
	G^A	FS *varieties:* 537,071		12.00	15.00	20.00	50.00
		2 over 1; normal date.					
		TB *varieties:* incl. above		60.00	100.00	150.00	225.00
		TB over FS; normal initials.					
	G^O	SB	2,015,000	12.00	15.00	20.00	50.00
	H̊	JA	⎫239,510	25.00	40.00	70.00	125.00
	H^O	JA	⎭	25.00	40.00	70.00	125.00
	M̊	MH *varieties:* 2,746,000		12.00	15.00	20.00	50.00
		2 over 1; normal date.					
	O^A	AE	99,950	25.00	40.00	60.00	125.00
	P^I	MH *varieties:* 1,602,000		12.00	15.00	20.00	75.00
		2 over 1; normal date.					

Straight J   Full J

Date	Mint	Assayer	Quantity Minted	F	VF	EF	Unc.
	Z^S	JS *varieties:* 2,484,600		12.00	15.00	20.00	50.00
		2 over 1; normal date; straight J; full J.					
1883	A^S	ML	464,345	12.00	15.00	20.00	100.00
	C^A	MM *varieties:* 817,833		12.00	15.00	20.00	50.00
		3 over M; normal date.					
	C^N	AM	333,192	12.00	15.00	20.00	50.00
	D^O	MC *varieties:* 451,798		12.00	15.00	20.00	60.00
		second 8 over 7; normal date.					
	G^A	TB	561,000	60.00	100.00	150.00	225.00
	G^O	SB	2,100,000	40.00	75.00	125.00	200.00
		BR *varieties:* incl. above		12.00	15.00	20.00	50.00
		B over S; BR over SB; normal initials.					
	H^O	JA *varieties:* 204,200		200.00	350.00	500.00	750.00
		3 over 2; normal date.					
		FM/JA, 3/2 incl. above		25.00	35.00	50.00	85.00

Date	Mint	Assayer	Quantity Minted	F	VF	EF	Unc.
	$\overset{\circ}{\text{M}}$	MH *varieties:*	2,726,000	$12.00	$15.00	$20.00	$50.00
		3 over 2; normal date.					
	O^A	AE	121,950	20.00	30.00	40.00	125.00
	P^I	MH	1,545,000	12.00	15.00	20.00	75.00
	Z^S	JS *varieties:*	2,563,200	12.00	15.00	20.00	50.00
		3 over 2; normal date.					
1884	A^S	ML		12.00	15.00	20.00	100.00

1884 over 3 C^A

Date	Mint	Assayer	Quantity Minted	F	VF	EF	Unc.
	C^A	MM *varieties:*		12.00	15.00	20.00	50.00
		4 over 3; normal date.					
	C^N	AM		12.00	15.00	20.00	50.00
	D^O	MC *varieties:*		12.00	15.00	20.00	60.00
		4 over 3; normal date.					
	G^A	TB		12.00	15.00	20.00	50.00
		AH		12.00	15.00	20.00	50.00
	G^O	BR *varieties:*		12.00	15.00	20.00	50.00
		84 over 73; 4 over 3; normal date.					
		RR *varieties:*		12.00	15.00	20.00	50.00
		8 over 7; normal date.					
	$\overset{\circ}{\text{H}}$	FM *varieties:*		15.00	20.00	25.00	75.00
		4 over 3; normal date.					
	$\overset{\circ}{\text{M}}$	MH *varieties:*		12.00	15.00	20.00	50.00
		4 over 3; normal date.					
	O^A	AE	142,450	17.50	35.00	60.00	100.00
	P^I	MH *varieties:*		12.00	15.00	20.00	75.00
		4 over 3; H over M; normal date and initials.					
	Z^S	JS		12.00	15.00	20.00	50.00
1885	A^S	ML	279,704	12.00	15.00	20.00	100.00
	C^A	MM *varieties:*	1,344,990	12.00	15.00	20.00	50.00
		5 over 4; 5 over 6; normal date.					

1885 Culiacán, mint mark G^N

Date	Mint	Assayer	Quantity Minted	F	VF	EF	Unc.
	C	AM (Culiacán)	227,442	125.00	200.00	300.00	450.00
	C^N	AM (Culiacán)					
		varieties: incl. above		12.00	15.00	20.00	50.00
		5 over 6; normal date.					
	G^N	AM (Culiacán - error) incl. above		60.00	100.00	150.00	300.00
	D^O	MC ⎫	547,410	12.00	15.00	20.00	60.00
		JB ⎭		40.00	60.00	80.00	120.00
	G^A	AH ⎫	443,007	12.00	15.00	20.00	50.00
		JS ⎭		17.50	25.00	40.00	75.00

Date	Mint	Assayer	Quantity Minted	F	VF	EF	Unc.
	G^O	RR *varieties:*	2,363,000	$12.00	$15.00	$20.00	$50.00
		second 8 over 7; 85 over 74; normal date.					
	H̊	FM	3,649,000	15.00	20.00	25.00	75.00
	M̊	MH	132,060	20.00	30.00	40.00	100.00
	O^A	AE	157,500	20.00	30.00	40.00	100.00
	P^I	MH *varieties:*	1,736,000	12.00	15.00	20.00	75.00
		5 over 4; 5 over 8; normal date.					
	P^I	LC		15.00	20.00	25.00	100.00
	Z^S	JS	2,252,000	12.00	15.00	20.00	50.00
1886	A^S	ML	857,439	12.00	15.00	20.00	100.00
	C^A	MM	2,482,979	12.00	15.00	20.00	50.00
	C^N	AM	570,510	12.00	15.00	20.00	50.00
	D^O	MC *varieties:*	954,916	12.00	15.00	20.00	60.00
		6 over 3; normal date.					
	G^A	JS	1,039,067	12.00	15.00	20.00	50.00
	G^O	RR *varieties:*	4,127,000	12.00	15.00	20.00	50.00
		86 over 75; second 8 over 7; normal date.					
	H^O	FM ⎱	224,900	25.00	35.00	50.00	100.00
		FG ⎰		15.00	20.00	25.00	90.00
	M̊	MH	7,558,000	12.00	15.00	20.00	50.00
	O^A	AE	120,200	20.00	30.00	40.00	100.00
	P^I	LC ⎱	3,346,500	12.00	15.00	20.00	75.00
		MR ⎰		12.00	15.00	20.00	75.00
	Z^S	JS *varieties:*	5,303,300	12.00	15.00	20.00	50.00
		6 over 8; 6 over 5; normal date.					
		FZ	incl. above	12.00	15.00	20.00	50.00
1887	A^S	ML	650,041	12.00	15.00	20.00	100.00
	C^A	MM	2,624,835	12.00	15.00	20.00	50.00
	C^N	AM	731,902	12.00	15.00	20.00	50.00
	D^O	MC	1,004,123	12.00	15.00	20.00	60.00
	G^A	JS	877,628	12.00	15.00	20.00	50.00
	G^O	RR	4,205,000	12.00	15.00	20.00	50.00
	H^O	FG	149,900	15.00	20.00	25.00	100.00
	M̊	MH	7,681,000	12.00	15.00	20.00	50.00
	O^A	AE *varieties:*	115,400	20.00	30.00	40.00	100.00
		7 over 6; normal date.					
	P^I	MR	2,922,360	12.00	15.00	20.00	75.00
	Z^S	FZ ⎱	4,733,000	12.00	15.00	20.00	50.00
	Z	FZ (error) ⎰		30.00	50.00	70.00	125.00
1888	A^S	ML	507,650	12.00	15.00	20.00	100.00
	C^A	MM *varieties:*	2,433,864	12.00	15.00	20.00	50.00
		8 over 7; normal date.					
	C^N	AM	768,358	12.00	15.00	20.00	50.00
	D^O	MC	995,830	12.00	15.00	20.00	60.00
	G^A	JS	1,159,019	12.00	15.00	20.00	50.00
	G^O	RR	3,985,000	12.00	15.00	20.00	50.00
	H^O	FG	364,180	15.00	20.00	25.00	75.00
	M̊	MH	7,179,000	12.00	15.00	20.00	50.00
	O^A	AE	144,550	20.00	30.00	40.00	100.00
	P^I	MR	2,438,300	12.00	15.00	20.00	75.00
	Z^S	FZ *varieties:*	5,132,000	12.00	15.00	20.00	50.00
		8 over 7; normal date.					
1889	A^S	ML	426,600	12.00	15.00	20.00	100.00

Date	Mint	Assayer	Quantity Minted	F	VF	EF	Unc.
	C^A	MM	2,680,629	$12.00	$15.00	$20.00	$50.00
	C^N	AM	1,074,773	12.00	15.00	20.00	50.00
	D^O	MC	873,988	12.00	15.00	20.00	60.00
	G^A	JS	1,582,578	12.00	15.00	20.00	50.00
	G^O	RR	3,646,000	12.00	15.00	20.00	50.00
	H^O	FG	490,350	15.00	20.00	25.00	75.00
	M̥	MH	7,332,000	12.00	15.00	20.00	50.00
	O^A	AE	150,000	20.00	30.00	40.00	100.00
	P^I	MR	2,103,140	12.00	15.00	20.00	75.00
	Z^S	FZ	4,344,000	12.00	15.00	20.00	50.00
1890	A^S	ML	450,200	12.00	15.00	20.00	100.00
	C^A	MM	2,137,473	12.00	15.00	20.00	50.00
	C^N	AM	874,127	12.00	15.00	20.00	50.00
	D^O	MC	} 1,119,108	12.00	15.00	20.00	60.00
		JP		12.00	15.00	20.00	60.00
	G^A	JS	1,657,932	12.00	15.00	20.00	50.00
	G^O	RR	3,615,000	12.00	15.00	20.00	50.00
	H^O	FG	565,175	15.00	20.00	25.00	75.00
	M̥	MH	} 7,412,000	12.00	15.00	20.00	50.00
		AM		12.00	15.00	20.00	50.00
	O^A	AE	181,400	20.00	30.00	40.00	100.00
	P^I	MR	1,562,000	12.00	15.00	20.00	75.00
	Z^S	FZ	3,887,000	12.00	15.00	20.00	50.00
1891	A^S	ML	532,800	12.00	15.00	20.00	100.00
	C^A	MM *varieties:* 2,268,051 1 over 0; normal date.		12.00	15.00	20.00	50.00
	C^N	AM	777,409	12.00	15.00	20.00	50.00
	D^O	JP	1,487,333	12.00	15.00	20.00	60.00
	G^A	JS	1,507,397	12.00	15.00	20.00	50.00
	G^O	RS	3,197,000 RR is a contemporary counterfeit.		12.00	15.00	20.00	50.00
	H^O	FG	738,200	15.00	20.00	25.00	50.00
	M̥	AM	8,076,000	12.00	15.00	20.00	50.00
	O^A	EN	160,400	20.00	30.00	40.00	100.00
	P^I	MR	1,184,200	12.00	15.00	20.00	75.00
	Z^S	FZ	4,113,500	12.00	15.00	20.00	50.00
1892	A^S	ML	465,340	12.00	15.00	20.00	100.00
	C^A	MM	2,527,362	12.00	15.00	20.00	50.00
	C^N	AM	681,018	12.00	15.00	20.00	50.00
	D^O	JP	} 1,596,548	12.00	15.00	20.00	60.00
		ND		40.00	75.00	125.00	175.00
	*G^A	JS *varieties:* 1,626,752 2 over 1; normal date.			12.00	15.00	20.00	50.00
	G^O	RS	3,672,000	12.00	15.00	20.00	50.00
	H^O	FG	643,000	15.00	20.00	25.00	50.00
	M̥	AM	9,392,000	12.00	15.00	20.00	50.00
	O^A	EN	120,200	20.00	30.00	40.00	100.00
	P^I	MR	1,336,480	12.00	15.00	20.00	75.00
	Z^S	FZ *varieties:* 4,237,500 2 over 1; normal date.			12.00	15.00	20.00	50.00

*A specimen in the collection of the Chase Manhattan Bank is struck over an 1875-S U.S. Trade Dollar.

Date	Mint	Assayer	Quantity Minted	F	VF	EF	Unc.
1893	A^S	ML	734,300	$12.00	$15.00	$20.00	$100.00
	C^A	MM	2,631,564	12.00	15.00	20.00	50.00
	C^N	AM	1,143,751	12.00	15.00	20.00	50.00
	D^O	ND	1,617,436	12.00	15.00	20.00	60.00
	G^A	JS	1,952,104	12.00	15.00	20.00	50.00
	G^O	RS	3,854,000	12.00	15.00	20.00	50.00
	H^O	FG	518,100	15.00	20.00	25.00	75.00
	M̊	AM	10,773,000	12.00	15.00	20.00	50.00
	O^A	EN	66,100	45.00	75.00	125.00	200.00
	P^I	MR	530,450	12.00	15.00	20.00	75.00
	Z^S	FZ	3,872,000	12.00	15.00	20.00	50.00
1894	A^S	ML	725,000	12.00	15.00	20.00	100.00
	C^A	MM	2,641,783	12.00	15.00	20.00	50.00
	C^N	AM	2,118,240	12.00	15.00	20.00	50.00
	D^O	ND	1,537,062	12.00	15.00	20.00	60.00
	G^A	JS	2,046,109	12.00	15.00	20.00	50.00
	G^O	RS	4,127,000	12.00	15.00	20.00	50.00
	H^O	FG	504,100	15.00	20.00	25.00	75.00
	M̊	AM	12,394,000	12.00	15.00	20.00	50.00
	Z^S	FZ	3,081,400	12.00	15.00	20.00	50.00
1895	A^S	ML	476,503	12.00	15.00	20.00	100.00
	C^A	MM	1,112,254	12.00	15.00	20.00	50.00
	C^N	AM	1,834,005	12.00	15.00	20.00	50.00
	D^O	ND *varieties:* 761,339		12.00	15.00	20.00	60.00
		5 over 3; normal date.					
	G^A	JS	1,146,152	12.00	15.00	20.00	50.00
	G^O	RS *varieties:* 3,768,060		12.00	15.00	20.00	50.00
		5 over 1; 5 over 3; normal date.					
	H^O	FG	320,005	15.00	20.00	25.00	75.00
	M̊	AM	⎫ 10,474,000	12.00	15.00	20.00	50.00
		AB	⎭	12.00	15.00	20.00	50.00
	Z^S	FZ	4,717,720	12.00	15.00	20.00	50.00
1896	C^N	AM	2,134,243	12.00	15.00	20.00	50.00
	G^O	RS *varieties:* 5,229,000					
		normal legend		12.00	15.00	20.00	50.00
		*G^O 1896 RS over A^S 1891 ML		13.50	16.50	22.50	55.00
	M̊	AB	⎫ 9,327,000	12.00	15.00	20.00	50.00
		AM	⎭	12.00	15.00	20.00	50.00
	Z^S	FZ	4,226,000	12.00	15.00	20.00	50.00
1897	C^N	AM	1,580,000	12.00	15.00	20.00	50.00
	G^O	RS	4,344,000	12.00	15.00	20.00	50.00
	M̊	AM	8,621,000	12.00	15.00	20.00	50.00
	Z^S	FZ	4,877,000	12.00	15.00	20.00	50.00

---

*T. V. Buttrey, "A Rare Variety of Mexican Eight Reales," in *The Numismatist*, vol. 73 no. 9 (September 1960) pp. 1326-1327; Edward Beals, "The Guanajuato 1896/1 8 Reales," in *Plus Ultra*, vol. 5 no. 40 (Jan. 27, 1967) pp. 3-5.

GOLD ISSUES — ½ ESCUDO
Facing Eagle Type 1825-1870

The obverse of all Republican gold of the *escudo* system is identical with that of the silver: the national emblem of the eagle, perched upon the cactus in the midst of the waters of Lake Texcoco, tearing a snake with his beak and claw. The reverse, however, was designed particularly for the gold: a hand, holding the Liberty cap upon a pole, points to an open book inscribed LEY *(Law)*. Above is the inscription LA LIBERTAD EN LA LEY; below, a legend similar to that of the silver affirms the coin's denomination, mint, date, assayers' initials, and fineness.

The ½ *escudo* was valued as the equivalent of the 8 *reales*, or later the 1 peso, in silver.

Diameter 15 mm; weight 1.692 grams; composition .875 gold, .125 copper; edge: obliquely reeded.

Date Mint Assayer			VG	F	VF	EF
1825	Gᴬ	FS............................	$50.00	$70.00	$115.00	$165.00
	M̥	JM *varieties:*................	35.00	50.00	70.00	125.00
		5 over 4; normal date.				
1827	M̥	JM *varieties:*...............	35.00	50.00	70.00	125.00
		7 over 6; normal date.				
1829	Gᴬ	FS............................	42.50	60.00	90.00	150.00
	M̥	JM............................	45.00	60.00	90.00	150.00
1831	Gᴬ	FS............................	55.00	85.00	115.00	165.00
	M̥	JM *varieties:*...............	30.00	40.00	60.00	100.00
		1 over 0; normal date.				
1832	M̥	JM............................	30.00	40.00	60.00	100.00
1833	Dᴼ	RM-M over L...............	35.00	55.00	80.00	135.00
	M̥	MJ olive and oak reversed.....	35.00	45.00	70.00	125.00

1834 Durango, 4 over 3

1835 Durango, 5 over 3

1834	Dᴼ	RM 4 over 3................	35.00	65.00	85.00	125.00
	Gᴬ	FS............................	47.50	80.00	90.00	150.00
	M̥	ML...........................	35.00	45.00	70.00	125.00
1835	Dᴼ	RM 5 over 3................	38.50	60.00	90.00	150.00

Date	Mint	Assayer	VG	F	VF	EF
	Gᴬ	FS	$42.50	$70.00	$90.00	$150.00
	M̊	ML	45.00	70.00	90.00	150.00
1836	Dᴼ	RM 6 over 4	38.50	60.00	90.00	150.00
1837	Dᴼ	RM	42.50	65.00	90.00	150.00
	Gᴬ	JG	55.00	85.00	115.00	165.00
1838	Dᴼ	RM	50.00	80.00	115.00	165.00
	Gᴬ	JG	55.00	85.00	115.00	165.00
	M̊	ML	70.00	90.00	125.00	175.00
1839	Gᴬ	JG	55.00	90.00	125.00	175.00
	M̊	ML	70.00	90.00	125.00	175.00
1840	M̊	ML	30.00	40.00	60.00	100.00
1841	M̊	ML	30.00	40.00	60.00	100.00
1842	Gᴬ	JG	55.00	90.00	125.00	175.00
	M̊	ML	40.00	50.00	80.00	135.00
		MM	40.00	50.00	80.00	135.00
1843	Dᴼ	RM	50.00	80.00	115.00	165.00
	GC	MP 3 over 2	—	—	—	—
	M̊	MM	35.00	45.00	70.00	125.00
1844	Dᴼ	RM 44 over 33	55.00	90.00	125.00	180.00
	M̊	MF	30.00	40.00	60.00	100.00
1845	G	PM	35.00	45.00	70.00	125.00
	M̊	MF	30.00	40.00	60.00	100.00
1846	Dᴼ	RM	50.00	80.00	115.00	165.00
	GC	MP	55.00	75.00	90.00	150.00
	M̊	MF *varieties:*	30.00	40.00	60.00	100.00
		6 over 5; normal date.				
1847	Gᴬ	JG	55.00	90.00	125.00	175.00
	GC	MP	50.00	65.00	90.00	150.00
1848	C	CE	40.00	60.00	85.00	150.00
	Dᴼ	RM	42.50	65.00	90.00	150.00

1848 GC. MP,			1850 Dᴼ JMR,		
8 over 7,			50 over 33,		
denomination ″¹/₂ F″			denomination ″¹/₁ E″		

Date	Mint	Assayer	VG	F	VF	EF
	GC	MP 8 over 7	55.00	70.00	100.00	165.00
	M̊	GC	35.00	45.00	70.00	125.00
1849	G	PF	35.00	45.00	70.00	125.00
1850	Dᴼ	JMR 50 over 33	50.00	80.00	115.00	165.00
	Gᴬ	JG	40.00	60.00	80.00	135.00
	M̊	GC	30.00	40.00	60.00	100.00
1851	Dᴼ	JMR	55.00	90.00	125.00	175.00
	GC	MP	55.00	75.00	90.00	150.00
	G	PF	35.00	40.00	60.00	100.00
	M̊	GC	30.00	40.00	60.00	100.00

Gold ½ Escudo

Date	Mint	Assayer	VG	F	VF	EF
1852	D^O	JMR	$55.00	$90.00	$125.00	$175.00
	G^A	JG	40.00	60.00	80.00	135.00
	G̊	PF	30.00	40.00	60.00	100.00
	M̊	GC	30.00	40.00	60.00	100.00
1853	C	CE	35.00	55.00	80.00	135.00
	D^O	CP	35.00	60.00	85.00	135.00
	G̊	PF	35.00	45.00	70.00	125.00
	M̊	GC	30.00	40.00	60.00	100.00
1854	C	CE	40.00	60.00	85.00	150.00
	D^O	CP	42.50	65.00	90.00	150.00
	M̊	GC	30.00	40.00	60.00	100.00
1855	D^O	CP	35.00	55.00	80.00	135.00
	G̊	PF	40.00	50.00	80.00	135.00
	M̊	GF	30.00	40.00	60.00	100.00
1856	C	CE	60.00	100.00	150.00	250.00
	M̊	GF 6 over 4	30.00	40.00	60.00	100.00
1857	C	CE	40.00	60.00	85.00	150.00
	G̊	PF	30.00	40.00	60.00	100.00
	M̊	GF	30.00	40.00	60.00	100.00
1858	G̊	PF 8 over 7	30.00	40.00	60.00	100.00
	M̊	FH	30.00	40.00	60.00	100.00
1859	C	CE	40.00	60.00	85.00	150.00
	D^O	CP	42.50	65.00	90.00	150.00
	G^A	JG	50.00	80.00	125.00	175.00
	G̊	PF	30.00	40.00	60.00	100.00
	M̊	FH	35.00	45.00	70.00	125.00
1860	C	CE	35.00	55.00	80.00	135.00
	G^O	PF	30.00	40.00	60.00	100.00
	M̊	FH 60 over 59	35.00	45.00	70.00	125.00
	Z^S	VL	35.00	50.00	70.00	125.00
1861	D^O	CP	40.00	60.00	85.00	135.00
	G^A	JG	35.00	55.00	80.00	135.00
	G^O	PF	30.00	40.00	60.00	100.00
	M̊	CH, C over F	40.00	50.00	80.00	135.00
1862	C	CE	30.00	50.00	70.00	125.00
	G^O	YE 2 over 1	32.50	45.00	65.00	110.00
	M̊	CH	35.00	45.00	70.00	125.00
	Z^S	VL *varieties:*	30.00	40.00	60.00	100.00
		2 over 1; normal date.				
1863	C	CE	30.00	50.00	70.00	125.00
	G^O	YF	30.00	40.00	60.00	100.00
	M̊	CH 63 over 57, CH over GF	30.00	40.00	60.00	100.00
1864	D^O	LT	55.00	85.00	125.00	175.00
1866	C	CE	45.00	75.00	100.00	150.00
1867	C	CE	35.00	55.00	75.00	125.00
1868	M̊	PH 6 over 5	50.00	70.00	90.00	150.00
1869	M̊	CH 6 over 5	50.00	70.00	90.00	150.00
1870	C	CE	—	—	—	—

1 ESCUDO
Facing Eagle Type 1825-1870

In appearance the 1 *escudo* is similar in all respects to the ½ *escudo*. It exchanged for two pesos, or sixteen *reales* in silver.

Diameter 18 mm; weight 3.384 grams; composition .875 gold, .125 copper; edge: obliquely reeded.

Date	Mint	Assayer	VG	F	VF	EF
1825	Gᴬ	FS	$75.00	$90.00	$125.00	$180.00
	M̥	JM	60.00	75.00	100.00	150.00
1826	Gᴬ	FS	85.00	100.00	150.00	200.00
1827	M̥	JM *varieties:*	60.00	75.00	100.00	150.00
		7 over 6; normal date.				
1830	M̥	JM 30 over 29	65.00	85.00	110.00	165.00
1831	Gᴬ	FS	85.00	100.00	150.00	200.00
	M̥	JM	60.00	75.00	100.00	150.00
1832	Dᴼ	RL	100.00	125.00	165.00	200.00
	M̥	JM	70.00	90.00	125.00	175.00
1833	Dᴼ	RM 3 over 2, M over L	100.00	125.00	175.00	225.00
	M̥	JM	65.00	80.00	110.00	160.00
	M̥	MJ	60.00	75.00	100.00	150.00
1834	Dᴼ	RM	90.00	125.00	150.00	185.00
	Gᴬ	FS	75.00	90.00	125.00	180.00
	M̥	ML	70.00	90.00	125.00	175.00
1836	Dᴼ	RM, M over L	80.00	100.00	140.00	175.00
1838	Dᴼ	RM	90.00	125.00	150.00	185.00
1841	M̥	ML	60.00	75.00	100.00	150.00
1842	Gᴬ	JG over MC	85.00	100.00	140.00	200.00
1843	Gᴬ	MC	75.00	90.00	125.00	180.00
	M̥	MM	60.00	75.00	100.00	150.00
1844	GC	MP	110.00	130.00	175.00	250.00
1845	GC	MP	100.00	120.00	165.00	225.00
	G̶	PM	60.00	75.00	100.00	150.00
	M̥	MF	60.00	75.00	100.00	150.00
1846	C	CE	75.00	90.00	125.00	175.00
	Dᴼ	RM 46 over 38	115.00	155.00	185.00	225.00
	GC	MP	110.00	130.00	175.00	250.00
	M̥	MF 6 over 5	65.00	85.00	110.00	165.00
1847	C	CE	75.00	90.00	125.00	175.00
	Gᴬ	JG	85.00	100.00	140.00	200.00
	GC	MP	100.00	120.00	165.00	225.00
	M̥	MM	65.00	80.00	110.00	160.00
1848	C	CE	75.00	90.00	125.00	175.00
	Gᴬ	JG 8 over 7	85.00	100.00	140.00	200.00
	GC	MP	100.00	120.00	165.00	225.00
	M̥	GC	70.00	90.00	125.00	175.00
1849	C	CE 9 over 8	85.00	115.00	155.00	225.00
	Gᴬ	JG	85.00	100.00	140.00	200.00
	GC	MP	110.00	130.00	175.00	250.00

REPUBLIC

Date	Mint	Assayer	VG	F	VF	EF
	G	PF........................	60.00	75.00	100.00	150.00
1850	C	CE........................	75.00	90.00	125.00	175.00
	D^O	JMR......................	$110.00	$135.00	$175.00	$225.00
	G^A	JG........................	85.00	100.00	140.00	200.00
	GC	MP.......................	100.00	120.00	165.00	225.00
	M̥	GC.......................	70.00	90.00	125.00	175.00
1851	C	CE 1 over 0..................	85.00	115.00	155.00	225.00
	D^O	JMR......................	110.00	135.00	175.00	225.00
	GC	MP.......................	110.00	130.00	175.00	225.00
	G	PF........................	60.00	75.00	100.00	150.00
1852	G^A	JG 2 over 1..................	85.00	100.00	140.00	200.00
1853	C	CE 3 over 1..................	85.00	115.00	155.00	225.00
	D^O	CP........................	100.00	125.00	165.00	200.00
	G	PF........................	60.00	75.00	100.00	150.00
	Z^S	OM.......................	100.00	125.00	175.00	250.00
1854	C	CE........................	85.00	100.00	135.00	185.00
	D^O	CP *varieties:*..............	100.00	135.00	175.00	225.00
		5 over 4, C over R; 5 over 3.				
1855	D^O	CP........................	100.00	125.00	165.00	200.00
1856	C	CE *varieties:*..............	75.00	90.00	125.00	165.00
		6 over 5 over 4; normal date.				
	G^A	JG........................	85.00	100.00	140.00	200.00
	M̥	GF *varieties:*..............	60.00	75.00	100.00	150.00
		6 over 4; 6 over 5; normal date.				
1857	C	CE *varieties:*..............	75.00	90.00	125.00	175.00
		7 over 1; normal date.				
	G^A	JG........................	75.00	90.00	125.00	180.00
1858	M̥	FH........................	70.00	90.00	125.00	175.00
1859	D^O	CP........................	100.00	125.00	165.00	200.00
	G^A	JG 9 over 7..................	85.00	100.00	140.00	200.00
	M̥	FH........................	60.00	75.00	100.00	150.00
1860	G^A	JG *varieties:*..............	75.00	90.00	125.00	180.00
		60 over 59; normal date.				
	G	PF........................	60.00	75.00	100.00	150.00
	M̥	TH........................	70.00	90.00	125.00	175.00
	Z^S	VL *varieties:*..............	75.00	100.00	125.00	175.00
		60 over 59, V is inverted A; normal die.				
1861	C	PV........................	85.00	100.00	135.00	185.00
	D^O	CP........................	100.00	125.00	165.00	200.00
	M̥	CH........................	60.00	75.00	100.00	150.00
1862	C	CE........................	85.00	100.00	135.00	185.00
	G	YE........................	60.00	75.00	100.00	150.00
	M̥	CH........................	70.00	90.00	125.00	175.00
	Z^S	VL........................	75.00	100.00	125.00	175.00
1863	C	CE........................	75.00	90.00	125.00	175.00
	M̥	TH........................	60.00	75.00	100.00	150.00
1864	D^O	LT over CP..................	100.00	125.00	165.00	200.00
1866	C	CE........................	85.00	100.00	135.00	185.00
1869	M̥	CH........................	60.00	75.00	100.00	150.00
1870	C	CE........................	85.00	100.00	135.00	185.00

2 ESCUDOS
Facing Eagle Type 1825-1870

The design of the 2 *escudos* issues conforms to that of the other fractional denominations in gold, and remains unchanged throughout. This denomination was struck only sporadically and usually in small quantities. It exchanged for 4 pesos in silver.

Diameter 23 mm; weight 6.768 grams; composition .875 gold, .125 copper; edge: obliquely reeded.

Date	Mint	Assayer	VG	F	VF	EF
1825	M̥	JM........................	$125.00	$175.00	$225.00	$275.00
1827	M̥	JM *varieties:*..............	125.00	175.00	225.00	275.00
		7 over 6; normal date.				
1828	E°M°	LF........................	700.00	1,000	1,750	2,500
1830	M̥	JM 30 over 29..............	140.00	190.00	250.00	300.00
1831	M̥	JM........................	125.00	175.00	225.00	275.00
1833	D°	RM........................	300.00	450.00	700.00	1,200
	M̥	ML........................	125.00	175.00	225.00	275.00
1835	G^A	FS........................	125.00	175.00	225.00	275.00
1836	G^A	JG 6 over 5................	140.00	190.00	250.00	300.00
1837	D°	....	—	—	—	—
1839	G^A	JG........................	125.00	175.00	225.00	275.00
1840	G^A	MC........................	125.00	175.00	225.00	275.00
1841	G^A	MC........................	125.00	175.00	225.00	275.00
	M̥	ML........................	125.00	175.00	225.00	275.00
1844	D°	RM........................	275.00	400.00	600.00	1,000
	GC	MP........................	150.00	200.00	275.00	400.00
	M̥	MF........................	125.00	175.00	225.00	275.00
1845	G̊	PM........................	125.00	175.00	225.00	275.00
	M̥	MF........................	125.00	175.00	225.00	275.00
1846	C	CE........................	125.00	175.00	225.00	325.00
	M̥	MF........................	125.00	175.00	225.00	275.00
1847	C	CE........................	125.00	175.00	225.00	325.00
	G^A	JG 7 over 6................	140.00	190.00	250.00	300.00
	GC	MP........................	125.00	175.00	350.00	500.00
1848	C	CE........................	125.00	175.00	225.00	325.00
	G^A	JG 8 over 7................	140.00	190.00	250.00	300.00
	GC	MP........................	150.00	200.00	350.00	450.00
	M̥	GC........................	125.00	175.00	225.00	275.00
1849	GC	MP....	150.00	200.00	300.00	400.00
	G̊	PF........................	125.00	175.00	225.00	275.00
1850	G^A	JG........................	125.00	175.00	225.00	275.00
	GC	MP........................	150.00	200.00	300.00	400.00
	M̥	GC........................	125.00	175.00	225.00	275.00
1851	G^A	JG........................	125.00	175.00	225.00	275.00
1852	C	CE........................	125.00	175.00	225.00	325.00
1853	G^A	JG........................	125.00	175.00	225.00	275.00
	G̊	PF........................	125.00	175.00	225.00	275.00
1854	G^A	JG........................	125.00	175.00	225.00	275.00
	C	CE........................	150.00	200.00	250.00	350.00
1856	C	CE 6 over 1................	165.00	225.00	275.00	375.00

Date	Mint	Assayer	VG	F	VF	EF
	G̥	PF	125.00	175.00	225.00	275.00
	M̥	GF *varieties:*	125.00	175.00	225.00	275.00
		6 over 5; normal date.				
1857	C	CE	$125.00	$175.00	$225.00	$325.00
1858	Gᴬ	JG	125.00	175.00	225.00	275.00
	M̥	FH	125.00	175.00	225.00	275.00
1859	Gᴬ	JG *varieties:*	125.00	175.00	225.00	275.00
		9 over 8; normal date.				
	G̥	PF	125.00	175.00	225.00	275.00
	M̥	FH	125.00	175.00	225.00	275.00
1860	Gᴬ	JG 6 over 5	140.00	190.00	250.00	300.00
	G̥	PF	125.00	175.00	225.00	275.00
	Zˢ	VL	125.00	175.00	225.00	350.00
1861	Gᴬ	JG *varieties:*	140.00	190.00	250.00	300.00
		61 over 59; 1 over 0.				
	Hᴼ	FM	500.00	1,000	1,500	2,000
	M̥	TH	125.00	175.00	225.00	275.00
		CH	125.00	175.00	225.00	275.00
1862	G̥	YE	125.00	175.00	225.00	275.00
	M̥	CH	125.00	175.00	225.00	275.00
	Zˢ	VL	125.00	175.00	225.00	350.00
1863	Gᴬ	JG 3 over 1	140.00	190.00	250.00	300.00
	M̥	TH	125.00	175.00	225.00	275.00
1864	Zˢ	MO	135.00	175.00	250.00	400.00
1868	M̥	PH	125.00	175.00	225.00	275.00
1869	M̥	CH	125.00	175.00	225.00	275.00
1870	Gᴬ	IC	125.00	175.00	225.00	275.00

4 ESCUDOS
Facing Eagle Type 1825-1869

The 4 *escudos* was the least popular of the gold denominations, as was the 4 *reales* of the silver. Aside from a fairly regular series from Guanajuato the denomination was struck only sporadically. The piece exchanged for 8 pesos in silver.

Diameter 30 mm; weight 13.536 grams; composition .875 gold, .125 copper; edge: obliquely reeded.

1825	M̥	JM		450.00	550.00	700.00	1,000
1827	M̥	JM		400.00	500.00	600.00	850.00
1829	G̥	MJ 9 over 8		400.00	500.00	675.00	950.00
		JM		350.00	450.00	600.00	850.00
1831	G̥	MJ		350.00	450.00	600.00	850.00
1832	Dᴼ	RM		650.00	850.00	1,250	1,800

Date	Mint	Assayer	VG	F	VF	EF
	G̵	MJ	350.00	450.00	600.00	850.00
	M̥	JM	450.00	550.00	700.00	1,000
1833	Dᴼ	RM	$350.00	$600.00	$850.00	$1,250
	G̵	MJ	350.00	450.00	600.00	850.00
1834	G̵	PJ	400.00	550.00	700.00	1,000
1835	G̵	PJ	400.00	550.00	700.00	1,000
1836	G̵	PJ	350.00	450.00	600.00	850.00
1837	G̵	PJ	350.00	450.00	600.00	850.00
1838	G̵	PJ	350.00	450.00	600.00	850.00
1839	G̵	PJ	400.00	550.00	700.00	1,000
1840	G̵	PJ	350.00	450.00	600.00	850.00
1841	G̵	PJ	400.00	550.00	700.00	1,000
1844	Gᴬ	MC	650.00	850.00	1,100	1,500
		JG	400.00	650.00	850.00	1,200
	GC	MP	400.00	700.00	850.00	1,250
	M̥	MF	450.00	550.00	700.00	1,000
1845	GC	MP	350.00	500.00	650.00	850.00
	G̵	PM	350.00	450.00	600.00	850.00
1846	GC	MP	400.00	700.00	850.00	1,200
1847	C	CE	400.00	650.00	850.00	1,200
	G̵	PM	400.00	550.00	700.00	1,000
1848	C	CE	650.00	850.00	1,100	1,500
	GC	MP	500.00	650.00	750.00	1,100
1849	G̵	PF	400.00	550.00	700.00	1,000
1850	GC	MP	600.00	850.00	1,100	1,500
	M̥	GC	450.00	550.00	700.00	1,000
1851	G̵	PF	400.00	550.00	700.00	1,000
1852	Dᴼ	JMR		Rare		
	G̵	PF	350.00	450.00	600.00	850.00
1855	G̵	PF	350.00	450.00	600.00	850.00
1856	M̥	GF	400.00	500.00	600.00	850.00
1857	G̵	PF	350.00	450.00	600.00	850.00
	M̥	GF	400.00	500.00	600.00	850.00
1858	G̵	PF	350.00	450.00	600.00	850.00
	M̥	FH	450.00	600.00	700.00	1,000
1859	G̵	PF	400.00	550.00	700.00	1,000
	M̥	FH 9 over 8	450.00	600.00	700.00	1,000
1860	G̵	PF	350.00	450.00	600.00	850.00
1861	Hᴼ	FM	1,000	1,500	2,500	3,500
	M̥	CH	450.00	600.00	700.00	1,000
	O	FR	1,500	2,500	4,000	6,500
1862	G̵	YE	350.00	450.00	600.00	850.00
	Zˢ	VL	400.00	600.00	700.00	1,000
1863	G̵	YF	350.00	450.00	600.00	850.00
	M̥	CH	400.00	500.00	600.00	850.00
1868	M̥	PH	400.00	500.00	600.00	850.00
1869	M̥	CH	400.00	500.00	600.00	850.00

8 ESCUDOS
Hooked Neck Eagle 1823

Of all the denominations of *escudo* gold, only the 8 *escudos* of the first year of the Republic was struck with the hooked neck eagle obverse. The reverse design illustrates its legend, LA LIBERTAD EN LA LEY, as a hand holding the

Liberty cap points to the book of Law. The denomination was equivalent to 16 pesos in silver.

Diameter 37 mm; weight 27.073 grams; composition .875 gold, .125 copper; edge: obliquely reeded.

Date	Mint	Assayer	F	VF	EF	Unc.
1823	M̊	JM..........................	$3,500	$6,500	$10,000	$22,500

Facing Eagle Type 1824-1873

The usual standing or upright eagle appears on the obverse, combined with the composite "hand on book" reverse. As in the case of the *real* silver, the largest denomination of the *escudo* gold is also the most commonly available.

Diameter 37 mm; weight 27.073 grams; composition .875 gold, .125 copper; edge: obliquely reeded.

1824	M̊	JM..........................	350.00	450.00	600.00	900.00
1825	G^A	FS..........................	500.00	750.00	1,000	1,750
	M̊	JM *varieties:*...............	350.00	450.00	600.00	900.00
		5 over 3; normal date.				
1826	G^A	FS..........................	600.00	900.00	1,250	2,000
	M̊	JM 6 over 5................	350.00	450.00	600.00	900.00
1827	M̊	JM..........................	350.00	450.00	600.00	900.00
1828	E^{O}M^O	LF......................	2,000	3,500	6,000	10,000
	G̊	MJ......................	375.00	475.00	650.00	1,000
	M̊	JM..........................	350.00	450.00	600.00	900.00
1829	E^{O}M^O	LF......................	2,000	3,500	6,000	10,000
	G̊	MJ......................	375.00	475.00	650.00	1,000
	M̊	JM..........................	350.00	450.00	600.00	900.00

Date	Mint	Assayer	F	VF	EF	Unc.
1830	G^A	FS	$500.00	$750.00	$1,000	$1,750
	G͜	MJ	375.00	475.00	650.00	1,000
	M̥	JM	350.00	450.00	600.00	900.00
1831	G͜	MJ	375.00	475.00	650.00	1,000
	M̥	JM	350.00	450.00	600.00	900.00
1832	D^O	RM	800.00	1,250	1,500	2,500
	G͜	MJ	375.00	475.00	650.00	1,000
	M̥	JM 2 over 1	350.00	450.00	600.00	900.00
1833	D^O	RM-M over L	400.00	500.00	750.00	1,000
	G͜	MJ	375.00	475.00	650.00	1,000
	M̥	MJ	350.00	450.00	600.00	900.00
		ML	350.00	450.00	600.00	900.00
1834	D^O	RM	400.00	500.00	750.00	1,000
	G͜	PJ	375.00	475.00	650.00	1,000
	M̥	ML	350.00	450.00	600.00	900.00
1835	D^O	RM	400.00	500.00	750.00	1,000
	G͜	PJ	375.00	475.00	650.00	1,000
	M̥	ML 5 over 4	350.00	450.00	600.00	900.00
1836	D^O	RM, M over L	400.00	500.00	750.00	1,000
	G^A	FS	1,200	1,500	2,000	3,000
	G͜	PJ	375.00	475.00	650.00	1,000
	M̥	ML	350.00	450.00	600.00	900.00
1837	D^O	RM	400.00	500.00	750.00	1,000
	G^A	JG	600.00	900.00	1,500.00	2,600
	G͜	PJ	375.00	475.00	650.00	1,000
	M̥	ML 7 over 6	350.00	450.00	600.00	900.00
1838	D^O	RM	400.00	500.00	750.00	1,000
	G͜	PJ 8 over 7	425.00	625.00	900.00	1,500.00
	M̥	ML	350.00	450.00	600.00	900.00
1839	D^O	RM	400.00	500.00	750.00	1,000
	G͜	PJ 9 over 8	425.00	625.00	900.00	1,500
	M̥	ML	350.00	450.00	600.00	900.00
1840	D^O	RM 4 over 3, M over L	450.00	650.00	1,000	1,500
	G^A	MC	1,200	1,500	2,000	3,000
	G͜	PJ	375.00	475.00	650.00	1,000
	M̥	ML	350.00	450.00	600.00	900.00
1841	C^A	RG	400.00	500.00	750.00	1,000
	D^O	RM *varieties:*	450.00	650.00	1,000	1,500
		4 over 3; 41 over 34, M over L.				
	G͜	PJ	375.00	475.00	650.00	1,000
	M̥	ML	350.00	450.00	600.00	900.00
1842	C^A	RG	400.00	500.00	750.00	1,000
	D^O	RM 4 over 3	450.00	650.00	1,000	1,500
	G͜	PJ	375.00	475.00	650.00	1,000
		PM	375.00	475.00	650.00	1,000
	M̥	ML	350.00	450.00	600.00	900.00
1843	C^A	RG	450.00	650.00	1,000	1,750
	D^O	RM 3 over 1	450.00	650.00	1,000	1,500
	G^A	MC	—	—	—	—
	G͜	PM	375.00	475.00	650.00	1,000
	M̥	MM	350.00	450.00	600.00	900.00
1844	C^A	RG	450.00	650.00	1,000	1,750.00
	D^O	RM *varieties:*	500.00	800.00	1,250	2,000
		first 4 over 3, M over L; normal die.				

Date	Mint	Assayer	F	VF	EF	Unc.
	GC	MP........................	$600.00	$800.00	$1,000	$1,750
	G̥	PM *varieties:*...............	375.00	475.00	650.00	1,000
		second 4 over 3; normal date				
	M̥	MF........................	350.00	450.00	600.00	900.00
1845	Cᴬ	RG........................	450.00	650.00	1,000	1,750
	Dᴼ	RM *varieties:*...............	500.00	800.00	1,250	2,000
		45 over 36; normal date.				
	Gᴬ	MC........................	400.00	500.00	750.00	1,000
	GC	MP........................	600.00	800.00	1,000	1,750
	G̥	PM........................	375.00	475.00	650.00	900.00
	M̥	MF........................	350.00	450.00	600.00	900.00
1846	Cᴬ	RG........................	400.00	500.00	750.00	1,000
	C	CE........................	400.00	500.00	750.00	1,000
	Dᴼ	RM........................	400.00	500.00	750.00	1,000
	GC	MP........................	600.00	800.00	1,000	1,750
	G̥	PM........................	375.00	475.00	650.00	900.00
	M̥	MF........................	350.00	450.00	600.00	900.00
1847	C	CE........................	400.00	500.00	750.00	1,000
	Dᴼ	RM........................	400.00	500.00	750.00	1,000
	GC	MP........................	600.00	800.00	1,000	1,750
	G̥	PM........................	375.00	475.00	650.00	900.00
	M̥	RC........................	350.00	450.00	600.00	900.00
1848	Cᴬ	RG........................	400.00	500.00	750.00	1,000
	C	CE........................	400.00	500.00	750.00	1,000
	Dᴼ	CM........................	400.00	500.00	750.00	1,000
	GC	MP........................	600.00	800.00	1,000	1,750
	G̥	PM *varieties:*...............	375.00	475.00	650.00	900.00
		8 over 7; normal date.				
		PF........................	375.00	475.00	650.00	900.00
	M̥	GC........................	350.00	450.00	600.00	900.00
1849	Cᴬ	RG........................	400.00	500.00	750.00	1,000
	C	CE........................	400.00	500.00	750.00	1,000
	Dᴼ	CM 4 over 3................	450.00	650.00	1,000	1,500
		JMR......................	450.00	650.00	1,000	1,500
	Gᴬ	JG........................	400.00	500.00	750.00	1,000
	GC	MP........................	600.00	800.00	1,000	1,750
	G̥	PF........................	375.00	475.00	650.00	900.00
	M̥	GC........................	350.00	450.00	600.00	900.00
1850	Cᴬ	RG 5 over 4................	450.00	650.00	1,000	1,500
	C	CE........................	400.00	500.00	750.00	1,000
	Dᴼ	JMR......................	450.00	650.00	1,000	1,500
	Gᴬ	JG........................	400.00	500.00	750.00	1,000
	GC	MP........................	600.00	800.00	1,000	1,750
	G̥	PF........................	375.00	475.00	650.00	900.00
	M̥	GC........................	350.00	450.00	600.00	900.00
1851	Cᴬ	RG 5 over 4................	450.00	650.00	1,000	1,500
	C	CE........................	400.00	500.00	750.00	1,000
	Dᴼ	JMR......................	450.00	650.00	1,000	1,500
	Gᴬ	JG........................	400.00	500.00	750.00	1,000
	GC	MP........................	600.00	800.00	1,000	1,750
	G̥	PF........................	375.00	475.00	650.00	900.00
	M̥	GC........................	350.00	450.00	600.00	900.00
1852	Cᴬ	RG 5 over 4................	450.00	650.00	1,000	1,500

Date	Mint	Assayer	F	VF	EF	Unc.
	C	CE	$400.00	$500.00	$750.00	$1,000
	D^O	JMR 2 over 1	500.00	750.00	1,100	1,925
		CP	500.00	800.00	1,250	2,000
	G^A	JG 2 over 1	500.00	650.00	1,000	1,500
	GC	MP	600.00	800.00	1,000	1,750
	G	PF	375.00	475.00	650.00	900.00
	M̊	GC	350.00	450.00	600.00	900.00
1853	C^A	RG 5 over 4	450.00	650.00	1,000	1,500
	C	CE 3 over 1	450.00	650.00	1,000	1,500
	D^O	CP	400.00	500.00	750.00	1,000
	G	PF	375.00	475.00	650.00	900.00
	M̊	GC	350.00	450.00	600.00	900.00
1854	C^A	RG 5 over 4	450.00	650.00	1,000	1,500
	C	CE	400.00	500.00	750.00	1,000
	D^O	CP	400.00	500.00	750.00	1,000
	G	PF	375.00	475.00	650.00	900.00
	M̊	GC *varieties:*	350.00	450.00	600.00	900.00
		5 over 4; 4 over 3.				
1855	C^A	RG 55 over 43	450.00	650.00	1,000	1,500
	C	CE 5 over 4	450.00	650.00	1,000	1,500
	D^O	CP 5 over 4	450.00	650.00	1,000	1,650
	G^A	JG	400.00	500.00	750.00	1,000
	G	PF *varieties:*	375.00	475.00	650.00	900.00
		5 over 4; normal date.				
	M̊	GF	350.00	450.00	600.00	900.00
1856	C^A	RG	400.00	500.00	750.00	1,000
	C	CE	400.00	500.00	750.00	1,000
	D^O	CP	400.00	500.00	750.00	1,000
	G^A	JG	400.00	500.00	750.00	1,000
	G	PF	375.00	475.00	650.00	900.00
	M̊	GF 6 over 5	350.00	450.00	600.00	900.00
1857	C^A	JC over RG	400.00	500.00	750.00	1,000
	C	CE	400.00	500.00	750.00	1,000
	D^O	CP	400.00	500.00	750.00	1,000
	G^A	JG	400.00	500.00	750.00	1,000
	G	PF	375.00	475.00	650.00	900.00
	M̊	GF	350.00	450.00	600.00	900.00
1858	C^A	JC	400.00	500.00	750.00	1,000
		BA over RG	400.00	500.00	750.00	1,000
	C	CE	400.00	500.00	750.00	1,000
	D^O	CP	400.00	500.00	750.00	1,000
	G	PF	375.00	475.00	650.00	900.00
	M̊	FH	350.00	450.00	600.00	900.00
	O^A	AE	2,000	3,000	4,000	6,000
	Z^S	MO	400.00	500.00	700.00	900.00
1859	C^A	JC-J over R	400.00	500.00	750.00	1,000
	C	CE	400.00	500.00	750.00	1,000
	D^O	CP	400.00	500.00	750.00	1,000
	G	PF	375.00	475.00	650.00	900.00
	M̊	FH	350.00	450.00	600.00	900.00
	O^A	AE	650.00	1,000	1,500	3,000
	Z^S	MO	400.00	500.00	700.00	900.00
1860	C^A	JC-J over R	400.00	500.00	750.00	1,000
	C	CE	400.00	500.00	750.00	1,000

Date	Mint	Assayer	F	VF	EF	Unc.
		PV	400.00	500.00	750.00	1,000
	G	PF *varieties:*	$375.00	$475.00	$650.00	$900.00
		60 over 59; normal date.				
	M̥	FH	350.00	450.00	600.00	900.00
		TH	350.00	450.00	600.00	900.00
	⊛	AE	650.00	1,000	1,500	3,000
	Zˢ	MO	400.00	500.00	700.00	900.00
1861	Cᴬ	JC	400.00	500.00	750.00	1,000
	C	PV	400.00	500.00	750.00	1,000
		CE	400.00	500.00	750.00	1,000
	Dᴼ	CP 1 over 0	450.00	650.00	1,000	1,650
	Gᴬ	JG 1 over 0	500.00	650.00	1,000	1,500
	G	PF *varieties:*	375.00	475.00	650.00	900.00
		1 over 0; normal date.				
	M̥	CH 6 over 5	350.00	450.00	600.00	900.00
	O	FR	600.00	900.00	1,500	3,000
	Zˢ	VL *varieties:*	400.00	500.00	700.00	900.00
		1 over 0; normal date.				
1862	Cᴬ	JC	400.00	500.00	750.00	1,000
	C	CE	400.00	500.00	750.00	1,000
	Dᴼ	CP	400.00	500.00	750.00	1,000
	G	YE *varieties:*	375.00	475.00	650.00	900.00
		2 over 1; normal date.				
	M̥	CH	350.00	450.00	600.00	900.00
	O	FR	600.00	900.00	1,500	3,000
	Zˢ	VL	400.00	500.00	700.00	900.00
1863	Cᴬ	JC	400.00	500.00	750.00	1,000
	C	CE	400.00	500.00	750.00	1,000
	Dᴼ	CP	400.00	500.00	750.00	1,000
	Gᴬ	JG 3 over 1	500.00	650.00	1,000	1,500
	G	YF	375.00	475.00	650.00	900.00
		PF	375.00	975.00	650.00	900.00
	Hᴼ	FM	650.00	800.00	1,000	1,750
	M̥	CH 6 over 5	350.00	450.00	600.00	900.00
		TH 6 over 5	350.00	450.00	600.00	900.00
	O	FR	600.00	900.00	1,500	3,000
	Zˢ	VL	400.00	500.00	700.00	900.00
	Zˢ	MO	400.00	500.00	700.00	900.00
1864	A	PG	650.00	1,000	1,500	2,500
	Cᴬ	JC	400.00	500.00	750.00	1,000
	C	CE	400.00	500.00	750.00	1,000
	Dᴼ	LT	600.00	900.00	1,250	2,000
	H̥	FM	900.00	1,250	2,000	3,000
		PR over FM	900.00	1,250	2,000	3,000
	O	FR	600.00	900.00	1,500	3,000
	Zˢ	MO	400.00	500.00	700.00	900.00
1865	Cᴬ	JC	400.00	500.00	750.00	1,000
	C	CE	400.00	500.00	750.00	1,000
	H̥	FM over PR	750.00	1,000	1,500	2,500
	Zˢ	MO	400.00	500.00	700.00	900.00
1866	Cᴬ	JC	400.00	500.00	750.00	1,000
		FP	500.00	750.00	1,200	2,500
		JG	500.00	750.00	1,200	2,500

Date	Mint	Assayer	F	VF	EF	Unc.
	C	CE *varieties:*	$400.00	$500.00	$750.00	$1,000
		6 over 5; normal date.				
	D^O	CM	400.00	500.00	750.00	1,000
	G^A	JG	400.00	500.00	750.00	1,000
1867	C^A	JG	400.00	500.00	750.00	1,000
	C	CE	400.00	500.00	750.00	1,000
	D^O	CP 7 over 6	450.00	650.00	1,000	1,650
	G	YF	375.00	475.00	650.00	900.00
	H̊	PR	750.00	1,000	1,500	2,500
	M̊	CH	350.00	450.00	600.00	900.00
	O	AE	600.00	900.00	1,500	3,000
1868	A	DL 8 over 7	1,500	2,250	3,000	3,750
	C^A	JG	400.00	500.00	750.00	1,000
	C	CE	400.00	500.00	750.00	1,000
	G	YF	375.00	475.00	650.00	900.00
	H̊	PR	750.00	1,000	1,500	2,500
	M̊	CH	350.00	450.00	600.00	900.00
		PH	350.00	450.00	600.00	900.00
	O	AE	600.00	900.00	1,500	3,000
	Z^S	JS	400.00	500.00	700.00	900.00
		YH	400.00	500.00	700.00	900.00
1869	A	DL	650.00	1,000	1,500	2,500
	C^A	MM	400.00	500.00	750.00	1,000
	C	CE	400.00	500.00	750.00	1,000
	D^O	CP	400.00	500.00	750.00	1,000
	H̊	PR	750.00	1,000	1,500	2,500
	M̊	CH	350.00	450.00	600.00	900.00
	O	AE	600.00	900.00	1,500	3,000
	Z^S	YH	400.00	500.00	700.00	900.00
1870	A	DL	1,500	2,250	3,000	3,750
	C^A	MM	400.00	500.00	750.00	1,000
	C	CE	400.00	500.00	750.00	1,000
	D^O	CP	400.00	500.00	750.00	1,000
	G	FR	375.00	475.00	650.00	900.00
	H̊	PR	750.00	1,000	1,500	2,500
	Z^S	YH	400.00	500.00	750.00	900.00
1871	C^A	MM 7 over 6	450.00	650.00	1,000	1,500
	H̊	PR	750.00	1,000	1,500	2,500
	Z^S	YH	400.00	500.00	700.00	900.00
1872	A	AM	1,500	2,250	3,200	4,000
	H̊	PR 2 over 1	825.00	1,100	1,650	2,750
1873	H̊	PR	750.00	1,000	1,500	2,500

4 | THE SECOND EMPIRE— MAXIMILIAN 1863-1867

A long series of civil struggles, combined with foreign exasperation at repeated defaults on the Mexican external debt, culminated in the invasion
of Mexico by the French in 1861. Encouraged by conservative elements they
captured Mexico City in 1863 and established a Mexican Empire. The Arch-
duke Maximilian of Austria was crowned Emperor in 1864 at the age of 32.
The Second Mexican Empire lasted a few years longer than the First, but it
was perhaps even less firmly founded. In spite of massive military support
from the French it never controlled all of Mexico. Withdrawal of that support
in 1867 doomed it to collapse. The execution of Maximilian at Querétaro
on June 19, 1867 was as much symbolic as vengeful; the Empire had fallen
and the world was put on notice not to try to resurrect it.

The coins in this section are those issued with the designs and legends of
the Empire. The head of the Emperor appears in accordance with kingly
usage in Europe and on the earlier Mexican coinages of the Spanish kings
and Agustín. The Imperial coat of arms includes as its central theme the
Mexican eagle and snake, under a crown and the legend IMPERIO MEXICANO.
On the smaller silver and the 1¢ copper the eagle itself is crowned (again
the type is reminiscent of the coins of Agustín). All denominations are decimal,
reminding us of the French passion for the metric system and all that it
implied; Republican efforts to introduce this system, including a decimal
coinage, had not been successful at the time of the French invasion. The
coins are usually well struck, save for the San Luis Potosí $1.

Maximilian's financial officials were determined to create a modern Mexican
coinage. However, the new coins were bound to be suspect given both their
origin and the curious decision by the government to decrease the flan diameter of the larger denominations. The Maximilian 50 centavos measured
30 millimeters as against the circulating Republican 4 *reales* at 32 mm,
the peso 37 mm as against the 8 *reales* 39 mm, and the $20 gold 35 mm as
against the Republican 8 *escudos* (=$16) 37 mm. Although the Imperial
coins contained proportionately the same amount of silver or gold as the
Republican, and were of the same alloy, the smaller flan size was psycholog-
ically wrong. Moreover the coin legends failed to indicate the fineness of any
of Maximilian's gold or silver. The *Diario del Imperio* of August 10, 1866
notes that some persons were refusing to accept coins of the Imperial type
on that account.

The pieces listed below are by no means the only coins struck under the
Empire. At one time or another most of the mints of the country were under
Imperial control, and many records exist to prove that they continued to
strike. Yet we have no other varieties of Maximilian's coins than these;
indeed there are none at all from most of the mints in question. It can only
be that these mints were continuing to strike with antedated Republican
dies, bearing both the designs and the denominations of the Republican system.
Thus production of 503,842 peso pieces is attested at Guadalajara in 1866,
but no coin is known of that mint and date; presumably, earlier Guadalajara
Republican dies were reused in the absence of current Imperial dies.

1 CENTAVO 1864

It would appear from existing coinage that all 1 centavo pieces for Maximilian were made at the Mexico City mint, and only during 1864. No actual records have been found to disprove this claim, but in 1876 a set of dies was found for the 1864-M Maximilian centavo at the Zacatecas mint.

The obverse shows a crowned eagle quite similar to the French Imperial eagle of the same period. The reverse has the value, date, and mint mark enclosed in a wreath.

Diameter 25.0-25.5 mm; weight 9.5 grams; pure copper; edge: reeded.

Date Mint	Quantity Minted	F	VF	EF	Unc.
1864 M......................		$30.00	$65.00	$275.00	$2,000

5 CENTAVOS 1864-1866

The first Mexican decimal coinage under Emperor Maximilian consisted of minor denominations only. Obverses for the 5 centavos show a crowned Imperial eagle, with inscription above. Reverses have the denomination, date, and mint mark enclosed in a wreath.

Diameter 15 mm; weight 1.35 grams; composition .9027 silver, .0973 copper; edge: reeded

1864 G.................90,000		17.50	35.00	75.00	325.00
M......................		11.00	22.00	50.00	275.00
P......................		225.00	375.00	1,250	2,750
1865 G......................		22.50	45.00	90.00	275.00
Z......................		20.00	45.00	135.00	475.00
1866 G......................		60.00	130.00	375.00	2,200
M *varieties*...............		22.00	45.00	90.00	475.00
6 over 4; normal date.					

10 CENTAVOS 1864-1866

The obverse of the 10 centavos issued during the reign of Maximilian shows a crowned Imperial eagle, with inscription above. The reverse has the value, date, and mint mark within a wreath.

Diameter 18 mm; weight 2.707 grams; composition .9027 silver, .0973 copper; edge: reeded.

10 CENTAVOS

Date	Mint	Quantity Minted	F	VF	EF	Unc.
1864	G	45,000	$17.50	$35.00	$80.00	$300.00
	M	....	12.50	20.00	60.00	275.00
	P	....	40.00	75.00	200.00	650.00
1865	G	....	12.50	20.00	60.00	275.00
	Z	....	20.00	45.00	120.00	475.00
1866	M *varieties:*.............		17.50	27.50	65.00	325.00
	6 over 4; normal date.					

1866 M, 6 over 4

50 CENTAVOS 1866

The first Mexican coinage of the 50 centavos denomination occurred under Maximilian in 1866 at the México mint. No other variety is known of this type.

The obverse shows a bust of the Emperor facing right, with surrounding inscription. The reverse bears the Imperial coat of arms, with the Mexican eagle in the center. Inscription is above, and value and mint mark below.

Designs for the 50 centavos, 1 peso and gold 20 pesos of Maximilian were made by a professor of engraving, Sebastian C. Navalón. He was assisted by two talented pupils, Cayetano Ocampo and Antonio Spíritu. The three initials N., O., and S. appear on the truncation of the bust.

Diameter 30 mm; weight 13.536 grams; composition .9027 silver, .0973 copper; edge: reeded.

1866 M⁰................31,150	30.00	75.00	300.00	1,250

1 PESO 1866-1867

The first coinage of the 1 peso denomination in Mexico occurred in 1866 as part of the issues of Maximilian. The obverse carries a portrait of the Emperor facing right, with surrounding inscription. There is a ribbon below his head, upon which are inscribed the last names of the three engravers who designed the coin — Navalón the teacher, and his pupils Ocampo and Spíritu.

The reverse shows the Imperial Mexican coat of arms, very closely resembling the contemporary French design. Value, date, and mint mark are at the bottom, and inscription at the top.

Diameter 37 mm; weight 27.07 grams; composition .9027 silver, .0973 copper; edge: reeded.

Date	Mint	Quantity Minted	F	VF	EF	Unc.
1866	G^O		$425.00	$650.00	$1,000	$2,500
	M̊	2,147,675	25.00	50.00	115.00	400.00
	P^I		50.00	100.00	200.00	750.00
1867	M̊	1,238,000	40.00	85.00	250.00	550.00

Contemporary French
Coin of Emperor
Napoleon III

GOLD 20 PESOS 1866

The first Mexican decimal gold coinage was also struck in 1866 under Maximilian. The design is similar to the silver 1 peso of the same type. The obverse shows a bust of the Emperor facing right. On a ribbon below his head are the

GOLD 20 PESOS

names of the three engravers who designed the coin — Navalón, Ocampo, and Spíritu. The reverse carries the Imperial coat of arms similar to the contemporary French style of Napoleon III.

Diameter 35 mm; weight 33.841 grams; composition .875 gold, .125 copper; edge: reeded.

Date	Mint	Quantity Minted	F	VF	EF	Unc.
1866	M̊	8,274	$800.00	$1,200	$1,800	$3,500

GOLD "1 PESO" FANTASIES

In recent years several tiny gold pieces have appeared on the market, bearing the head of Maximilian in a style similar to that of his portrait gold and silver. Allegedly "gold Pesos," these thin flan imitations are modern fabrications which have no connection with the genuine Maximilian coinage at all. The first type, which bears no mark of value, exists with two obverse dies, one with light lettering and small ribbon, the other with heavy lettering and large ribbon. It is known also in silver.

A second type includes the purported denomination and a fineness designation, LEY • ORO • K 22 (i.e., "Gold fineness 22 carats"). Both details are historically impossible: the gold peso would have weighed 1.69 grams, while the imitation weighs but ca. 0.50 grams; and no indication of fineness appears on the gold of Maximilian, which was 21 carats fine in any case.

A third type carries the jugate busts of Maximilian and Carlota, with a reverse of the imperial arms and the dates 1866-1867 but no denomination.

5 | THE MEXICAN REPUBLIC — DECIMAL SYSTEM 1863-1905

The Mexican government first attempted to introduce a decimal system of coinage in the 1850's. Internal political difficulties complicated a problem already confused by poor communications, the private leasing of the mints and a shortage of resources, so that it was not until 1863 that the first decimal coins were struck for circulation (the 1¢, 5¢ and 10¢ of México and San Luis Potosí). In the following year the Maximilian government introduced its own decimal types, and presently an entirely decimal coinage was being uttered in the name of the Empire.

However, the realities of the case were that these first decimal coins were struck in small numbers and must have taken years to penetrate the currency. Further, the lowest denominations — 1¢, 5¢, and 10¢ — were incommensurate with the denominations of the *real* silver coinage. The *real* and decimal systems exchanged theoretically as follows:

$$8 \ reales = \$1.00 \qquad 2 \ reales = 25¢ \qquad \tfrac{1}{2} \ real = 6\tfrac{1}{4}¢$$
$$4 \ reales = 50¢ \qquad 1 \ real = 12\tfrac{1}{2}¢ \qquad \tfrac{1}{4} \ real = 3\tfrac{1}{8}¢$$

Thus, given a decimal system including no denomination under 1¢, exact exchange between the two systems was impossible under 2 *reales* = 25¢. This must have inhibited the use of the small decimal coins. Finally, the reluctance to accept Maximilian's silver for its want of fineness indication, and later the withdrawal of his coin for political reasons after the restoration of the Republic, meant that a true decimalization of the currency was delayed for years. The last non-commensurate *real* issues of which we know were the ½ and 1 *reales* struck at Culiacán and Zacatecas in 1869. Yet 1 *real* hacienda tokens are known from at least the 1880's, confirming that the earlier system of accounting was still in use.

This exchange difficulty did not arise with the gold coinage. The smallest denomination, the ½ *escudo,* had always exchanged for the silver 8 *reales* = $1.00. Thus the *escudo* denominations, while not the usual multiples of a decimal system, were easily tariffed at $16, $8, $4, $2, and $1.

Some of the earliest decimal silver, the 5¢ and 10¢ of México and San Luis Potosí 1867-69, bore the same eagle/Liberty cap design as the *real* silver. This was no doubt a source of confusion; at the same time silver coins of identical type worth 5¢, 6¼¢, 10¢, and 12½¢ were in circulation. Beginning in 1869, when all denominations of decimal silver and gold began to issue from México and to a certain extent from the branch mints, new reverse designs were developed by which to distinguish the two coinage systems. The small size coins — silver 5¢, 10¢, gold $1, $2½ — bore simply the mark of value within a wreath. The larger size denominations — silver 25¢, 50¢, $1, gold $5, $10, $20 — bore a grouping of small Liberty cap upon a burst of rays, sword, the scroll of the Constitution, and a balance scale from which the peso of this type gets its name, the *balanza* peso. This type system was used with small modification until its complete reform in 1905, save for one piece. As indicated elsewhere, the peso was of a different diameter from the earlier 8 *reales,* 37 as against 39 millimeters, though both were of the same intrinsic content. This, along with the change in type, rendered the new coin suspect in the China trade. Consequently the *balanza* peso was abandoned in 1873 and the earlier 8 *real* dollar reinstituted.

1 CENTAVO
Seated Liberty Type 1863

The first regular 1 centavo coinage began in 1863. Pattern centavos had been prepared as early as 1841 (see Pattern 64 in chapter 7), of the same type as the ⅛ *real* first struck at México in that year, and this pattern was closely followed in the regular coinage of 1863. The obverse bears a seated figure of Liberty, and inscription LIBERTAD Y REFORMA. The reverse design is a wreath enclosing the denomination and date, with mint mark below.

The México mint issues bear two varieties of the date, with round top 3 or flat top 3. Edges are plain or reeded on the former, reeded on the latter. The engraver's name PAREDES appears in the exergue of the obverse.

The San Luis Potosí coinage differs from that of México in some respects. There is one style of date, the edge is coarsely reeded, and the engraver's name SANABRIA appears in the exergue.

The 1 centavo of 1863 is the only Mexican decimal coin which does not carry an inscription denoting the country of origin. In this it followed the ⅛ *real* of México, which also had omitted the national legend.

Diameter 26 mm (actual planchet size varies from less than 26 to 27½ mm); weight 8.0 grams; pure copper; edge: plain or reeded.

		Round Top 3		Flat Top 3	
Date Mint	Quantity Minted	F	VF	EF	Unc.
1863 Ṁ *varieties:*..............					
round top 3...........		$10.00	$15.00	$30.00	$150.00
flat top 3..............		8.00	12.50	25.00	150.00
S.L.P. 1,024,813		10.00	25.00	65.00	300.00

Standing Eagle Type 1869-1881

A new design marked the resumption of Republican coinage in 1869. On the obverse is a standing eagle with serpent, in a style typical of the later 19th century Mexican coat of arms. On the reverse is the value, date and mint mark enclosed in a wreath.

Usual 1 centavo mint marks include small letter superscript.

Only the Guanajuato issues include small letter adjacent.

1 CENTAVO

Note: In all cases except the Guanajuato issues of 1874-81 the mint mark appears with its small superscript letter *above* the large initial letter. Superscript letters are placed at the side in the listings below because of space limitations.

Diameter 25 mm; weight 8.0 grams; pure copper; edge: plain (Culiacán 1874-81) or reeded.

				1874 $\overset{s}{Z}$	
				4 over 3	
Date	Mint	Quantity Minted	F	VF	EF	Unc.

Date	Mint	Quantity Minted	F	VF	EF	Unc.
1868	M^O	$200.00	—	—	—
1869	M^O*............1,874,320	$7.50	$15.00	$35.00	$75.00
1870	M^O.............1,200,000	8.00	11.00	35.00	75.00
1871	M^O..............917,500	8.00	11.00	30.00	70.00
	P^I		Rare		
1872	G^A..............262,500	7.00	10.00	30.00	100.00
	M^O *varieties:*....1,625,000	6.00	9.00	25.00	75.00
	2 over 1; normal date.				
	O^A...............15,724	300.00	500.00	1,200	—
	Z^S...............55,000	22.50	30.00	100.00	300.00
1873	G^A..............333,228	6.00	9.00	25.00	100.00
	M^O.............1,605,000	4.00	5.50	12.50	50.00
	O^A...............10,787		Rare		
	Z^S.............1,460,000	4.00	6.00	20.00	100.00
1874	C^N..............265,853	6.00	9.00	20.00	100.00
	G^A...............76,355	6.00	9.00	20.00	100.00
	G^O....................	15.00	30.00	75.00	200.00
	M^O *varieties*.....1,700,000	3.00	5.50	12.50	50.00
	4 over 3; normal date; period after date.				
	O^A................4,835		Rare		
	Z^S *varieties:*.......685,000	4.00	6.00	20.00	100.00
	4 over 3; normal date.				
1875	C^N *varieties:*.......152,520	8.00	11.00	14.00	100.00
	5 over 4; normal date.				
	G^A....................	4.00	6.00	20.00	100.00
	G^O..............190,000	11.50	20.00	60.00	150.00
	H^O................3,500		Rare		
	M^O.............1,495,000	6.00	8.00	20.00	50.00
	O^A................2,860		Rare		
	Z^S *varieties:*.......200,000	7.00	10.00	30.00	100.00
	5 over 4; normal date.				
1876	A^S...............49,500	40.00	60.00	150.00	600.00
	C^N..............153,875	5.00	8.00	15.00	80.00
	G^A..............302,500	3.00	6.00	17.50	100.00
	G^O....................	100.00	150.00	350.00	750.00

*The 1869 M^O is known with plain edge (trial?).

1 CENTAVO

Date	Mint	Quantity Minted	F	VF	EF	Unc.
	H^O	8,508	$35.00	$75.00	$200.00	$500.00
	M^O	1,600,000	3.00	5.50	12.50	50.00
	Z^S		5.00	8.00	20.00	100.00
1877	C^N	993,088	6.00	9.00	13.50	100.00
	G^A	107,500	4.00	6.00	18.50	100.00
	G^O			Rare		
	M^O	1,270,000	3.00	5.50	13.50	50.00
	P^I	248,900	10.00	13.50	25.00	100.00
	Z^S		50.00	125.00	300.00	750.00
1878	G^A	542,500	4.00	6.00	15.00	100.00
	G^O	576,400	8.00	11.00	30.00	125.00
	M^O *varieties:*	1,900,000	6.00	9.00	13.50	50.00
	8 over 5; 8 over 7; normal date.					
	P^I	751,100	8.00	10.00	20.00	100.00
	Z^S		4.50	7.00	20.00	100.00
1879	D^O	109,900	10.00	17.50	35.00	125.00
	M^O *varieties:*	1,505,000	3.00	5.50	11.50	40.00
	9 over 8; normal date.					
1880	A^S		20.00	40.00	100.00	350.00
	C^N	141,684	7.50	10.00	12.50	100.00
	D^O	68,600	35.00	70.00	150.00	500.00
	G^O	890,000	6.00	10.00	25.00	125.00
	H^O *varieties:*	102,400	6.75	10.00	35.00	100.00
	short H, round ^{O}; tall H, oval ^{O}.					
	M^O *varieties:*	1,130,000	4.25	6.00	12.50	40.00
	second 8 over 7; normal date.					
	Z^S	100,000	5.00	8.00	25.00	100.00
1881	A^S		30.00	60.00	125.00	200.00
	C^N	166,700	7.50	10.00	21.50	125.00
	G^A *varieties:*	974,785	7.00	9.00	18.50	125.00
	second 8 over 7; normal date.					
	H^O	458,600	5.00	10.00	25.00	100.00
	M^O	1,060,000	4.50	7.00	15.00	40.00
	Z^S	1,200,000	4.25	6.00	20.00	100.00

Copper-nickel Coinage 1882-1883

In 1882, an attempt was made to provide a more suitable minor coinage than the large copper centavos in use at that time. Denominations of 1, 2, and 5 centavos were introduced in a copper-nickel alloy.

The 2 centavos coin was a new denomination in the Mexican decimal series. For the 1 and 5 centavos, extreme changes were evident in size and design. The obverse showed a quiver with arrows tied with a ribbon, a bow, and an Aztec club. The reverse expressed the value as a Roman numeral enclosed within a wreath. No mint mark or assayer's initial was placed on the copper-nickel coinage, though all were struck at the México mint. All the dies and flans of this issue were of European manufacture.

The new issues proved to be highly controversial, and finally were discounted by the populace. As a result, coinage was forced to a halt during 1883.

Diameter 16 mm; weight 2.0 grams; composition .750 copper, .250 nickel; edge: plain.

1 CENTAVO

Date	Mint	Quantity Minted	F	VF	EF	Unc.
1882	(México)	} 99,954,500	$8.00	$12.00	$18.50	$35.00
• 1883	(México)		.50	.75	1.00	1.50

Standing Eagle Type Resumed 1886-1897

In 1886, coinage of large copper centavos similar to issues of 1869-1881 was resumed. Blanks for the México mint pieces were provided by the Heaton mint of Birmingham, England until the introduction of the reduced size centavo in 1899.

1893 M^O
3 over 2

1886 M^O 12,687,314	1.50	2.00	8.50	40.00
1887 M^O 7,292,304	1.50	2.00	5.00	35.00
1888 M^O *varieties:*.....9,984,389	1.50	2.00	8.50	25.00
second 8 over 7; third 8 over 7; normal date.				
1889 G^A over M^O.........———	3.50	5.00	15.00	80.00
M^O 19,969,525	2.00	3.00	8.00	25.00
1890 G^A ....———	4.00	5.75	18.50	90.00
M^O *varieties:*....18,726,326	1.50	2.00	8.50	25.00
9 over 8; 90 over 89; normal date.				
1891 D^O *varieties:*........———	8.00	11.00	30.00	100.00
D^O over M^O; normal mint mark.				
M^O 14,544,143	1.50	2.00	8.50	25.00
P^I *varieties:*........———	8.00	11.00	25.00	80.00
P^I over M^O; normal mint mark.				
1892 M^O 12,907,603	1.50	2.00	8.50	25.00
1893 M^O *varieties:*.....5,077,559	1.50	2.00	8.50	25.00
3 over 2; normal date.				
1894 M^O 1,895,740	2.00	3.00	10.00	27.50
1895 M^O 3,452,500	2.00	3.00	8.50	25.00
1896 M^O 3,075,000	2.00	3.00	8.50	25.00
1897 C^N *varieties:*.......300,000	2.50	5.00	12.00	50.00
large ^{N} in mint mark; small ^{N} in mint mark.				
M^O 4,150,000	1.50	2.00	8.50	25.00

1 CENTAVO

Restyled Eagle Issue 1898

In 1898, an important modification was made on the obverse of many denominations. The eagle is restyled to appear taller and more elegant. The reverse remains similar to the previous issue.

Date Mint	Quantity Minted	F	VF	EF	Unc.
1898 M̥............... 1,529,400		$4.00	$6.00	$15.00	$50.00

Reduced Size Coinage 1899-1905

By 1898 the large copper centavos had become more valuable as bullion than as circulating coins. The need for a smaller 1 centavo coin was apparent.

In November of 1899, a new issue of 1 centavo pieces substantially reduced in size was proposed. Anticipating quick approval, the mint made preparations for immediate coinage of these pieces. Striking commenced upon formal acceptance of the new coin December 21, 1899, but continued for only three days.

The obverse shows the perched eagle as the main device, and the reverse has the value as a monogram within a wreath. The mint mark appears below, as a single letter.

Diameter 20 mm; weight 3.0 grams; composition .950 copper, .040 tin, .010 zinc; edge: plain.

Date Mint	Quantity	F	VF	EF	Unc.
1899 M*................. 51,000		125.00	175.00	300.00	800.00
1900 M.............. 4,010,000		2.00	3.00	7.50	25.00
1901 C................. 220,000		17.50	25.00	40.00	80.00
M.............. 1,494,000		4.00	6.50	15.00	45.00
1902 C................. 320,000		15.00	22.50	45.00	85.00
M normal date.... 2,090,000		2.00	3.00	8.50	26.50
902 over 899...incl. above		—	—	—	—
1903 C................. 536,200		8.00	12.00	20.00	35.00
M.............. 8,400,000		1.50	2.00	5.00	12.50

1 CENTAVO

1902 M, 902 over 899		1904 C, 4 over 3	

Date	Mint	Quantity Minted	F	VF	EF	Unc.
1904	C-4 over 3	147,500	$32.50	$40.00	$65.00	$100.00
	M	10,250,000	1.50	2.00	5.00	15.00
1905	C*	110,000	75.00	125.00	225.00	500.00
	M	3,643,000	2.00	3.00	10.00	37.50

*Beware of counterfeits and altered dates or mint marks. For illustration of a struck counterfeit see chapter 8.

2 CENTAVOS
Copper-nickel Coinage 1882-1883

In 1882, the 2 centavos denomination was introduced as part of the Mexican decimal system. It was issued in conjunction with the 1 and 5 centavos coins of the same composition and design. The obverse shows a quiver and arrows, bow, and Aztec club. The reverse carries the value as a Roman numeral.

All were coined at the México mint without assayer's initial or mint mark.

Diameter 18 mm; weight 3.0 grams; composition .750 copper, .250 nickel; edge: plain.

Date	Mint	Quantity Minted				
1882	(México)	} 50,022,750	2.00	3.00	7.50	15.00
1883	(México)		.50	.75	1.50	2.50

5 CENTAVOS
Eagle/Wreath Type 1863-1870

In October, 1863, coinage of silver 5 and 10 centavos was authorized by the Juárez government for all the mints of the nation (part of which was actually under the control of the French). The decree was issued at the provisional capital of San Luis Potosí, and this mint became the first to strike decimal

5 CENTAVOS

silver for the Republic. The reverse design of value and date in wreath was new, although it recalls the copper issues struck at México in 1829-37. The mint mark appears below. The mint at Chihuahua began its coinage of similarly designed pieces in 1868 and continued their production through 1870.

Diameter 14 mm; weight 1.353 grams; composition .9027 silver, .0973 copper; edge: obliquely reeded.

Date	Mint	Quantity Minted	F	VF	EF	Unc.
1863	S.L.P.		$100.00	$150.00	$375.00	$1,200
1868	C^A		35.00	65.00	125.00	300.00
1869	C^A	*30,000*	25.00	40.00	100.00	250.00
1870	C^A	35,200	25.00	40.00	100.00	250.00

Cap and Rays Type 1867-1869

This new decimal issue retained the design of the fractional *real* silver still in circulation in spite of Maximilian's decimal attempts. The obverse shows the standing eagle, facing, with inscription above; the reverse bears the Phrygian Liberty cap and rays with value, date, and mint mark below.

Diameter 14 mm; weight 1.353 grams; composition .9027 silver, .0973 copper; edge: ornamented.

1867	M̊ *varieties:* 7 over 3; normal date.		20.00	40.00	100.00	250.00
1868	M̊		20.00	40.00	100.00	250.00
	P	34,360	20.00	45.00	100.00	250.00
1869	P	13,960	27.50	65.00	150.00	400.00

Standing Eagle Type 1869-1881

A new issue of 5 centavos coins appeared in 1869. The obverse bears a redesigned coat of arms, with inscription above. The reverse carries the denomination inside a half wreath. Mint mark, assayer's initial and silver content are at the top.

Occasional mulings occur with obverse dies of the gold 1 peso.

Diameter 14 mm; weight 1.353 grams; composition .9027 silver, .0973 copper; edge: reeded (rarely plain).

5 CENTAVOS

Date	Mint	Assayer	Quan. Minted	F	VF	EF	Unc.
1869	G^O	S..............	80,000	$15.00	$30.00	$60.00	$150.00
	M^O	C 9 over 8.....	*40,000*	8.00	15.00	40.00	100.00
	P^I	S.................		25.00	40.00	75.00	200.00
1870	M^O	C............	140,005	4.00	6.00	20.00	50.00
	P^I	G over M^OC... ⎫		25.00	40.00	75.00	200.00
		O............ ⎭	}19,640	25.00	40.00	75.00	200.00
	Z^S	H............	40,000	11.00	20.00	45.00	90.00
1871	CH.	M............	14,260	17.50	40.00	100.00	250.00
	C^N	P................		15.00	40.00	75.00	150.00
	G^O	S............	100,000	5.00	10.00	25.00	65.00
	M^O	C............ ⎫		9.00	20.00	40.00	90.00
		M............ ⎭	}103,303	7.50	12.00	25.00	60.00
	P^I	O............	5,400		Rare		
	Z^S	H............	40,000	6.00	12.00	20.00	50.00
1872	G^O	S............	30,000	30.00	60.00	125.00	250.00
	M^O	M...........	266,000	5.00	8.00	20.00	50.00

1873 CH. M very crude date

1874 CH. M
crude date

Date	Mint	Assayer	Quan. Minted	F	VF	EF	Unc.
	P^I	O............	——	60.00	85.00	150.00	350.00
	Z^S	H............	40,000	8.00	15.00	30.00	60.00
1873	CH.	M very crude date....		60.00	125.00	200.00	450.00
	C^N	P............	4,992	40.00	75.00	125.00	250.00
	G^O	S............	*40,000*	11.00	17.50	35.00	90.00
	M^O	M............	*20,000*	7.00	15.00	35.00	75.00
	P^I	....	*5,000*		Rare		
	Z^S	H *varieties*:...*20,000*		10.00	20.00	45.00	90.00
		3 over 2; normal date.					
1874	A^S	DL................		7.50	10.00	25.00	80.00
	CH.	M crude date.......		7.50	17.50	35.00	90.00
	C^N	P................		12.50	30.00	50.00	100.00
	D^O	M................		90.00	150.00	225.00	500.00
	G^O	S................		7.00	12.00	25.00	60.00

H^O, 74 over 69

Horizontal ○ occurs on both varieties

Normal date

5 CENTAVOS

Date	Mint	Assayer	Quantity Minted	F	VF	EF	Unc.
	H^O	R *varieties:*		$9.00	$20.00	$40.00	$100.00
		74 over 69; normal date.					
	M^O	M *varieties:*		4.00	6.50	17.50	45.00
		74 over 69; normal date.					
	M^O	B		5.00	7.50	22.50	50.00
	P^I	H		20.00	35.00	60.00	150.00
	Z^S	H		8.00	10.00	16.50	40.00
		A		40.00	75.00	150.00	300.00
1875	A^S	DL		7.50	10.00	25.00	80.00
	C^N	P			Rare		
	G^O	S		8.00	15.00	27.00	65.00
	M^O	B *varieties:*		4.00	6.50	15.00	35.00
		B over M; normal initial.					
	P^I	H		6.50	10.00	25.00	60.00
	Z^S	A		6.00	10.00	25.00	50.00
1876	A^S	L		12.50	20.00	35.00	100.00
	C^N	P		10.00	25.00	50.00	100.00
	G^O	S		8.00	15.00	27.00	65.00
	M^O	B *varieties:*		4.00	6.00	12.00	30.00
		6 over 5; normal date.					
	P^I	H		10.00	20.00	45.00	90.00
	Z^S	A		9.00	15.00	30.00	60.00
		S		10.00	15.00	30.00	65.00
1877	D^O	P 4,795		30.00	45.00	100.00	200.00
	G^A	A		8.50	15.00	40.00	80.00
	G^O	S		7.00	12.00	20.00	55.00
	M^O	M *varieties:* ... 80,000		4.00	6.00	12.00	30.00
		7 over 6; normal date.					
	P^I	H		8.00	12.00	17.50	45.00
	Z^S	S		3.00	5.00	10.00	27.50

1878 Alamos mule	Normal obverse	1878 H^O A	Mule obverse

				F	VF	EF	Unc.
1878	A^S	L mule, gold peso obv.			Rare		
	D^O	E-8/7, E/P 4,300		38.50	65.00	140.00	275.00
	G^O	S-8 over 7 20,000		8.50	15.00	25.00	65.00
	H^O	A *varieties:* 22,000					
		regular obverse		8.00	17.50	35.00	80.00
		mule, gold peso obv.		15.00	35.00	75.00	150.00
	M^O	M *varieties:* .. 100,000		2.50	4.00	12.00	30.00
		8 over 7; normal date.					
	P^I	H		50.00	75.00	100.00	250.00
	Z^S	S 60,000		3.00	6.00	12.00	30.00
1879	A^S	L mule, gold peso obv.		15.00	30.00	75.00	200.00
	D^O	B		35.00	60.00	125.00	250.00

5 CENTAVOS

Date	Mint	Assayer Quantity Minted	F	VF	EF	Unc.
	G^O	S....................	$8.00	$12.00	$22.50	$60.00
	M^O	M *varieties:*.........	4.50	7.00	15.00	35.00
		9 over 8; 9 over inverted 9; normal date.				
	Z^S	S *varieties:*.........	2.00	6.00	12.00	30.00
		9 over 8; normal date.				
1880	A^S	L mule, gold peso				
		obverse......*12,289*	25.00	50.00	90.00	250.00
	D^O	B....................		Rare		
	G^O	S.............*55,000*	15.00	35.00	75.00	200.00
	H^O	A............*43,000*	4.50	9.00	20.00	55.00
	M^O	M *varieties:*.........	4.00	6.00	12.00	30.00
		80/76, M/B; 80/76, normal initial; normal date and initial.				
	P^I	H.............*6,200*	15.00	30.00	50.00	100.00
	Z^S	S *varieties:*...*130,000*	4.50	7.50	15.00	35.00
		80 over 79; normal dat(				
1881	D^O	P.............*3,020*	75.00	150.00	300.00	750.00
	G^A	S.............*156,208*	3.00	6.00	12.00	30.00
	G^O	S *varieties:*...*160,000*	4.00	6.00	12.00	30.00
		1 over 0; normal date.				
	M^O	M *varieties:*...*180,000*	3.00	4.50	9.00	22.50
		1 over 0; normal date.				
	P^I	H.............*4,500*		Rare		
	Z^S	S.............*210,000*	2.75	4.50	9.00	22.50
1882	H^O	A -2 over 1............		Rare		
		some authorities question existence.				

Copper-nickel Coinage 1882-1883

The highest denomination of the copper-nickel coinage introduced in 1882 was the 5 centavos. Apparently only those dated 1882 were released to circulation, as most pieces of the 1883 coinage appear to be specimen strikes and are quite rare.

The design is similar to the 1 and 2 centavos — the quiver, arrows, and club on the obverse, and a Roman numeral as the value on the reverse. All were struck at the México mint.

Diameter 20 mm; weight 5.0 grams; composition .750 copper, .250 nickel; edge: plain.

Date	Mint	Quantity Minted				
1882	(México)...............	} *40,000,000*	.75	1.50	3.00	5.00
1883	(México)...............		25.00	75.00	125.00	350.00

Standing Eagle Type Resumed 1886-1897

On May 10, 1886, the coinage of silver 5 centavos pieces was again authorized. Coinage identical to the 1869-1881 issues was then resumed.

5 CENTAVOS

1886 Alamos mule

Date	Mint	Assayer	Quantity Minted	F	VF	EF	Unc.
1886	Aˢ	L *varieties:*	43,342				
			normal obverse.....	$10.00	$15.00	$35.00	$100.00
			mule, gold peso obv.	25.00	40.00	90.00	150.00
	CH.	M	24,540	6.00	8.50	20.00	55.00
	Cᴺ	M	10,240	15.00	40.00	75.00	125.00
	Gᴬ	S	86,857	1.75	3.00	6.00	15.00
	Gᴼ	R	230,000	1.50	3.00	6.00	15.00
	Hᴼ	G	44,000	4.50	6.00	12.00	40.00
	Mᴼ	M *varieties:*	..398,000	1.75	2.25	6.00	15.00
		6 over 0; 6 over 1; normal date.					
	Pᴵ	R	33,000	8.00	12.00	17.50	45.00
	Zˢ	S.............\	} 360,000	1.75	2.25	4.50	11.50
		Z.........../		5.00	9.00	22.50	45.00
1887	Aˢ	L	20,000	8.50	12.50	25.00	50.00
	Cᴬ	M, Cᴬ over Mᴼ	.37,020	7.00	10.00	20.00	55.00
	Cᴺ	M	10,400	15.00	40.00	75.00	125.00
	Dᴼ	C	42,040	5.00	8.00	17.50	40.00
	Gᴼ	R	230,000	1.50	2.50	5.00	15.00
	Hᴼ	G	20,000	5.75	8.50	17.50	50.00
	Mᴼ	M *varieties:*	..720,000	1.75	2.00	5.00	15.00
		small initial M; large over small M.					
	Pᴵ	R	169,300	3.00	5.00	9.00	22.50
	Zˢ	Z	400,000	1.75	2.25	4.50	11.50
1888	Aˢ	L	32,000	6.50	10.00	20.00	50.00
	Cᴬ	M	144,600	2.00	3.00	6.00	12.50
	Cᴺ	M	119,160	1.50	2.50	6.00	15.00
	Dᴼ	C	91,275	4.00	7.00	15.00	35.00
	Gᴬ	S *varieties:*	...262,244	1.75	3.00	7.50	17.50
		large G; small G.					
	Gᴼ	R	320,000	1.50	2.50	5.00	12.50
	Hᴼ	G	12,000	7.50	12.00	20.00	60.00
	Mᴼ	M *vars.:*	1,360,000	1.75	2.00	5.00	12.50
		8 over 7; normal date.					
	Pᴵ	R	210,300	1.75	3.75	7.50	17.50
	Zˢ	Z *varieties:*	...500,000	1.75	2.25	4.50	11.50
		third 8 over 7; normal date.					
1889	Aˢ	L	16,000	8.50	12.50	30.00	75.00
	Cᴬ	M	44,020	4.00	5.00	10.00	25.00
	Cᴺ	M	66,220	4.00	6.00	12.50	35.00
	Dᴼ	C	48,637	3.50	6.00	12.00	30.00
	Gᴬ	S	178,350	1.25	2.00	6.00	15.00
	Gᴼ	R	60,000	4.00	6.00	12.00	30.00
	Hᴼ	G	67,100	3.00	6.00	12.00	30.00
	Mᴼ	M	1,242,000	1.75	2.00	5.00	12.50
	Pᴵ	R *varieties:*	...197,000	1.75	3.75	7.50	17.50
		9 over 7; normal date.					

5 CENTAVOS

Date	Mint	Assayer	Quantity Minted	F	VF	EF	Unc.
	Z^S	Z *varieties:*...520,000		$1.75	$2.25	$4.50	$11.50
		9 over inverted 9; Z^{S}Z over M^{O}M; normal date and mint mark.					
1890	A^S	L...............30,000		14.00	22.00	45.00	125.00
	C^A	M............101,740		1.50	2.50	5.00	12.50
	C^N	M............⎫179,680		1.50	2.50	5.00	12.00
		D............⎭		7.00	12.00	30.00	65.00
	D^O	C............⎫136,356		4.50	7.00	15.00	35.00
		P............⎭		5.00	8.00	17.50	40.00
	G^A	S.............68,000		3.50	5.00	10.00	25.00
	G^O	R...........250,000		1.50	2.50	5.00	12.50
	H^O	G............50,000		3.00	6.00	12.00	30.00
	M^O	M *vars.:*...1,694,000		1.50	2.00	5.00	12.50
		9 over 0; normal date.					
	O^A	E............⎫48,000			Rare		
		N............⎭		65.00	125.00	200.00	350.00
	P^I	R...........221,400		1.75	2.50	5.00	12.50
	Z^S	Z *varieties:*...580,000		1.75	2.25	4.50	11.50
		Z^S over M^O, Z over M; normal die.					
1891	A^S	L...............8,000		30.00	40.00	75.00	300.00
	C^A	M............164,440		1.50	2.50	5.00	12.50
	C^N	M............87,220		2.00	3.00	6.00	15.00
	D^O	P *varieties:*....47,984		3.00	5.00	10.00	25.00
		1 over 0; normal date.					
	G^A	S.............50,000		3.00	4.50	9.00	22.50
	G^O	R *varieties:*...168,000		1.50	2.50	5.00	12.50
		1 over 0; normal date.					
	H^O	G............46,000		3.00	4.00	9.00	22.50
	M^O	M.........1,030,000		1.75	2.00	5.00	12.50

1894 Z^o mint mark

← 1891 P^I
91 over 89 →

	P^I	R *varieties:*...176,000		1.75	2.50	4.50	12.50
		91 over 89, R over B; normal date and initial.					
	Z^S	Z............420,000		1.75	2.25	4.50	11.50
1892	A^S	L.............13,200		7.50	10.00	20.00	55.00
	C^A	M *varieties:*...84,520		1.50	2.50	5.00	12.50
		9 over inverted 9; normal date.					
	G^A	S.............78,000		2.00	3.00	6.00	15.00
	G^O	R...........138,000		1.50	3.00	6.00	15.00
◂	M^O	M *vars.:*.....1,400,000		1.75	2.00	5.00	12.50
		9 over inverted 9; normal date.					
	P^I	R *varieties:*...182,000		1.75	2.50	4.50	12.50
		92 over 89; 2 over 0; normal date.					
	Z^S	Z............346,000		1.75	2.25	4.50	11.50
1893	A^S	L.............24,000		6.50	10.00	20.00	55.00
	C^A	M............133,020		1.50	2.50	5.00	12.50
	G^A	S.............44,000		3.00	6.00	12.00	30.00
	G^O	R...........200,000		1.25	2.50	5.00	12.50
	H^O	G............84,400		2.50	3.50	9.00	22.50

5 CENTAVOS

Date	Mint	Assayer	Quantity Minted	F	VF	EF	Unc.
	M^O	M	220,000	$1.75	$2.00	$5.00	$11.50
	P^I	R	41,000	5.00	10.00	20.00	50.00
	Z^S	Z	258,000	1.75	2.25	4.50	11.50
1894	C^A	M	107,620	1.50	2.50	5.00	12.50
	C^N	M	23,820	4.00	7.00	15.00	35.00
	D^O	D	37,660	3.50	6.00	12.00	30.00
	G^O	R	200,000	1.25	2.50	5.00	12.50
	H^O	G	68,140	2.00	2.75	6.00	15.00
	M^O	M	320,000	1.75	2.00	5.00	11.50
	Z^S	Z *varieties:*	228,000	1.75	2.50	5.00	12.50
		normal mint mark; Z^O mint mark (error).					
1895	A^S	L	20,000	5.50	7.50	15.00	40.00
	C^A	M	73,640	2.00	3.00	6.00	15.00
	M^O	M	78,000	3.00	5.00	8.00	20.00
	Z^S	Z	260,000	1.75	2.25	4.50	11.50
1896	C^N	M	16,340	7.00	12.00	25.00	60.00
	G^O	R	525,000	1.25	2.00	4.00	10.00
	M^O	B	80,000	1.75	2.00	5.00	12.50
	Z^S	Z *varieties:*	200,000	1.75	2.25	4.50	11.50
		6 over inverted 6; normal date.					
1897	C^N	M	223,180	1.50	2.50	5.00	12.50
	G^O	R	596,000	1.50	2.00	4.00	10.00
	M^O	M	160,000	1.75	2.00	5.00	11.50
	Z^S	Z *varieties:*	200,000	1.75	2.25	4.50	11.50
		7 over 6; normal date.					

Restyled Eagle Type 1898-1905

In 1898, the eagle on the obverse of the 5 centavos was restyled to correspond with changes made on many denominations that year. The reverse design is similar to the previous issue.

1898 G^O mule—obverse eagle
of 1 peso gold

				F	VF	EF	Unc.
1898	C^N	M	44,000	1.75	4.00	8.00	20.00
	G^O	R mule, gold peso obverse	180,000	7.50	15.00	30.00	75.00
	M^O	M	80,000	2.00	4.00	7.00	25.00
	Z^S	Z	100,000	1.75	2.25	4.50	11.50
1899	C^N	M	}110,600	5.50	8.50	20.00	50.00
		Q		1.75	2.25	4.50	11.50
	G^O	R	260,000	1.75	2.25	4.50	11.50
	M^O	M	168,000	1.75	2.25	4.50	11.50
	Z^S	Z	50,000	2.00	3.00	7.00	20.00
1900	C^N	Q *varieties:*	239,400 →	1.75	2.50	6.00	15.00
		round Q, single tail; narrow C, oval Q; wide C, oval Q.					

5 CENTAVOS

Date	Mint	Assayer	Quantity Minted	F	VF	EF	Unc.
	G^O	R............200,000		$1.75	$2.25	$4.50	$11.50
	M^O	M...........300,000		1.75	2.25	4.50	11.50
	Z^S	Z............55,000		1.75	2.50	5.00	15.00
1901	C^N	Q............148,000		1.75	2.25	4.50	11.50
	M^O	M...........100,000		1.75	2.25	4.50	11.50
	Z^S	Z............40,000		1.75	2.50	5.00	15.00
1902	C^N	Q *varieties:*...262,000		1.75	2.50	6.00	15.00
		narrow C, heavy serifs; wide C, light serifs.					
	M^O	M...........144,000		1.25	2.00	3.75	9.00
	Z^S	Z *varieties:*....34,000		1.75	3.75	7.50	17.50
		2 over 1; normal date.					

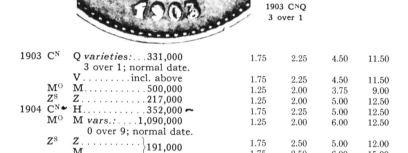

1903 C^{N}Q
3 over 1

Date	Mint	Assayer	Quantity Minted	F	VF	EF	Unc.
1903	C^N	Q *varieties:*...331,000		1.75	2.25	4.50	11.50
		3 over 1; normal date.					
		V.........incl. above		1.75	2.25	4.50	11.50
	M^O	M...........500,000		1.25	2.00	3.75	9.00
	Z^S	Z...........217,000		1.25	2.00	5.00	12.50
1904	C^N◆	H...........352,000 ⌐		1.75	2.25	5.00	12.50
	M^O	M *vars.:*....1,090,000		1.25	2.00	6.00	12.50
		0 over 9; normal date.					
	Z^S	Z..........⎱191,000		1.75	2.50	5.00	12.00
		M..........⎰		1.75	2.50	6.00	15.00
1905	M^O	M...........344,000		1.75	3.75	7.50	17.50
	Z^S	M.:..........46,000		2.00	4.50	9.00	22.50

10 CENTAVOS

Eagle/Wreath Type 1863-1870

The San Luis Potosí mint began production of this denomination along with the new 5 centavos, both authorized in October, 1863. A new design of value and date within wreath, mint mark below, was introduced to avoid confusion with the 1 *real,* of nearly the same size but worth 12½¢.

This type of 10 centavos was struck at San Luis Potosí only in 1863, but the same type is found from the Chihuahua mint for the years 1868-70.

Diameter 18 mm; weight 2.707 grams; composition .9027 silver, .0973 copper; edge: obliquely reeded.

10 CENTAVOS

Date	Mint	Quantity Minted	F	VF	EF	Unc.
1863	S.L.P.		$100.00	$225.00	$400.00	$900.00
1868	C^A	*varieties:*............	25.00	50.00	135.00	500.00
	8 over 7; normal date.					
1869	C^A.................15,000		20.00	40.00	125.00	450.00
1870	C^A.................17,400		17.50	35.00	100.00	400.00

Cap and Rays Type 1867-1869

The design of this 10 centavos group, like that of the concurrent 5 centavos, is almost identical to the silver of the *real* system. Obverses show a rather small eagle with inscription above. Reverses have a Phrygian Liberty cap and rays in the center, below which are the denomination, date, and mint mark.

Diameter 18 mm; weight 2.707 grams; composition .9027 silver, .0973 copper; edge: ornamented.

1867, 7 over 3

1867	M^O *varieties:*............		18.50	37.50	75.00	225.00
	7 over 3; normal date.					
1868	M^O *varieties:*............		18.50	37.50	75.00	225.00
	8 over 7; normal date.					
	P *varieties:*.........38,210		20.00	40.00	100.00	500.00
	8 over 7; normal date.					
1869	P 9 over 7...........4,900		25.00	50.00	150.00	600.00

Standing Eagle Type 1869-1897

A new issue of 10 centavos coins began in 1869. The obverse shows a redesigned eagle on cactus. The reverse has the value inside a partial wreath, with the mint mark, assayer's initial and fine silver content at the top.

Mulings occur at Culiacán with obverse dies of the gold 2½ pesos.

Diameter 17 mm; weight 2.707 grams; composition .9027 silver, .0973 copper; edge: reeded (rarely plain).

Date	Mint	Assayer	Quantity Minted	F	VF	EF	Unc.
1869	G^O	S 7,000		9.00	20.00	40.00	80.00
	M^O	C *varieties:*....30,001		8.00	17.50	35.00	75.00
		9 over 8; normal date.					

10 CENTAVOS

Date	Mint	Assayer	Quantity Minted	F	VF	EF	Unc.
	P^I	S 9 over 8.......4,000		$25.00	$50.00	$90.00	$175.00
1870	M^O	C...........110,000		3.00	9.00	15.00	35.00
	P^I	G............⎫	⎫	25.00	50.00	90.00	175.00
		O 70 over 69...⎬17,950			Rare		
	Z^S	H...........20,000		15.00	30.00	60.00	125.00
1871	CH.	M............8,150		10.00	15.00	30.00	60.00
	C^N	P.................		300.00	400.00	600.00	800.00
	G^A	C............4,734		17.50	25.00	75.00	150.00
	G^O	S-1 over 0......60,000		13.50	22.50	45.00	90.00
	M^O	C............⎫	⎫	12.00	17.50	45.00	100.00
		M............⎬84,003		12.00	17.50	45.00	100.00
	P^I	O............20,900		15.00	30.00	60.00	125.00
	Z^S	H *varieties:*...10,000		10.00	20.00	45.00	90.00
		1 over 0; normal date.					
1872	G^O	S............60,000		11.00	17.00	32.50	65.00
	M^O	M...........198,000		3.50	9.00	15.00	37.50
	P^I	O...........16,150		15.00	30.00	60.00	125.00
	Z^S	H...........10,000			Rare		

1873 CH. M, crude date

1874 CH. M, large 74

1873	CH.	M crude date........		10.00	15.00	35.00	75.00
	C^N	P............8,732		15.00	30.00	60.00	125.00
	G^A	C............25,330		7.50	10.00	30.00	65.00
	G^O	S............50,000		11.00	17.00	32.50	65.00
	M^O	M............40,000		7.00	12.00	22.50	45.00
	P^I	O............4,750		17.50	35.00	75.00	140.00
	Z^S	H............10,000		10.00	20.00	45.00	90.00
1874	A^S	DL...............		7.50	12.00	35.00	80.00
	CH.	M.................		10.00	20.00	40.00	80.00
	G^A	C.................		11.00	15.00	35.00	75.00
	G^O	S.................		11.00	17.00	32.50	65.00
	H^O	R.................		9.00	15.00	25.00	60.00
	M^O	M.................		3.50	10.00	20.00	40.00
		B *varieties:*........		3.00	7.50	12.50	30.00
		B over M; 7 over 6; normal date and initial.					
	P^I	H.................		15.00	30.00	60.00	125.00
	Z^S	H.................		10.00	20.00	45.00	90.00
		A.................		40.00	75.00	150.00	300.00
1875	A^S	L.................		4.00	8.00	20.00	50.00
	G^O	S.................		10.00	21.00	45.00	90.00
	M^O	B.................		3.50	7.50	12.50	30.00
	P^I	H.................		11.00	25.00	50.00	100.00
	Z^S	A.................		3.50	8.00	20.00	40.00
1876	A^S	L.................		8.00	12.00	35.00	80.00

10 CENTAVOS

Date	Mint	Assayer	Quantity Minted	F	VF	EF	Unc.
	G^O	S	....	$9.00	$15.00	$30.00	$65.00
	H^O	F	3,140	20.00	35.00	65.00	150.00
	M^O	B *varieties:*	....	2.00	3.75	7.50	17.50
			6 over 5, B over M; 6 over 5, normal initial;				
			normal date and initial.				
	P^I	H	....	15.00	30.00	60.00	125.00
	Z^S	A	....	4.00	7.00	17.50	35.00
		S	....	8.00	14.00	30.00	70.00
1877	G^A	A	....	9.00	12.00	30.00	65.00
	G^O	S	....	25.00	45.00	80.00	150.00
	M^O	M *varieties:*	....	2.00	4.00	8.00	20.00
			7/6, M over B; 7/6, normal M; normal date.				
	P^I	H	....	11.00	25.00	50.00	100.00
	Z^S	S *varieties:*	....	5.50	8.00	20.00	45.00
			regular initial S; small initial S.				
1878	A^S	L *varieties:*	....	5.00	10.00	30.00	60.00
			8 over 5; normal date.				
	D^O	E	...............*2,500*	30.00	50.00	100.00	300.00
	G^O	S *varieties:*	....*10,000*	7.50	12.00	20.00	50.00
			8 over 7; normal date.				
	H^O	A	....	3.00	5.00	10.00	25.00
	M^O	M *varieties:*	..*100,000*	2.00	4.00	8.00	20.00
			8 over 7; normal date.				
	P^I	H	....	35.00	60.00	110.00	200.00
	Z^S	S *varieties:*	....*30,000*	3.00	6.00	15.00	30.00
			8 over 7; normal date.				
1879	A^S	L	....	7.50	12.00	35.00	70.00
	D^O	B	....	65.00	100.00	225.00	500.00
	G^O	S	....	7.50	12.00	20.00	45.00
	H^O	A	....	9.00	15.00	25.00	60.00
	M^O	M *varieties:*	....	2.00	4.00	8.00	20.00
			7 over 6; normal date, M over C.				
	P^I	H	....	35.00	60.00	110.00	200.00
	Z^S	S	....	3.00	6.00	15.00	27.50
1880	A^S	L	...........*13,115*	4.50	8.00	20.00	50.00
	CH.	G-lg. G over					
		sm. G	.......*7,620*	15.00	30.00	55.00	100.00
	D^O	B 80 over 79	....		Rare		
	G^O	S	....	15.00	22.00	40.00	65.00
	H^O	A	....	3.00	5.00	10.00	25.00
	M^O	M 80 over 79	....	2.50	5.00	9.00	22.50
	P^I	H	....	30.00	55.00	100.00	175.00
	Z^S	S	....	3.00	6.00	12.00	22.50
1881	CH.		340		Rare		
	C^N	D	9,440	40.00	65.00	100.00	250.00
	G^A	A	...........⎫	40.00	60.00	150.00	300.00
		S	...........⎭115,447	3.50	5.00	15.00	30.00
	G^O	S *varieties:*	...100,000	2.00	5.00	10.00	20.00
			1 over 0; second 8 over 7; normal date.				
	H^O	A	28,300	4.00	7.00	15.00	35.00
	M^O	M *varieties:*	..510,000	1.50	2.50	8.00	17.50
			1 over 0; normal date.				

10 CENTAVOS

Date	Mint	Assayer	Quantity Minted	F	VF	EF	Unc.
	P^I	H 7,600		$30.00	$55.00	$100.00	$175.00
	Z^S	S *varieties:* . . .120,000		2.00	4.00	8.00	20.00
		1 over 0; normal date.					
1882	A^S	L 21,511		4.00	12.00	35.00	70.00
	C^N	D 12,230		20.00	40.00	80.00	150.00
	G^O	S 2 over 1 . . . . .*40,000*		2.50	6.00	12.00	22.00
	H^O	A *varieties:* 25,200		4.00	7.00	15.00	35.00
		2 over 1, large A; 2 over 1, small A; normal date.					
	M^O	M *varieties:* . . .*550,000*		1.50	3.00	7.00	17.50
		2 over 1; normal date					
	P^I	H *4,000*		15.00	30.00	60.00	125.00
	Z^S	S *varieties:* *64,000*		10.00	20.00	45.00	90.00
		2 over 1; normal date.					
1883	A^S	L *8,520*		9.00	17.50	40.00	100.00
	CH.	M *9,000*		10.00	17.50	35.00	75.00
	G^A	B *90,000*		3.50	5.00	15.00	30.00
	G^O	B *30,000*		2.50	5.00	10.00	25.00
	H^O	. . . .*7,000*		65.00	100.00	200.00	350.00
	M^O	M 3 over 2 . . . .*250,000*		2.50	5.00	9.00	25.00
	P^I	H		15.00	30.00	60.00	125.00
	Z^S	S *varieties:* . . .*102,000*		1.50	2.50	5.00	17.00
		second 8 over 7; normal date.					
1884	A^S	L		4.00	10.00	30.00	60.00
	CH.	M		11.00	15.00	30.00	75.00
	D^O	C		10.00	15.00	35.00	75.00
	G^A	B *varieties:*		5.00	8.00	20.00	45.00
		B over S; normal initial.					
		H		3.00	4.00	10.00	25.00
	G^O	B		1.50	3.00	6.00	15.00
		S		6.00	10.00	20.00	45.00
	H^O	A		6.00	10.00	20.00	40.00
		M		3.75	7.50	15.00	30.00
	M^O	M		1.50	2.50	7.00	15.00
	P^I	H		7.00	12.00	20.00	45.00

1884 Z^S,
4 over 3

	Z^S	S *varieties:*		1.50	2.50	5.00	15.00
		4 over 3; normal date.					
1885	A^S	L 15,420		4.00	8.00	20.00	50.00

1885 C^N M mule

1886 C^N M mule

10 CENTAVOS

Date	Mint	Assayer	Quantity Minted	F	VF	EF	Unc.
	C^N	M mule, gold $2\frac{1}{2}$					
		peso obv. ...18,240		$17.50	$40.00	$80.00	$150.00
	G^A	H.............93,412		2.50	5.00	10.00	25.00
	G^O	R............100,000		1.50	3.00	6.00	15.00
	H^O	M............20,500		12.00	20.00	35.00	75.00
	M^O	M...........470,000		1.50	2.50	7.00	15.00
	P^I	H............ ⎫51,000		10.00	20.00	45.00	90.00
		C............ ⎭		10.00	20.00	45.00	90.00
	Z^S	S *varieties*:...297,000		1.50	2.50	5.00	15.00
		normal ^{S} in mint mark; small ^{S} in mint mark; no assayer's initial (err					
1886	A^S	L.............44,739		4.50	8.00	20.00	50.00
	CH.	M.............45,250		4.50	6.00	12.00	30.00
	C^N	M mule, gold $2\frac{1}{2}$					
		peso obv. ...12,880		20.00	40.00	80.00	150.00
	D^O	C.............12,726		15.00	25.00	70.00	150.00
	G^A	S............151,405		2.50	5.00	10.00	25.00
	G^O	R.............95,000		3.00	5.00	8.50	20.00
	H^O	M............ ⎫10,000			Rare		
		G............ ⎭		7.50	12.50	22.50	50.00
	M^O	M...........603,000		1.50	2.50	7.00	15.00
	P^I	C............ ⎫52,400		6.50	8.00	16.00	40.00
		R............ ⎭		2.50	4.00	8.00	20.00
	Z^S	S............ ⎫274,000		1.50	2.50	5.00	12.00
		Z............ ⎭		12.00	25.00	45.00	90.00
1887	A^S	L.............15,000		5.00	7.50	25.00	60.00
	C^A	M.............96,070		3.00	4.00	8.00	20.00
	C^N	M.............10,820		8.00	20.00	35.00	75.00
	D^O	C.............81,480		3.00	6.00	12.00	25.00
	G^A	S............162,418		1.50	3.00	6.00	15.00
	G^O	R............330,000		2.50	5.00	10.00	25.00
	H^O	G............—		15.00	22.50	45.00	90.00
	M^O	M...........580,000		1.50	2.50	7.00	15.00
	P^I	R............118,450		1.50	2.50	5.00	15.00
	Z^S	Z *varieties*:...233,000		1.50	2.50	5.00	15.00
		normal mint mark; mint mark Z (error).					
1888	A^S	L.............38,300		3.50	5.00	20.00	50.00
	C^A	M *varieties*:...298,800		1.50	2.50	5.00	12.00
		C^A over M^O; normal mint mark.					
	C^N	M.............56,360		4.00	6.00	10.00	25.00
	D^O	C.............31,375		4.00	9.00	20.00	40.00
	G^A	S *varieties*:...225,000		1.50	3.00	6.00	15.00
		G^AS over H^OG; normal mint mark.					
	G^O	R............270,000		1.50	3.00	6.00	15.00
	H^O	G.............24,800		6.00	10.00	20.00	40.00
	M^O	M *varieties*:...710,000		1.50	3.00	7.00	16.50
		8/7, small ^{O} in mint mark; normal date, small ^{O}; large ^{O} in mint mark.					
	P^I	R............135,650		1.50	2.50	5.00	15.00
	Z^S	Z *varieties*:...270,000		1.50	2.50	5.00	15.00
		normal mint mark; mint mark Z (error).					
1889	A^S	L.............19,500		4.50	6.00	20.00	55.00

10 CENTAVOS

Date	Mint	Assayer	Quantity Minted	G-VG	F	VF	EF	Unc.
	C^A	M *varieties:*..114,770		$ .60	$2.00	$4.00	$8.00	$20.00
		9 over 8; small 89 (5¢ font).						
	C^N	M.............42,090		1.25	2.50	4.00	8.00	20.00
	D^O	C.............55,223		1.50	3.00	6.00	12.00	25.00
	G^A	S............310,092		.40	1.50	3.00	6.00	15.00
	G^O	R *varieties:*...205,000		.85	2.00	3.00	6.00	15.00
		G^{O}R over H^{O}G; *normal mint mark.						
	H^O	G.............42,400		1.50	3.00	6.00	10.00	25.00
	M^O	M............622,000		.40	1.50	2.50	7.00	15.00
	O^A	E.............21,000		——		Rare		
	P^I	R 9 over 7....131,000		3.25	6.00	8.00	16.00	40.00
	Z^S	Z *varieties:*...240,000		.40	1.50	2.50	5.00	15.00
		9/7, Z/S; normal date, Z/S; normal date and initial.						
1890	A^S	L.............40,000		1.50	3.00	4.00	20.00	40.00
	C^A	M *varieties:*..139,640		.60	1.50	3.00	7.00	15.00
		9 over 8; normal date.						
	C^N	M............131,920		.75	1.50	3.00	6.00	15.00
	D^O	C............50,021		1.50	3.00	6.00	12.00	25.00
	G^A	S............303,185		.40	1.50	3.00	6.00	15.00
	G^O	R............270,000		.40	1.50	3.00	6.00	15.00
	H^O	G.............48,000		1.25	3.00	4.50	8.00	20.00
	M^O	M *varieties:*..815,000		.40	1.50	2.50	7.00	15.00
		90 over 89; normal date.						
	O^A	E............⎫31,000		45.00	75.00	125.00	200.00	400.00
		N............⎭		——		Rare		
	P^I	R............204,100		.60	1.50	2.50	5.00	12.50
	Z^S	Z *varieties:*...410,000		.40	1.50	2.50	5.00	15.00
		normal mint mark; mint mark Z (error).						
1891	A^S	L.............38,000		2.75	4.00	5.00	20.00	50.00
	C^A	M............162,990		.60	1.50	3.00	7.00	15.00
	C^N	M............84,140		.95	4.00	7.00	12.50	25.00
	D^O	P............138,861		.95	2.00	4.00	8.00	17.50
	G^A	S............199,000		.40	5.00	10.00	20.00	35.00
	G^O	R............523,000		.40	1.50	3.00	6.00	15.00

1891 H^O
1 over 0

	H^O	G *varieties:*...136,000		1.00	3.00	4.50	8.00	20.00
		91 over 80; normal date.						
	M^O	M............859,000		.40	1.50	2.50	7.00	15.00
	P^I	R *varieties:*...163,000		.60	1.50	3.50	6.00	15.00
		91 over 89; normal date.						
	Z^S	Z *vars.:*.....1,105,000		.40	1.50	2.50	5.00	15.00
		normal mint mark; double S in mint mark.						
1892	A^S	L.............57,000		1.50	2.75	5.00	20.00	40.00
	C^A	M *varieties:*..169,110		.60	1.50	3.00	7.00	15.00
		9 over inverted 9; normal date.						

*Some reverse dies of Guanajuato, 1889 to 1893, show the initial R deformed by a chip so as to appear a B.

10 CENTAVOS

Date	Mint	Assayer	Quantity Minted	G-VG	F	VF	EF	Unc.
	C^N	M varieties:	...36,540	$1.25	$2.50	$5.00	$10.00	$20.00
		2 over 1; normal date.						
	D^O	P............	} 212,257	.85	2.00	4.00	8.00	17.50
		D............		.75	2.00	4.00	8.00	17.50
	G^A	S............329,435		.40	1.50	3.00	6.00	15.00
	G^O	R............440,000		.40	1.50	3.00	6.00	15.00
	H^O	G............66,600		1.25	3.00	4.50	9.00	22.50
	M^O	M.........1,030,000		.40	1.50	2.50	7.00	15.00
	P^I	R varieties:...200,250		.60	1.50	2.50	5.00	15.00
		2 over 0; normal date.						
	Z^S	Z............1,102,000		.40	1.50	2.50	5.00	15.00
1893	A^S	L............70,000		4.50	7.50	11.50	35.00	70.00
	C^A	M............246,100		.40	1.50	3.00	7.00	15.00
	D^O	D varieties:...257,902		.60	2.00	2.50	6.00	15.00
		D over C; normal initial.						
	G^A	S............225,000		.40	1.50	3.00	6.00	15.00
	G^O	R varieties:...389,000		.40	1.50	3.00	6.00	15.00
		3 over 1; normal date.						
	H^O	G............67,000		1.25	3.00	4.50	9.00	22.50
	M^O	M varieties:..310,200		.40	1.50	2.50	7.00	15.00
		M over C; normal initial.						
	P^I	R............47,500		.95	6.00	8.00	15.00	40.00
	Z^S	Z............1,011,000		.40	1.50	2.50	5.00	15.00
1894	C^A	M............162,960		.60	1.50	3.00	7.00	15.00
	C^N	M............43,100		1.10	2.00	4.00	8.00	20.00
	D^O	D............183,713		.60	1.50	2.50	6.00	15.00
	G^A	S............243,000		1.10	3.00	6.00	12.00	22.00
	G^O	R............400,000		.40	1.50	2.50	5.00	12.00
	M^O	M............350,000		.60	5.00	10.00	20.00	35.00
	Z^S	Z............892,000		.40	1.50	2.50	5.00	12.00
1895	C^A	M............127,400		.60	1.50	3.00	7.00	15.00
	C^N	M............22,880		1.25	2.50	5.00	11.00	22.50
	D^O	D............142,030		.60	1.50	2.50	6.00	15.00
	G^A	S............80,000		.75	1.50	3.00	6.50	16.00
	G^O	R............355,000		.40	1.50	2.50	5.00	12.00
	M^O	M............320,000		.60	1.50	2.50	7.50	15.00
	Z^S	Z............920,000		.40	1.50	2.50	5.00	12.00
1896	C^N	M............120,870		.65	1.50	2.50	5.00	12.00
	G^O	R............190,000		.40	1.50	2.50	5.00	12.00
	M^O	B varieties:...340,000		.60	2.00	3.00	6.00	14.00
		B over C; normal initial.						
		M.........incl. above		5.00	10.00	20.00	35.00	90.00
	Z^S	Z varieties:...700,000		.40	1.50	2.50	5.00	12.00
		normal mint mark; mint mark Z (error).						
1897	G^O	R............205,000		.40	1.50	2.50	5.00	12.00
	M^O	M............170,000		.65	1.50	2.50	5.00	12.00
	Z^S	Z varieties:...900,000		.40	1.50	2.50	5.00	12.00
		7 over 6; 7/6, mint mark Z (error); normal date.						

Restyled Eagle Type 1898-1905

As with other denominations, the eagle on the obverse of the 10 centavos is changed to appear taller and more elegant in 1898. The reverse design is similar to the previous issue.

10 CENTAVOS

Date	Mint	Assayer	Quan. Minted	F	VF	EF	Unc.
1898	C^N	M.............9,870		$35.00	$65.00	$100.00	$200.00
	G^O	R............435,000		1.50	2.50	5.00	15.00
	M^O	M...........130,000		1.50	2.50	5.00	15.00
	Z^S	Z............240,000		1.50	2.50	7.50	20.00
1899	C^N	Q *varieties:*....79,700		5.00	7.50	15.00	35.00
		round Q, single tail; oval Q, double tail.					
	G^O	R............270,000		1.50	2.50	5.50	17.00
	M^O	M...........190,000		1.50	2.50	5.00	15.00
	Z^S	Z............105,000		1.50	3.00	10.00	22.00
1900	C^N	Q............159,900		1.50	2.50	5.00	15.00
	G^O	R............130,000		7.00	12.00	22.50	50.00
	M^O	M...........311,000		1.50	2.50	5.00	15.00
	Z^S	Z............219,000		7.50	10.00	20.00	45.00
1901	C^N	Q............235,000		1.50	2.50	5.00	15.00
	M^O	M............80,000		2.50	3.50	7.00	17.00
	Z^S	Z............70,000		2.50	5.00	10.00	25.00
1902	C^N	Q............186,000		1.50	2.50	5.00	16.00
	M^O	M...........181,000		1.50	2.50	5.00	15.00
	Z^S	Z............120,000		2.50	5.00	10.00	25.00
1903	C^N	Q........... ⎫ 256,000		1.50	2.50	6.00	18.00
		V........... ⎭		1.50	2.50	5.00	12.00
	M^O	M...........581,000		1.50	2.50	5.00	15.00
	Z^S	Z............227,500		1.50	3.00	10.00	20.00
1904	C^N	H............307,000		1.50	2.50	5.00	12.00
	M^O	M *vars.:*....1,266,000		1.25	2.00	4.50	12.00
		mint mark M^O; mint mark M (error).					
	Z^S	Z........... ⎫ 367,500		1.50	3.00	10.00	20.00
		M........... ⎭		1.50	3.00	10.00	25.00
1905	M^O	M...........266,000		2.50	3.75	7.50	18.00
	Z^S	M............66,250		7.50	15.00	30.00	60.00

20 CENTAVOS

Restyled Eagle Type 1898-1905

The law of December 12, 1892 authorized the issuance of 20 centavos coins to replace the 25 centavos pieces then in circulation. Unaccountably, actual coinage and release of 20 centavos coins did not take place at any mint until 1898.

The obverse eagle is in the tall, elegant style characteristic of all coinage of 1898. The reverse has the value in the center with a wreath below, and mint mark, assayer's initial and silver content above.

Diameter 22 mm; weight 5.415 grams; composition .9027 silver, .0973 copper; edge: reeded.

20 CENTAVOS

Date	Mint	Assayer	Quan. Minted	F	VF	EF	Unc.
1898	C^N	M............113,790		$5.00	$10.00	$25.00	$75.00
	G^O	R............135,000		4.00	8.00	22.00	75.00
	M^O	M............150,000		4.00	7.50	20.00	40.00
	Z^S	Z............195,000		6.00	10.00	20.00	60.00
1899	C^N	M............ } 44,200		12.00	20.00	35.00	125.00
		Q............ }		20.00	35.00	75.00	225.00
	G^O	R............215,000		4.00	7.50	20.00	75.00
	M^O	M............425,000		4.00	6.50	15.00	35.00
	Z^S	Z............210,000		6.00	10.00	20.00	60.00
1900	C^N	Q............67,950		6.50	10.00	25.00	65.00
	G^O	R-9 over 8.....37,500		10.00	20.00	35.00	110.00
	M^O	M............294,500		4.00	6.50	15.00	35.00
	Z^S	Z-9 over 8......96,750		4.00	7.50	20.00	75.00
1901	C^N	Q............185,000		4.00	7.50	20.00	60.00
	M^O	M............110,000		4.00	7.50	20.00	40.00
	Z^S	Z *varieties* 130,000		4.00	7.50	20.00	60.00
		1 over 0; normal date.					
1902	C^N	Q *varieties:*....97,500		4.00	8.00	22.00	60.00
		9 over 8; normal date.					
	M^O	M............119,500		4.00	6.50	15.00	35.00
	Z^S	Z............105,000		4.00	8.00	17.50	80.00
1903	C^N	Q............92,500		4.00	7.50	20.00	40.00
	M^O	M............212,500		5.00	10.00	25.00	50.00
	Z^S	Z............143,000		5.00	9.00	20.00	75.00
1904	C^N	H............257,700		5.00	10.00	25.00	50.00
	M^O	M............275,500		5.00	10.00	20.00	45.00
	Z^S	Z............ } 246,000		6.00	10.00	25.00	55.00
		M............ }		5.00	9.00	20.00	75.00
1905	M^O	M............117,000		6.50	20.00	35.00	80.00
	Z^S	M............59,000		10.00	20.00	45.00	125.00

25 CENTAVOS

Balance Scale Type 1869-1892

The first coinage of the 25 centavos denomination occurred in 1869. The obverse shows an eagle on cactus, with inscription above and date below.

The three branches of government are represented on the reverse. An unsheathed sword symbolizes Executive Power. The scroll with the. word LEY indicates the Legislative Power and the Constitution. The balances themselves stand for the equity of the Judicial Power. Above is the Phrygian Liberty cap with rays. Below are the value, mint, assayer's initial, and silver content.

This design became the standard for other larger-size gold and silver coins issued during the same years.

25 CENTAVOS

Diameter 25 mm; weight 6.768 grams; composition .9027 silver, .0973 copper; edge: reeded.

Date	Mint	Assayer	Quantity Minted	F	VF	EF	Unc.
1869	M^O	C *76,000*		$10.00	$25.00	$55.00	$120.00
	P^I	S		25.00	75.00	150.00	300.00
1870	G^O	S 128,000		5.00	15.00	45.00	100.00
	M^O	C 136,000		6.00	12.00	30.00	90.00
	P^I	G	49,560	10.00	30.00	75.00	150.00
		O		10.00	30.00	75.00	150.00
	Z^S	H *152,000*		6.00	15.00	50.00	110.00
1871	CH.	M 17,564		12.00	25.00	60.00	150.00
	C^N	P			Rare		
	G^O	S 172,000		5.00	15.00	45.00	100.00
	M^O	M 137,651		6.00	12.00	30.00	90.00
	P^I	O 30,116		10.00	30.00	75.00	150.00
	Z^S	H 250,000		6.00	15.00	50.00	100.00

1872 CH.M
very crude date

Date	Mint	Assayer	Quantity Minted	F	VF	EF	Unc.
1872	CH.	M v. crude date .24,000		20.00	40.00	80.00	225.00
	C^N	P *2,780*			Rare		
	G^O	S *varieties:* . . .178,000		5.00	16.00	45.00	100.00
		2 over 1; normal date.					
	M^O	M 219,520		6.00	12.00	30.00	90.00
	P^I	O 46,000		10.00	30.00	75.00	150.00
	Z^S	H 260,000		6.00	15.00	50.00	100.00
1873	C^N	P *19,586*		30.00	70.00	150.00	300.00
	D^O	P *892*			Rare		
	G^O	S *120,000*		10.00	20.00	45.00	100.00
	M^O	M *varieties:* . . .*48,000*		6.00	12.00	30.00	90.00
		3 over 1; normal date.					
	P^I	O *12,880*		8.00	20.00	60.00	125.00
	Z^S	H *132,000*		6.00	15.00	50.00	100.00
1874	A	L		10.00	25.00	50.00	125.00
	C^N	P		17.50	45.00	110.00	250.00
	G^O	S		15.00	25.00	45.00	110.00
	H^O	R 22,824		8.00	15.00	40.00	100.00

25 CENTAVOS

Date	Mint	Assayer	Quantity Minted	F	VF	EF	Unc.
	M^O	M varieties:.........		$6.00	$12.00	$30.00	$90.00
		4 over 3; normal date.					
	M^O	B-74/69, B/M........		10.00	20.00	60.00	110.00
	P^I	H....................		15.00	40.00	90.00	200.00
	Z^S	H....................		10.00	20.00	60.00	110.00
		A....................		10.00	20.00	60.00	110.00
1875	A	L....................		10.00	25.00	50.00	125.00
	C^N	P....................			Rare		
	G^O	S varieties:.........		6.00	18.00	45.00	100.00
		5 over 4; normal date.					
	H^O	R....................			Rare		
	M^O	B....................		6.00	12.00	30.00	90.00
	P^I	H....................		8.00	20.00	60.00	125.00
	Z^S	A....................		7.00	20.00	60.00	110.00
1876	A	L....................		15.00	35.00	75.00	150.00
	C^N	P....................			Rare		
	G^O	S....................		6.00	18.00	45.00	100.00
	H^O	F varieties:....34,332		10.00	18.00	50.00	125.00
		6/4, F/R; normal date, F/R.					
	M^O	B varieties:.........		6.00	12.00	30.00	90.00
		6 over 5; normal date.					
	P^I	H varieties:.........		10.00	22.50	65.00	135.00
		6 over 5; normal date.					
	Z^S	A....................		6.00	15.00	50.00	100.00
		S....................		6.00	15.00	50.00	100.00
1877	A	L............11,402		25.00	50.00	125.00	250.00
	D^O	P....................		8.00	35.00	75.00	175.00
	G^O	S.........124,000		6.00	18.00	45.00	100.00
	H^O	F....................		10.00	20.00	50.00	120.00
	M^O	M...........56,000		6.00	12.00	30.00	90.00
	P^I	H...........19,100		10.00	22.50	65.00	135.00
	Z^S	S..........350,000		6.00	15.00	50.00	100.00
1878	A	L...........25,365		8.00	20.00	45.00	100.00
	C^N	D....................		15.00	30.00	75.00	150.00
	D^O	E-8 over 7..........			Rare		
		B....................			Rare		
	G^O	S.........146,000		6.00	18.00	45.00	100.00
	H^O	A...........22,636		10.00	20.00	50.00	110.00
	M^O	M varieties:..120,000		6.00	12.00	30.00	90.00
		8 over 1; 8 over 7; normal date.					
	P^I	H....................		12.50	27.50	50.00	110.00
	Z^S	S..........252,000		6.00	15.00	50.00	100.00
1879	A	L....................		8.00	25.00	50.00	125.00
	C^N	D....................		10.00	20.00	45.00	100.00
	D^O	B....................		17.50	35.00	75.00	175.00
	G^O	S....................		6.00	18.00	45.00	100.00
	H^O	A....................		10.00	20.00	50.00	110.00
	M^O	M....................		6.00	12.00	30.00	90.00
	P^I	H....................		8.00	20.00	60.00	125.00
		E....................			Rare		
	Z^S	S....................		6.00	15.00	50.00	100.00
1880	A	L....................		8.00	20.00	45.00	100.00

25 CENTAVOS

Date	Mint	Assayer	Quantity Minted	F	VF	EF	Unc.
	C^N	D	....		Rare		
	D^O	B	....		Rare		
	G^A	A	............*37,639*	$8.00	$15.00	$45.00	$100.00
	G^O	S	....	12.00	22.50	50.00	120.00
	H^O	A	....	8.00	15.00	40.00	100.00
	M^O	M	....	6.00	12.00	30.00	90.00
	P^I	H	....	12.50	27.50	50.00	110.00
	Z^S	S	....	6.00	15.00	50.00	100.00
1881	A	L	..............*8,800*		Rare		
	C^N	D-1 over 0	.....*18,164*	12.50	25.00	50.00	120.00
	G^A	S	............*39,094*	8.00	15.00	45.00	100.00
	G^O	S	............*408,000*	6.00	18.00	45.00	100.00
	H^O	A	............*19,360*	8.00	15.00	40.00	100.00
	M^O	M *varieties:*	..*300,000*	6.00	12.00	30.00	90.00
		1 over 0; normal date.					

1881 P^I E

	P^I	H	...........⎱ *49,880*	10.00	22.50	65.00	135.00
		E	...........⎰		Rare		
	Z^S	S	............*570,000*	6.00	15.00	50.00	100.00
1882	A	L	..............*7,777*	12.50	30.00	70.00	150.00
	C^N	D	....		Rare		
		M	....		Rare		
	D^O	C	............*17,142*	12.50	25.00	50.00	150.00
	G^A	S	............*17,772*	8.00	15.00	45.00	100.00
	G^O	S	............*204,000*	6.00	18.00	45.00	100.00
	H^O	A	............*8,120*	8.00	15.00	40.00	100.00
	M^O	M	...........*212,000*	6.00	12.00	30.00	90.00
	P^I	H	............*20,000*	8.00	20.00	60.00	125.00

1882 Z^S,
2 over 1

	Z^S	S *varieties:*	...*300,000*	6.00	15.00	50.00	100.00
		2 over 1; normal date.					
1883	A	L	............*28,148*	10.00	25.00	50.00	125.00
	CH.	M	............*11,888*	10.00	22.50	45.00	100.00
	C^N	M	............*15,368*	10.00	20.00	50.00	120.00

25 CENTAVOS

Date	Mint	Assayer Quantity Minted	F	VF	EF	Unc.
	G^A	B-3/2, B/S..........	$10.00	$18.50	$55.00	$125.00
	G^O	B............168,000	6.00	18.00	45.00	100.00
	H^O	M............2,000	10.00	20.00	50.00	120.00
	M^O	M............108,000	6.00	12.00	30.00	90.00
	P^I	H............16,800	10.00	22.50	65.00	135.00
	Z^S	S *varieties:*...193,200	6.00	15.00	50.00	100.00
		3 over 2; normal date.				
1884	A	L..................	10.00	25.00	50.00	125.00
	C^N	M..................	12.50	25.00	50.00	120.00
	D^O	C 4 over 3...........	17.50	35.00	75.00	175.00
	G^A	B..................	12.00	22.50	50.00	120.00
	G^O	B *varieties:*.........	5.00	16.00	45.00	100.00
		84 over 69; normal date.				
	H^O	M..................	12.00	30.00	75.00	150.00
	M^O	M..................	6.00	12.00	30.00	90.00
	P^I	H..................	10.00	20.00	60.00	125.00
	Z^S	S *varieties:*.........	6.00	15.00	50.00	100.00
		4 over 3; normal date.				
1885	A	L..................	15.00	35.00	75.00	150.00
	CH.	M............34,599	10.00	22.50	45.00	100.00
	C^N	M-5 over 4.....18,580	12.50	25.00	50.00	120.00
	D^O	C............15,023	10.00	25.00	50.00	150.00
	G^O	R *varieties:*..300,000	5.00	16.00	45.00	100.00
		85 over 69; second 8 over 6; normal date.				
	H^O	M..................	10.00	20.00	50.00	110.00
	M^O	M............216,000	6.00	12.00	30.00	90.00
	P^I	H............42,800	8.00	20.00	50.00	110.00
	Z^S	S............309,200	6.00	15.00	50.00	100.00
1886	A	L............45,662	8.00	20.00	45.00	100.00
	CH.	M............22,121	12.00	25.00	60.00	150.00
	C^N	M............21,888	10.00	17.50	50.00	120.00
	D^O	C............32,552	9.00	17.50	45.00	120.00
	G^O	R *varieties:*...322,000	5.00	10.00	25.00	75.00
		86 over 65 (actually 86/85/69); 86 over 69, R over S; second 8 over 6; normal date.				
	H^O	G............6,400	12.00	30.00	75.00	150.00
	M^O	M *varieties:*..436,000	6.00	12.00	30.00	90.00
		6 over 5; normal date.				
	P^I	C...........}78,400	11.00	28.00	70.00	140.00
		R *varieties:*...}	7.00	18.00	50.00	110.00
		6 over inverted 6; normal date.				
	Z^S	S *varieties:*...613,200	6.00	15.00	50.00	100.00
		6 over 5; normal date.				
		Z.........incl. above	6.00	15.00	50.00	100.00
1887	A^S	L............12,320	8.00	20.00	45.00	100.00
	C^A	M............26,300	8.00	12.00	25.00	75.00
	C^N	M............32,220	10.00	17.50	50.00	120.00
	D^O	C............27,117	8.00	15.00	45.00	120.00
	G^O	R............254,000	5.00	10.00	25.00	75.00
	H^O	G............11,600	15.00	40.00	90.00	225.00
	M^O	M............376,000	6.00	12.00	30.00	90.00
	P^I	R, P^I over Z^S..}91,700	7.00	18.00	50.00	110.00
		B, P^I over Z^S..}	75.00	125.00	200.00	350.00

25 CENTAVOS

Date	Mint	Assayer	Quantity Minted	G-VG	F	VF	EF	Unc.
	Z^S	Z 388,800		$1.50	$6.00	$15.00	$50.00	$100.00
1888	A^S	L 19,880		2.25	8.00	20.00	45.00	100.00
	C^A	M 14,192		7.50	10.00	22.50	45.00	100.00
	C^N	M 86,308		2.00	5.00	10.00	25.00	75.00
	D^O	C 25,005		4.25	8.00	15.00	45.00	120.00
	G^O	R 312,000		1.50	5.00	10.00	25.00	75.00
	H^O	G 19,760		1.75	8.00	15.00	40.00	100.00
	M^O	M 192,000		1.00	6.00	12.00	30.00	90.00
	P^I	R *varieties:*. . .106,380		1.00	6.00	15.00	35.00	100.00

P^I over Z^S; R over B; normal mint mark and initial.

Date	Mint	Assayer	Quantity Minted	G-VG	F	VF	EF	Unc.
	Z^S	Z 408,000		1.50	6.00	15.00	50.00	100.00
1889	A^S	L 14,200		3.75	10.00	25.00	50.00	125.00
	C^A	M 50,112		2.00	8.00	12.00	25.00	75.00
	C^N	M 50,324		2.25	10.00	20.00	50.00	120.00
	D^O	C 28,904		2.25	8.00	15.00	45.00	120.00
	G^A	S 30,400		2.00	8.00	15.00	45.00	100.00
	G^O	R *varieties:*. . .304,000		1.50	5.00	10.00	25.00	75.00

9 over 8; normal date.

1889 G^O
9 over 8

Date	Mint	Assayer	Quantity Minted	G-VG	F	VF	EF	Unc.
	H^O	G 28,400		2.00	8.00	15.00	40.00	100.00
	M^O	M 132,000		2.00	6.00	12.00	30.00	90.00
	P^I	R *varieties:*. . .115,240		6.00	5.00	12.00	40.00	90.00

P^I over Z^S; R over B; normal mint mark and initial.

Date	Mint	Assayer	Quantity Minted	G-VG	F	VF	EF	Unc.
	Z^S	Z 400,000		1.50	6.00	15.00	50.00	100.00
1890	A^S	L 23,200		2.50	8.00	20.00	45.00	100.00
	C^N	M 90,796		2.25	7.50	17.50	50.00	120.00
	D^O	C 68,432		2.25	5.00	12.00	40.00	120.00
	G^O	R 236,400		1.00	5.00	10.00	25.00	75.00
	H^O	G 18,000		9.00	10.00	20.00	50.00	120.00
	M^O	M 60,000		1.75	6.00	12.00	30.00	90.00
	P^I	R *varieties:*. . . . 64,100		1.75	6.00	12.00	40.00	90.00

P^I/Z^S, R/B; normal mint mark, R/B;
normal mint mark and initial.

Date	Mint	Assayer	Quantity Minted	G-VG	F	VF	EF	Unc.
	Z^S	Z 269,200		1.50	6.00	15.00	50.00	100.00
1892	C^N	M 16,068		2.50	10.00	20.00	50.00	125.00

50 CENTAVOS

Balance Scale Type 1869-1895

The balance scale 50 centavos coin employs the standard design introduced in 1869 on all large-size gold and silver coins. Obverses carry the typical coat of arms. Reverses show the symbolizations of the three branches of government as the sword, the scroll, and the balances.

Diameter 30 mm; weight 13.536 grams; composition .9027 silver, .0973 copper; edge: reeded.

50 CENTAVOS

Date	Mint	Assayer	Quantity Minted	G-VG	F	VF	EF	Unc.
1869	G^O	S.................		$2.75	$15.00	$30.00	$75.00	$350.00
	M^O	C.............46,000		6.50	15.00	30.00	75.00	300.00
1870	G^O	S.............*166,000*		2.50	12.00	25.00	50.00	250.00
	M^O	C.............52,000		2.50	12.00	25.00	50.00	250.00
	P^I	G *varieties:*....50,280		2.75	15.00	40.00	100.00	450.00
		87 over 78; normal date.						
		O........incl. above		2.75	15.00	40.00	100.00	450.00
	Z^S	H.............*86,000*		2.50	12.00	25.00	50.00	250.00
1871	C^N	P.................		6.50	50.00	100.00	250.00	1,200
	D^O	P.............591		——		Rare		
	G^O	S.............148,000		2.50	12.00	25.00	50.00	250.00
	M^O	C.............⎫13,600		6.50	20.00	40.00	100.00	350.00
		M over C.....⎭		4.00	20.00	40.00	100.00	350.00
	P^I	O over G......63,840		2.75	12.00	30.00	80.00	400.00
	Z^S	H.............146,000		2.50	12.00	25.00	50.00	250.00
1872	G^O	S *varieties:*...144,000		5.50	12.00	25.00	50.00	250.00
		2 over 1; normal date.						
	M^O	M *varieties:*...60,000		2.75	12.00	25.00	50.00	250.00
		2 over 1; normal date.						
	P^I	O *varieties:*....51,500		2.75	12.00	30.00	80.00	400.00
		O over G; normal initial.						
	Z^S	H.............132,000		2.50	12.00	25.00	50.00	250.00
1873	C^N	P.................		12.50	60.00	120.00	300.00	1,200
	D^O	P.............⎫4,010		15.00	30.00	75.00	175.00	750.00
		M over P.....⎭		3.50	30.00	75.00	175.00	750.00
	G^O	S.............*50,000*		2.50	12.00	25.00	50.00	250.00
	M^O	M.............*6,000*		3.00	15.00	30.00	60.00	400.00
	P^I	O.............⎫31,780		6.50	15.00	40.00	100.00	450.00
		H.............⎭		7.50	20.00	50.00	125.00	550.00
	Z^S	H.............*56,000*		2.50	12.00	25.00	50.00	250.00
∕1874	C^N	P.................		——		Rare		
	D^O	M.................		9.00	15.00	40.00	175.00	750.00
	G^O	S.................		2.50	12.00	25.00	50.00	250.00
	H^O	R.................		2.75	12.00	35.00	100.00	600.00

1874 M^O B
4 over 2

50 CENTAVOS

Date	Mint	Assayer Quantity Minted	G-VG	F	VF	EF	Unc.
	M^O	M 4 over 3..........	$6.50	$30.00	$60.00	$125.00	$600.00
		B *varieties:*.........	2.75	12.00	25.00	50.00	250.00
		4 over 2; 4 over 3, B over M; normal date.					
	P^I	H over O............	2.75	12.00	30.00	80.00	400.00
•	Z^S	H...................	3.75	12.00	25.00	50.00	250.00
1875	A^S	L..................	3.75	12.00	25.00	60.00	350.00
	C^N	P..................	5.50	12.00	25.00	50.00	250.00
	D^O	M..................	3.75	12.00	25.00	60.00	300.00
		H..................	15.00	50.00	100.00	250.00	800.00
	G^O	S..................	2.50	12.00	25.00	50.00	250.00
	H^O	R *varieties:*.........	2.75	12.00	25.00	75.00	400.00
		5 over 4; normal date.					
	M^O	B..................	6.50	15.00	30.00	60.00	350.00
	P^I	H..................	2.75	12.00	30.00	80.00	400.00
	Z^S	A..................	2.50	12.00	25.00	50.00	250.00
1876	A^S	L..................	5.50	12.00	25.00	60.00	350.00
	C^N	P..................	3.75	12.00	25.00	50.00	250.00
	D^O	M *varieties:*.........	5.50	12.00	30.00	75.00	400.00
		6 over 5; normal date.					
	G^O	S..................	2.75	12.00	25.00	50.00	250.00
	H^O	F *varieties:*.........	6.50	12.00	25.00	50.00	400.00
		6 over 5, F over R; normal date and initial.					
	M^O	B *varieties:*.........	2.75	12.00	25.00	50.00	250.00
		6 over 5; normal date.					
	P^I	H..................	7.50	25.00	60.00	150.00	700.00
	Z^S	A *varieties:*.........	2.50	12.00	25.00	50.00	250.00
		6 over 5; normal date.					
		S..................	2.50	12.00	25.00	50.00	250.00
1877	A^S	L..............26,162	6.00	15.00	30.00	75.00	400.00
	C^N	G *varieties:*.........	2.75	12.00	25.00	50.00	250.00
		7 over 6; normal date.					
	D^O	P..............2,000	3.50	12.00	30.00	75.00	400.00
	G^O	S.............76,000	2.50	12.00	25.00	50.00	250.00
	H^O	F..................	2.75	12.00	25.00	75.00	400.00
	M^O	M *varieties:*.........	2.75	12.00	30.00	75.00	300.00
		second 7 over 2; normal date.					
	P^I	H.............34,180	2.75	12.00	30.00	80.00	400.00
	Z^S	S............100,000	2.50	12.00	25.00	50.00	250.00
1878	A^S	L..................	2.75	12.00	25.00	60.00	350.00
	C^N	G............ ⎫	3.50	15.00	30.00	60.00	300.00
		D............ ⎬18,160	6.50	15.00	35.00	75.00	350.00
	D^O	B..................	——		Rare		
	G^O	S.............37,000	2.50	15.00	30.00	75.00	350.00
	M^O	M *varieties:*....8,000	4.00	15.00	30.00	90.00	350.00
		8 over 7; normal date.					
	P^I	H.............9,700	2.75	15.00	40.00	100.00	450.00
	Z^S	S *varieties:*...254,000	4.00	12.00	25.00	50.00	250.00
		8 over 7; normal date.					
1879	A^S	L..................	3.75	12.00	25.00	60.00	350.00
	C^N	D *varieties:*.........	2.75	12.00	25.00	50.00	250.00
		D over G; normal D.					

50 CENTAVOS

Date	Mint	Assayer Quantity Minted	G-VG	F	VF	EF	Unc.
	D^O	B..................	——		Rare		
	G^O	S..................	$2.50	$12.00	$25.00	$50.00	$250.00
	M^O	M..................	6.50	15.00	30.00	90.00	350.00
	P^I	H *varieties:*.........	2.75	15.00	35.00	90.00	450.00
		9 over 7; normal date.					
	Z^S	S..................	2.50	12.00	25.00	50.00	250.00
1880	A^S	L...........*56,630*	2.75	12.00	25.00	60.00	350.00
	C^N	D..................	2.75	12.00	25.00	50.00	250.00
	D^O	P..................	6.50	15.00	40.00	100.00	500.00
	G^O	S..................	2.50	12.00	25.00	50.00	250.00
	H^O	A *varieties:*.........	6.50	12.00	25.00	75.00	400.00
		second 8 over 7; normal date.					
	M^O	M..................	13.00	25.00	50.00	150.00	500.00
	P^I	H..................	2.75	12.00	30.00	80.00	400.00
	Z^S	S..................	2.50	12.00	25.00	50.00	250.00
1881	A^S	L............*17,910*	6.50	15.00	30.00	75.00	400.00
	C^N	D *varieties:*...*187,927*	2.75	12.00	25.00	50.00	250.00
		1 over 0; normal date.					
		G.........incl. above	15.00	45.00	90.00	175.00	350.00
	D^O	P.............*10,282*	6.50	15.00	40.00	100.00	500.00
	G^O	S *varieties:*....*32,000*	2.75	12.00	25.00	50.00	250.00
		81 over 79; normal date.					
	H^O	A.............*13,000*	3.75	12.00	25.00	75.00	400.00
	M^O	M.............*16,000*	6.75	15.00	30.00	90.00	350.00
	P^I	H.............*27,660*	4.00	15.00	30.00	80.00	400.00
	Z^S	S.............*201,000*	2.50	12.00	25.00	50.00	250.00
1882	C^N	D..................	——		Rare		
		G..................	——		Rare		
	D^O	C............. *8,957*	15.00	30.00	75.00	200.00	800.00
	G^O	S............. *18,000*	2.50	12.00	25.00	50.00	250.00
	H^O	A..................	5.50	12.00	30.00	90.00	450.00
	M^O	M-2 over 1...... *2,000*	6.75	18.50	35.00	110.00	425.00
	P^I	H.............*21,680*	2.50	15.00	30.00	80.00	400.00
	Z^S	S *2,000*	6.75	25.00	50.00	150.00	450.00

50 centavos showing CH^A mint mark used 1883-86

Date	Mint	Assayer Quantity Minted	G-VG	F	VF	EF	Unc.
1883	CH^A	M.............*11,888*	6.00	20.00	40.00	100.00	400.00
	C^N	D.............18,634	6.50	20.00	40.00	100.00	500.00
	G^O	S..................	3.50		Rare		
		B *varieties:*.........	2.75	12.00	25.00	50.00	250.00
		3 over 2, B over S; normal date and initial.					
	M^O	M.............*4,000*	——		Rare		
		beware of contemporary counterfeits.					
	P^I	H.............*29,200*	3.50	15.00	30.00	80.00	400.00
	Z^S	S-s/A in mmk. .*30,600*	2.50	12.00	25.00	50.00	250.00

50 CENTAVOS

Date	Mint	Assayer	Quantity Minted	G-VG	F	VF	EF	Unc.
1884	A^S	L..............6,286		$19.50	$30.00	$60.00	$150.00	$600.00
	CH^A	M.................		3.75	25.00	50.00	125.00	500.00
	D^O	C *varieties:*.........		2.75	15.00	40.00	100.00	500.00
		4 over 2; normal date.						
	G^O	B over S.............		2.50	12.00	25.00	75.00	300.00
	M^O	M.................		——	40.00	100.00	300.00	1,000
	P^I	H..................		2.50	15.00	30.00	80.00	400.00
	Z^S	S *varieties:*..........		2.50	12.00	25.00	50.00	250.00
		4 over 3; normal date.						
1885	A^S	L-A^S over H^O....20,538		6.50	15.00	30.00	75.00	400.00
	CH^A	M.............*13,068*		4.00	15.00	35.00	90.00	350.00
	C^N	M-5/3, M/G....*9,254*		3.50	20.00	40.00	85.00	250.00
	D^O	B..................		6.00	15.00	40.00	100.00	500.00
	G^O	R.............*53,000*		2.50	12.00	25.00	50.00	250.00
	M^O	M.............*12,000*		4.00	12.00	25.00	50.00	250.00
	P^I	H *varieties:*...*44,800*		2.75	15.00	30.00	80.00	400.00
		5 over 0; 5 over 4; normal date.						
		C.........incl. above		2.75	15.00	30.00	80.00	400.00
	Z^S	S *varieties:*.....*2,000*		6.50	12.00	25.00	50.00	250.00
		5 over 4; normal date.						
1886	CH^A	M.............18,161		5.50	20.00	40.00	100.00	400.00
	C^N	M.............7,030		19.50	30.00	60.00	150.00	800.00
	D^O	C.............15,590		6.50	15.00	40.00	100.00	500.00
	G^O	R *varieties:*....*59,000*		2.50	12.00	25.00	50.00	250.00
		6 over 5, R over S; 6 over 5, R over B; normal date.						
	M^O	M *varieties:*...66,000		5.50	12.00	25.00	50.00	200.00
		6 over 5; normal date.						
	P^I	C............\}91,500		4.00	15.00	30.00	80.00	400.00
		R *varieties:*...\/		4.00	15.00	30.00	80.00	400.00
		6 over 1; normal date.						
	Z^S	Z.............2,000		——		Rare		
1887	C^A	M.............26,272		9.00	25.00	60.00	125.00	450.00
	C^N	M.............75,802		3.50	12.00	25.00	50.00	250.00
	D^O	C-D^O over M^O..28,133		15.00	15.00	40.00	90.00	350.00
	G^O	R.............18,000		3.50	12.00	30.00	75.00	350.00
	M^O	M *varieties:*...88,000		2.75	12.00	25.00	50.00	200.00
		7 over 6; normal date.						
	P^I	R.............32,400		6.75	15.00	30.00	80.00	400.00
	Z^S	Z.............63,000		6.00	15.00	30.00	75.00	250.00
1888	A^S	L		—		Rare		
1888	C^N	M.................		——		Rare		
	G^O	R.................				Rare		
	H^O	G.................				Rare		
	M^O	M.................				Rare		
	P^I	R*.................		——		Counterfeit		
1892	C^N	M.............8,200		15.00	30.00	60.00	150.00	800.00
1894	H^O	G.............59,200		4.00	12.00	25.00	75.00	400.00
1895	H^O	G.............8,000		22.50	75.00	150.00	350.00	1,200

1 PESO
Balance Scale Type 1869-1873

The balance scale 1 peso coin appeared in 1869, along with other similarly designed coins. It combines the standing eagle on the obverse, with the sword,

---

*This piece, not in mint reports, in my judgement, is a contemporary counterfeit.   TVB

1 PESO

ind balances representing the three branches of government on the

1 peso coin is very slightly smaller than the old-style 8 *reales* Liberty cap piece, though the weight and silver content are the same.

Diameter 37 mm; weight 27.073 grams; composition .9027 silver, .0973 copper; edge: reeded.

Date	Mint	Assayer	Quantity Minted	F	VF	EF	Unc.
1869	M^O	C.........................		$30.00	$60.00	$125.00	$500.00
	O^A	E.........................		300.00	450.00	750.00	2,000
1870	C^N	E.........................		40.00	65.00	125.00	475.00
	D^O	P.........................		35.00	60.00	125.00	500.00
	G^A	C.........................		400.00	850.00	2,000	6,000
	M^O	C *varieties:*.........5,115,000		12.00	20.00	40.00	200.00
		70 over 69; normal date.					
		M *varieties:*.......incl. above		20.00	30.00	50.00	250.00
		M over C; normal initial.					
	O^A	E *varieties:*.........176,704		15.00	35.00	75.00	400.00
		large ^{A} in mint mark; small ^{A} in mint mark.					
	P^I	S *varieties:*.........1,967,410		150.00	250.00	450.00	1,000
		S over A; normal initial.					
		G.................incl. above		20.00	30.00	65.00	300.00
		H.................incl. above			Rare		
		believed to be a contemporary counterfeit.					
		O *varieties:*.......incl. above		20.00	30.00	65.00	300.00
		O over G; normal initial.					
	Z^S	H...................4,518,800		15.00	30.00	55.00	300.00
1871	C^N	P *varieties:*..........478,354		20.00	35.00	65.00	300.00
		7 over 1; normal date.					
	D^O	P...................426,574		20.00	35.00	65.00	300.00
	G^A	C...................828,901		35.00	70.00	150.00	600.00
	G^O	S *varieties:*.........3,946,000		12.00	20.00	40.00	190.00
		1 over 0; normal date.					
	M^O	M *varieties:*.........6,974,148		12.00	20.00	40.00	200.00
		1 over 0; normal date.					
	O^A	E *varieties:*..........139,768		15.00	25.00	50.00	300.00
		71 over 69; large A in mint mark; small A in mint mark.					
	P^I	O *varieties:*.........2,103,070		17.50	30.00	60.00	300.00
		71 over 69; normal date, O over G.					
	Z^S	H...................4,459,080		12.00	20.00	40.00	200.00

1 PESO

Date	Mint	Assayer	Quantity Minted	F	VF	EF	Unc.
1872	CH.	P over M	} 747,000	$1,500	$2,000	$3,000	$4,000
		M		20.00	30.00	50.00	250.00
	C^N	P	209,330	25.00	45.00	75.00	350.00

1872 D^o peso
showing P.^{T} initials

Date	Mint	Assayer	Quantity Minted	F	VF	EF	Unc.
	D^O	P	} 296,058	25.00	40.00	75.00	350.00
		P$_T$		75.00	150.00	275.00	750.00
	G^A	C	485,331	30.00	60.00	125.00	500.00
	G^O	S	4,067,000	12.00	20.00	40.00	200.00
	M^O	M *varieties:*	4,801,006	12.00	20.00	40.00	200.00
		2 over 1; normal date.					
	O^A	E *varieties:*	179,911	15.00	30.00	60.00	300.00
		large A in mint mark; small A in mint mark.					
	P^I	O	1,872,620	15.00	30.00	55.00	300.00
	Z^S	H	4,038,806	12.00	20.00	40.00	200.00
1873	CH.	M *varieties:*	320,000	20.00	30.00	50.00	250.00
		M over P; normal initial.					
	C^N	P	526,755	20.00	35.00	65.00	300.00
	D^O	P	203,191	25.00	40.00	75.00	350.00
	G^A	C *varieties:*	276,662	35.00	70.00	150.00	600.00
		3 over 2; normal date.					
	G^O	S *varieties:*	1,560,000	12.00	20.00	40.00	200.00
		3 over 2; G^O over M^O, S over M; normal date and initials.					
	M^O	M	1,764,793	12.00	20.00	40.00	200.00
	O^A	E	105,101	20.00	35.00	65.00	350.00
	P^I	O	} 893,100	15.00	30.00	55.00	300.00
		H		17.50	30.00	65.00	350.00
	Z^S	H	1,781,640	12.00	20.00	40.00	200.00

Liberty Cap Type 1898-1909

On May 27, 1897, a new coinage of 1 peso pieces was authorized to begin in 1898 as a permanent replacement for the historic 8 *reales* coin.* This action restored the true name to the unit for the first time since coinage of the balance scale peso was suspended in 1873.

The basic design of the new peso piece is similar to the 8 *reales* coinage. The obverse eagle is redesigned to show the more majestic coat of arms typical

---

*An eccentric 1898 8 *reales* (i.e., not Un Peso) of México is illustrated and discussed by Miguel L. Muñoz, "El Columnario de 1772 y el Ocho Reales de 1898," in *Gaceta Numismática 28* (March, 1973), pp. 23-29.

1 PESO

of 1898. The reverse has a larger Liberty cap, the words UN PESO, and the silver content expressed as 902.7.

Liberty cap peso pieces were coined in 1908 and 1909 with the old REPUBLICA MEXICANA obverse, the only coins to be regularly struck with this inscription after the monetary reform of 1905.

In 1949, a total of 10,250,000 pieces of 1 peso dated 1898 M^O AM were produced for the Republic of China. The México mint struck 8,250,000 pieces; the balance of 2,000,000 pieces was struck in the U.S. mint at San Francisco. These pieces can properly be called restrikes and trade coins. Restrikes can be distinguished from originals in that the beaded rim of the reverse contains 134 beads, while the rim of the original contains 139 beads. There are also small differences in the punches: the numeral 1, for example, which on the original has a straight serif and tapers to a short base, on the restrike has a curved serif and sits directly on a long thin base.

Diameter 39 mm; weight 27.073 grams; composition .9027 silver, .0973 copper; edge: reeded.

Date	Mint	Assayer	Quantity Minted	F	VF	EF	Unc.
1898	C^N	AM *varieties:*	1,720,000	$10.00	$15.00	$30.00	$75.00
		C^N over M^O; normal mint mark.					
	G^O	RS *varieties:*	4,256,000	16.00	25.00	40.00	100.00
		G^O over M^O; normal mint mark.					
	M^O	AM original	10,156,000	10.00	12.50	20.00	65.00
		*restrike (1949)	10,250,000	10.00	12.50	20.00	50.00
	Z^S	FZ	5,714,000	10.00	12.50	22.50	70.00
1899	C^N	AM	⎫ 1,722,000	30.00	65.00	125.00	225.00
		JQ	⎭	10.00	17.50	35.00	100.00
	G^O	RS	3,207,000	12.00	16.00	22.00	75.00
	M^O	AM	7,930,000	10.00	12.50	22.50	70.00
	Z^S	FZ	5,618,000	10.00	12.50	22.50	70.00
1900	C^N	JQ	1,804,000	10.00	15.00	25.00	75.00
	G^O	RS	1,489,000	20.00	45.00	85.00	250.00
	M^O	AM	8,226,000	10.00	12.50	22.50	70.00
	Z^S	FZ	5,357,000	10.00	12.50	22.50	70.00
1901	C^N	JQ	1,473,000	10.00	15.00	25.00	75.00
	M^O	AM	14,505,000	10.00	12.50	22.50	70.00

*Dr. A. F. Pradeau, "The San Francisco, California, Mexican Pesos of 1898," in *Plus Ultra* vol. 5 no. 60 (September 27, 1968) p. 3.

1 PESO

Date	Mint	Assayer	Quantity Minted	F	VF	EF	Unc.
	Z^S	AZ.................... —		—	—	Rare	—
		FZ................5,706,000		$10.00	$12.50	$22.50	$70.00
1902	C^N	JQ................1,194,000		10.00	15.00	25.00	75.00
	M^O	AM *varieties:*......16,224,000		10.00	12.50	22.50	70.00
		2 over 1; normal date.					
	Z^S	FZ................7,134,000		10.00	12.50	22.50	70.00
1903	C^N	JQ..............} 1,514,000		10.00	15.00	25.00	100.00
		FV..............}		30.00	65.00	150.00	250.00
	M^O	AM..............} 22,396,000		10.00	12.50	22.50	70.00
		MA (error).......}					
	Z^S	FZ *varieties:*........3,080,000		10.00	12.50	22.50	70.00
		3 over 2; normal date.					
1904	C^N	MH..............} 1,554,000		10.00	15.00	25.00	75.00
		RP..............}		75.00	125.00	225.00	350.00
	M^O	AM..............14,935,000		10.00	12.50	22.50	70.00
	Z^S	FZ..............} 2,423,000		10.00	15.00	25.00	70.00
		FM..............}		10.00	15.00	40.00	100.00
1905	C^N	RP................598,000		30.00	65.00	125.00	225.00
	M^O	AM................3,557,000		15.00	22.50	55.00	125.00
	Z^S	FM................995,000		30.00	60.00	95.00	150.00
1908	M^O	AM..............} 7,575,000		10.00	12.50	20.00	55.00
		GV..............}		10.00	12.50	20.00	55.00
1909	M^O	GV................2,924,000		10.00	12.50	20.00	55.00

GOLD 1 PESO

Standing Eagle Type 1870-1905

The first coinage of 1 peso gold pieces took place in 1870. They were coined simultaneously with the silver 8 *reales* and pesos through their entire period of issue. The obverse shows a standing eagle different from that appearing on silver coinage, with inscription above and date below. The reverse bears the value in a wreath, and assayer's initial, gold content, and mint mark at the top.

A mule with the silver 5¢ obverse had been noted at Guanajuato for 1898.

Diameter 15 mm; weight 1.692 grams; composition .875 gold, .125 copper; edge: reeded.

1873 M^O
3 over 1

Date	Mint	Assayer	Quantity Minted	VF	EF	Unc.
1870	G^O	S...........................100.00		125.00	150.00	250.00
	M^O	C...........................50.00		80.00	125.00	200.00
1871	G^O	S...........................100.00		150.00	200.00	400.00
	M^O	M over C....................50.00		80.00	125.00	200.00
1872	M^O	M over C....................50.00		80.00	125.00	200.00
	Z^S	H...........................125.00		150.00	175.00	250.00
1873	C^N	P...........................75.00		100.00	150.00	250.00

GOLD 1 PESO

Date	Mint	Assayer	Quantity Minted	F	VF	EF	Unc.
	M^O	M 3 over 1	*2,900*	$50.00	$80.00	$125.00	$200.00
1874	M^O	M		50.00	80.00	125.00	200.00
1875	C^N	P		85.00	125.00	150.00	250.00
	H^O	R	310		Rare		
	M^O	B over M		50.00	80.00	125.00	200.00
	Z^S	A 5 over 3		125.00	150.00	200.00	250.00
1876	H^O	F			Rare		
	M^O	B over M, 6 over 5		50.00	80.00	125.00	200.00
1877	M^O	M		50.00	80.00	125.00	200.00
1878	C^N	G	248	100.00	175.00	225.00	450.00
	M^O	M	*2,000*	50.00	80.00	125.00	200.00
	Z^S	S		125.00	150.00	175.00	250.00
1879	C^N	D		100.00	150.00	175.00	275.00
	M^O	M		50.00	80.00	125.00	200.00
1880	M^O	M second 8 over 7		50.00	80.00	125.00	200.00
1881	C^N	D 1 over 0	338	100.00	150.00	175.00	275.00
	M^O	M second 8 over 7	1,000	50.00	80.00	125.00	200.00
1882	C^N	D	340	100.00	150.00	175.00	275.00
	M^O	M second 8 over 7		50.00	80.00	125.00	200.00
1883	C^N	D		100.00	150.00	175.00	275.00
	M^O	M-83 over 72	*1,000*	50.00	80.00	125.00	200.00
1884	C^N	M		100.00	150.00	175.00	275.00
	M^O	M		50.00	80.00	125.00	200.00
1885	M^O	M *varieties:*		50.00	80.00	125.00	200.00
		85 over 71; normal date.					
1886	C^N	M 6 over 4	277	100.00	150.00	225.00	450.00
	M^O	M	1,700	50.00	80.00	125.00	200.00
1887	M^O	M	2,200	50.00	80.00	125.00	200.00
1888	A^S	L *varieties:*	——		Rare		
		A^{S}L over M^{O}M; normal mint mark and initial.					
	C^A	M-C^A over M^O	104		Rare		
	C^N	M	2,586	65.00	100.00	150.00	250.00
	G^O	R	210	125.00	175.00	225.00	450.00
	H^O	G over M^O M	——		Rare		
	M^O	M	1,000	50.00	80.00	125.00	200.00
	Z^S	Z	280	175.00	225.00	300.00	650.00
1889	C^N	M			Rare		
	M^O	M	500	100.00	150.00	200.00	275.00
	Z^S	Z	492	150.00	175.00	225.00	450.00
1890	M^O	M	570	100.00	150.00	200.00	275.00
	G^O	R	1,916	75.00	100.00	150.00	250.00
	Z^S	Z	738	150.00	175.00	225.00	450.00
1891	C^N	M 91 over 89	969	75.00	100.00	150.00	250.00
	M^O	M	746	100.00	150.00	200.00	275.00
1892	C^N	M	780	75.00	100.00	150.00	250.00
	G^O	R	533	100.00	150.00	175.00	275.00
	M^O	M 2 over 0	2,895	50.00	80.00	125.00	200.00
1893	C^N	M	498	85.00	125.00	150.00	250.00
	M^O	M	5,917	50.00	80.00	125.00	200.00
1894	C^N	M	493	80.00	125.00	150.00	250.00
	G^O	R	180	150.00	200.00	250.00	500.00
	M^O	M	6,244	50.00	80.00	125.00	200.00

GOLD 1 PESO

Date	Mint	Assayer	Quantity Minted	F	VF	EF	Unc.
1895	C^N	M	1,143	$65.00	$100.00	$150.00	$250.00
	G^O	R	676	100.00	150.00	175.00	275.00
	M^O	M	} 8,994	50.00	80.00	125.00	200.00
		B		50.00	80.00	125.00	200.00
1896	C^N	M 6 over 5	1,028	65.00	100.00	150.00	250.00
	G^O	R 6 over 5	4,671	75.00	100.00	150.00	250.00
	M^O	B	} 7,166	50.00	80.00	125.00	200.00
		M		50.00	80.00	125.00	200.00
1897	C^N	M	785	65.00	100.00	150.00	250.00
	G^O	R *varieties:*	4,280	65.00	100.00	150.00	250.00
		7 over 6; normal date.					
	M^O	M	5,131	50.00	80.00	125.00	200.00

1898 Peso,
Mint Mark C^N over M^O

1898 G^O mule

Date	Mint	Assayer	Quantity Minted	F	VF	EF	Unc.
1898	C^N	M *varieties:*	3,521	65.00	100.00	150.00	250.00
		C^N over M^O; normal mint mark.					
	G^O	R *varieties:*	5,193				
		regular obverse		65.00	100.00	150.00	250.00
		mule, 5¢ obverse		75.00	100.00	150.00	250.00
	M^O	M 8 over 7	5,368	50.00	80.00	125.00	200.00
1899	C^N	Q	2,000	65.00	100.00	150.00	250.00
	G^O	R	2,748	65.00	100.00	150.00	250.00
	M^O	M	9,515	50.00	80.00	125.00	200.00
1900	G^O	R 9 over 8	864	75.00	125.00	150.00	250.00
	M^O	M *varieties:*	9,301	50.00	80.00	125.00	200.00
		90 over 89; 9 over 8; normal date.					
1901	C^N	Q 1 over 0	2,350	65.00	100.00	150.00	250.00
	M^O	M	8,293	50.00	80.00	125.00	200.00
1902	C^N	Q *varieties:*	2,480	65.00	100.00	150.00	250.00
		C^N over M^O, Q over C; normal die.					
	M^O	M *varieties:*	11,018	50.00	80.00	125.00	200.00
		large date; small date.					
1903	M^O	M	10,369	50.00	80.00	125.00	200.00
1904	C^N	H *varieties:*	3,614	65.00	100.00	150.00	250.00
		C^N over M^O; normal mint mark.					
	M^O	M	9,845	50.00	80.00	125.00	200.00
1905	C^N	P	1,000	Reported not confirmed			
	M^O	M	3,429	50.00	80.00	125.00	200.00

GOLD 2½ PESOS

Standing Eagle Type 1870-1893

The 2½ pesos gold piece was first coined in 1870, and only sparingly made over a period of 23 years. The design consists of a standing eagle on the ob-

GOLD 2½ PESOS

verse and the denomination in a wreath on the reverse, similar to the 1 peso
gold coin of the same years.

Diameter 18 mm; weight 4.23 grams; composition .875 gold, .125 copper; edge: reeded.

Date	Mint	Assayer	Quantity Minted	F	VF	EF	Unc.
1870	M^O	C	820	$150.00	$300.00	$450.00	$850.00
1871	G^O	S	600	1,250	2,000	2,500	3,250
1872	M^O	M over C	800	150.00	300.00	450.00	750.00
	Z^S	H	1,300	150.00	300.00	450.00	750.00
1873	M^O	M-3 over 2		150.00	300.00	450.00	750.00
	Z^S	H		150.00	300.00	450.00	750.00
1874	H^O	R	——		Rare		
	M^O	M		150.00	300.00	450.00	750.00
		B over M		150.00	300.00	450.00	750.00
1875	M^O	B		150.00	300.00	450.00	750.00
	Z^S	A 5 over 3		150.00	300.00	450.00	750.00
1876	M^O	B		150.00	300.00	450.00	750.00
1877	M^O	M		150.00	300.00	450.00	750.00
	Z^S	S		150.00	300.00	550.00	850.00
1878	M^O	M	*400*	150.00	300.00	450.00	750.00
	Z^S	S	*300*	150.00	300.00	450.00	750.00
1879	M^O	M		150.00	300.00	450.00	750.00
1880	M^O	M-80 over 79		175.00	350.00	550.00	850.00
1881	M^O	M	*400*	150.00	300.00	450.00	750.00
1882	M^O	M		150.00	300.00	450.00	750.00
1883	M^O	M second 8 over 7	*400*	150.00	300.00	450.00	750.00
1884	M^O	M		150.00	300.00	450.00	750.00
1885	M^O	M		150.00	300.00	450.00	750.00
1886	M^O	M	400	150.00	300.00	450.00	750.00
1887	M^O	M	400	150.00	300.00	450.00	750.00
1888	A^S	L-A^S over M^O	——		Rare		
	D^O	C	——		Rare		

1888 2½ Pesos,
Mint Mark G^O over M^O

	G^O	R-G^O over M^O	110	1,750	2,250	2,750	3,500
	H^O	G	——		Rare		
	M^O	M	540	150.00	300.00	450.00	750.00
	Z^S	Z-Z^S over M^O	80	300.00	500.00	1,000	1,750
1889	M^O	M	240	150.00	300.00	525.00	850.00
	Z^S	Z-Z^S over M^O	184	225.00	425.00	750.00	1,200
1890	M^O	M	420	150.00	300.00	450.00	750.00

GOLD 2½ PESOS

Date	Mint	Assayer	Quantity Minted	F	VF	EF	Unc.
	Z^S	Z	326	$175.00	$300.00	$525.00	$850.00
1891	M^O	M	188	200.00	350.00	750.00	1,200
1892	M^O	M	240	200.00	350.00	750.00	1,200
1893	C^N	M	141	1,500	2,000	2,500	3,500

GOLD 5 PESOS

Balance Scale Type 1870-1905

The first issue of a 5 pesos gold coin took place in 1870. The obverse carries the typical coat of arms of the period. The reverse shows the balance scale design symbolizing the three branches of government. This design is carried by all larger gold and silver coins of similar years of issue.

As the 2½ pesos, the early issues of the 5 pesos gold coins were never made in quantity.

Diameter 22 mm; weight 8.46 grams; composition .875 gold, .125 copper; edge: reeded.

Date	Mint	Assayer	Quantity Minted	F	VF	EF	Unc.
1870	M^O	C	550	200.00	400.00	500.00	750.00
1871	G^O	S	1,600	375.00	600.00	900.00	1,500
	M^O	M varieties: 71 over 69;	1,600	200.00	400.00	500.00	825.00
1872	M^O	M	1,600	200.00	400.00	500.00	750.00
1873	C^N	P		250.00	400.00	500.00	750.00
	D^O	P 3 over 2		725.00	1,325	1,875	2,750
	M^O	M 3 over 2		200.00	400.00	500.00	750.00
1874	C^N	P		—	—	—	—
	H^O	R		1,750	2,500	3,000	4,500
	M^O	M		200.00	400.00	500.00	750.00
	Z^S	A		200.00	400.00	500.00	750.00
1875	A^S	L		—	—	—	—
	C^N	P		250.00	400.00	500.00	750.00
	M^O	B		200.00	400.00	500.00	750.00
	Z^S	A		200.00	400.00	500.00	850.00
1876	C^N	P		250.00	400.00	500.00	750.00
	M^O	B over M, 6 o...		200.00	400.00	500.00	750.00
1877	C^N	G		250.00	400.00	500.00	750.00
	D^O	P		650.00	1,200	1,700	2,500
	H^O	R	⎫	750.00	1,250	2,000	3,000
		A	⎬ 990	650.00	1,100	1,750	2,800
	M^O	M	⎭	250.00	450.00	700.00	1,000
	Z^S	S over A		200.00	400.00	500.00	750.00
1878	A^S	L	383	900.00	1,500	2,000	2,750
	D^O	E		650.00	1,200	1,700	2,500
	M^O	M varieties: 8 over 7; normal date.	400	200.00	400.00	500.00	750.00
	Z^S	S over A, 8 over 7		200.00	400.00	500.00	850.00

GOLD 5 PESOS

Date	Mint	Assayer	Quantity Minted	F	VF	EF	Unc.
1879	D^O	B varieties:................		$650.00	$1,200	$1,700	$2,500
		9 over 7; normal date.					
	M^O	M-9 over 8................		200.00	400.00	500.00	825.00
1880	M^O	M........................		200.00	400.00	500.00	750.00
1881	M^O	M........................		200.00	400.00	500.00	750.00
1882	C^N	174			Rare		
	M^O	M.....................200		250.00	450.00	700.00	1,000
1883	M^O	M.....................*200*		250.00	450.00	700.00	1,000
	Z^S	S........................		200.00	400.00	500.00	850.00
1884	M^O	M........................		200.00	400.00	500.00	750.00
1886	M^O	M.....................200		250.00	450.00	700.00	1,000
1887	G^O	R.....................140		600.00	1,250	1,500	2,200
	M^O	M.....................200		250.00	450.00	700.00	1,000
1888	C^A	M.....................120			Rare		
	G^O	R......................65			Rare		
	H^O	G........................——			Rare		
	M^O	M.....................250		200.00	400.00	500.00	800.00
	Z^S	Z......................70		750.00	1,250	2,000	3,000
1889	M^O	M.....................190		250.00	450.00	750.00	1,250
	Z^S	Z.....................373		200.00	400.00	500.00	850.00
1890	C^N	M.....................435		250.00	400.00	500.00	750.00
	M^O	M.....................149		250.00	450.00	725.00	1,150
1891	C^N	M...................1,390		250.00	400.00	500.00	750.00
	M^O	M.....................156		250.00	450.00	700.00	1,000
1892	M^O	M.....................214		250.00	450.00	700.00	1,000
	Z^S	Z...................1,229		200.00	400.00	500.00	750.00
1893	G^O	R......................16			Rare		
	M^O	M...................1,058		200.00	400.00	500.00	750.00
1894	C^N	M.....................484		250.00	400.00	500.00	750.00
1895	C^N	M.....................142		500.00	750.00	1,500	2,500
1897	M^O	M.....................370		200.00	400.00	500.00	800.00
1898	M^O	M.....................376		200.00	400.00	500.00	800.00
1900	C^N	Q...................1,536		250.00	400.00	500.00	750.00
	M^O	M...................1,014		200.00	400.00	500.00	750.00
1901	M^O	M...................1,071		200.00	400.00	500.00	750.00
1902	M^O	M...................1,478		200.00	400.00	500.00	750.00
1903	C^N	Q...................1,000		450.00	900.00	1,500	2,250
	M^O	M...................1,162		200.00	400.00	500.00	750.00
1904	M^O	M...................1,415		200.00	400.00	500.00	750.00
1905	M^O	M.....................563		225.00	425.00	525.00	800.00

GOLD 10 PESOS

Balance Scale Type 1870-1905

The first coinage of the 10 pesos gold piece took place in 1870. The obverse carries the eagle on cactus similar to other contemporary issues. The reverse shows the design of the balance scales, symbolizing the three branches of government. This design is uniformly found on the larger gold and silver issues of the period.

10 pesos pieces of this type were made in greater quantity than the early 2½ and 5 pesos coins, though no single issue was very large.

GOLD 10 PESOS

Diameter 27 mm; weight 16.92 grams; composition .875 gold, .125 copper; edge: reeded.

Date	Mint	Assayer	Quantity Minted	F	VF	EF	Unc.
1870	G^A	C	490	$400.00	$600.00	$1,000	$1,600
	M^O	C	480	550.00	900.00	1,200	2,000
	O^A	E	4,614	400.00	600.00	950.00	1,450
1871	G^A	C	1,910	400.00	600.00	1,000	1,600
	O^A	E	2,705	400.00	600.00	950.00	1,450
	Z^S	H	2,000	400.00	600.00	950.00	1,450
1872	D^O	P	1,755	400.00	600.00	950.00	1,450
	G^A	C	780	400.00	600.00	1,000	1,600
	G^O	S	1,400	800.00	1,500	2,000	3,000
	M^O	M 2 over 1	2,100	400.00	600.00	950.00	1,450
	O^A	E	5,897	400.00	600.00	950.00	1,450
	Z^S	H	3,092	400.00	600.00	950.00	1,450
1873	D^O	P 3 over 2	⎱ 1,091	400.00	600.00	950.00	1,450
		M over P, 3 over 2	⎰	400.00	600.00	950.00	1,450
	G^A	C	422	400.00	600.00	1,000	1,600
	M^O	M		400.00	600.00	950.00	1,450
	O^A	E	3,537	400.00	600.00	950.00	1,450
	Z^S	H	936	400.00	600.00	950.00	1,450
1874	A^S	DL			Rare		
	D^O	M		400.00	600.00	950.00	1,450
	G^A	C 4 over 3	477	500.00	850.00	1,250	1,800
	H^O	R			Rare		
	M^O	M 4 over 3		400.00	600.00	950.00	1,450
	O^A	E	2,205	400.00	600.00	950.00	1,450
	Z^S	H		400.00	600.00	950.00	1,450
1875	A^S	L	642	600.00	1,000	1,500	2,000
	D^O	M		400.00	600.00	950.00	1,450
	G^A	C	710	400.00	600.00	1,000	1,600
	M^O	B over M		400.00	600.00	950.00	1,450
	O^A	E	312	400.00	600.00	950.00	1,450
	Z^S	A-5 over 3		400.00	600.00	950.00	1,450
1876	D^O	M		500.00	850.00	1,250	2,000
	H^O	F	357		Rare		
	M^O	B			Rare		
	O^A	E	766	400.00	600.00	950.00	1,450
	Z^S	S 6 over 5		400.00	600.00	950.00	1,450
1877	D^O	P		400.00	600.00	950.00	1,450
	O^A	E	463	400.00	600.00	950.00	1,450
	Z^S	S over H	506	400.00	600.00	950.00	1,450
1878	A^S	L	977	400.00	600.00	950.00	1,450
	D^O	E	582	400.00	600.00	950.00	1,450

Decimal Gold

GOLD 10 PESOS

Date	Mint	Assayer	Quantity Minted	F	VF	EF	Unc.
	G^A	A	183	$600.00	$950.00	$1,350	$2,000
	H^O	A	814	1,750	3,000	3,500	5,000
	M^O	M	*300*	400.00	600.00	950.00	1,450
	O^A	E	229	400.00	600.00	950.00	1,450
	Z^S	S	*711*	400.00	600.00	950.00	1,450
1879	A^S	L	1,078	400.00	600.00	950.00	1,450
	D^O	B		400.00	600.00	950.00	1,450
	G^A	A	200	600.00	950.00	1,350	2,000
	H^O	A		1,000	2,000	2,500	3,500
	O^A	E	210	400.00	600.00	950.00	1,450
	Z^S	S		400.00	600.00	950.00	1,450
1880	A^S	L	2,629	400.00	600.00	950.00	1,450
	D^O	P	*2,030*	400.00	600.00	950.00	1,450
	G^A	S	404	500.00	850.00	1,250	1,800
	H^O	A		1,000	2,000	2,500	3,500
	O^A	E	238	400.00	600.00	950.00	1,450
	Z^S	S	2,089	400.00	600.00	950.00	1,450
1881	A^S	L	2,574	400.00	600.00	950.00	1,450
	C^N	D		400.00	600.00	1,000	1,600
	D^O	P 81 over 79	2,617	600.00	950.00	1,350	2,000
	G^A	S	239		Rare		
	H^O	A		600.00	1,000	1,600	2,500
	M^O	M	100	400.00	600.00	950.00	1,450
	O^A	E	961	400.00	600.00	950.00	1,450
	Z^S	S	736	400.00	600.00	950.00	1,450
1882	A^S	L	3,403	400.00	600.00	950.00	1,450
	C^N	E	874	400.00	600.00	950.00	1,450
	D^O	P	} 1,528		Rare		
		C		400.00	600.00	950.00	1,450
	M^O	M		400.00	600.00	950.00	1,450
	O^A	E	170	550.00	900.00	1,200	2,000
	Z^S	S	1,599	400.00	600.00	950.00	1,450
1883	A^S	L	3,597	400.00	600.00	950.00	1,450
	C^N	M	*221*	400.00	600.00	950.00	1,450
	D^O	C	793	500.00	850.00	1,250	2,000
	M^O	M	*100*	600.00	1,000	1,600	2,500
	O^A	E	111	550.00	900.00	1,200	2,000
	Z^S	S-3 over 2	*256*	500.00	750.00	1,100	1,650
1884	A^S	L			Rare		
	C^N	D		400.00	600.00	950.00	1,450
		M		400.00	600.00	950.00	1,450
	D^O	C	108	500.00	850.00	1,250	2,000
	M^O	M		600.00	1,000	1,600	2,500
	O^A	E	325	400.00	600.00	950.00	1,450
	Z^S	S 4 over 3		400.00	600.00	950.00	1,450
1885	A^S	L	4,562	400.00	600.00	950.00	1,450
	C^N	M	*1,235*	400.00	600.00	950.00	1,450
	M^O	M		400.00	600.00	950.00	1,450
	O^A	E	370	400.00	600.00	950.00	1,450
	Z^S	S	1,588	400.00	600.00	950.00	1,450
1886	A^S	L	4,643	400.00	600.00	950.00	1,450
	C^N	M	981	400.00	600.00	950.00	1,450
	M^O	M	100	600.00	1,000	1,600	2,500
	O^A	E	400	400.00	600.00	950.00	1,450

GOLD 10 PESOS

Date	Mint	Assayer	Quantity Minted	F	VF	EF	Unc.
	Z^S	S.	5,364	$400.00	$600.00	$950.00	$1,450
1887	A^S	L.	3,667	400.00	600.00	950.00	1,450
	C^N	M.,	2,289	400.00	600.00	950.00	1,450
	G^O	R.	80	1,250	2,000	2,500	3,500
	M^O	M.	100	600.00	1,000	1,625	2,750
	O^A	E.	—	700.00	1,250	2,250	3,750
	Z^S	Z.	2,330	400.00	600.00	950.00	1,450
1888	A^S	L.	4,521	400.00	600.00	950.00	1,450
	C^A	M.	175		Rare		
	C^N	M.	767	400.00	600.00	950.00	1,450
	G^O	R.	68	1,500	2,500	3,000	4,000
	M^O	M.	144	450.00	750.00	1,200	2,000
	Z^S	Z.	4,810	400.00	600.00	950.00	1,450
1889	A^S	L.	5,615	400.00	600.00	950.00	1,450
	C^N	M.	859	400.00	600.00	950.00	1,450
	M^O	M.	88	600.00	1,000	1,600	2,500
	Z^S	Z.	6,154	400.00	600.00	950.00	1,450
1890	A^S	L.	4,920	400.00	600.00	950.00	1,450
	C^N	M.	1,427	400.00	600.00	950.00	1,450
	M^O	M.	137	600.00	1,000	1,600	2,500
	Z^S	Z.	1,321	400.00	600.00	950.00	1,450
1891	A^S	L.	568	400.00	600.00	950.00	1,450
	C^N	M.	670	400.00	600.00	950.00	1,450
	G^A	S.	196	600.00	950.00	1,350	2,000
	M^O	M.	133	600.00	1,000	1,600	2,500
	Z^S	Z.	1,930	400.00	600.00	950.00	1,450
1892	A^S	L.		—	—	—	—
	C^N	M.	379	400.00	600.00	950.00	1,450
	M^O	M.	45	600.00	1,000	1,600	2,500
	Z^S	Z.	1,882	400.00	600.00	950.00	1,450
1893	A^S	L.	817	400.00	600.00	950.00	1,450
	C^N	M.	1,806	400.00	600.00	950.00	1,450
	M^O	M.	1,361	400.00	600.00	950.00	1,450
	Z^S	Z.	2,899	400.00	600.00	950.00	1,450
1894	A^S	L.	1,658	400.00	600.00	950.00	1,450
	Z^S	Z.	2,501	400.00	600.00	950.00	1,450
1895	A^S	L.	1,237	400.00	600.00	950.00	1,450
	C^N	M.	179	500.00	850.00	1,250	2,000
	Z^S	Z.	1,217	400.00	600.00	950.00	1,450
1897	M^O	M.	239	400.00	600.00	950.00	1,450
1898	M^O	M-8 over 7	244	425.00	625.00	1,000	1,750
1900	M^O	M.	733	400.00	600.00	950.00	1,450
1901	M^O	M.	562	400.00	600.00	950.00	1,450
1902	M^O	M.	719	400.00	600.00	950.00	1,450
1903	C^N	Q.	774	400.00	600.00	950.00	1,450
	M^O	M.	713	400.00	600.00	950.00	1,450
1904	M^O	M.	694	400.00	600.00	950.00	1,450
1905	M^O	M.	401	400.00	600.00	950.00	1,450

GOLD 20 PESOS
Balance Scale Type 1870-1905

The second issue of the 20 pesos conforms closely in appearance with other large-size silver and gold coins of the same years. Main devices include the standing eagle on the obverse, and the balance scale design representing the three branches of government on the reverse.

Large bank transactions probably account for the quantity of 20 pesos coins struck during this period.

Diameter 34 mm; weight 33.841 grams; composition .875 gold, .125 copper; edge: reeded.

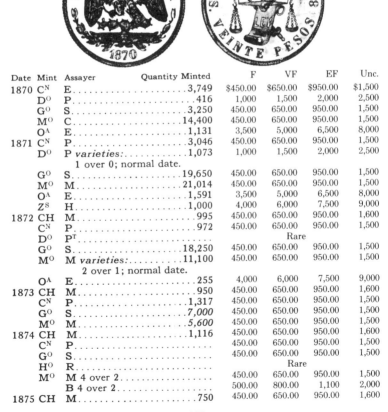

Date	Mint	Assayer	Quantity Minted	F	VF	EF	Unc.
1870	C^N	E	3,749	$450.00	$650.00	$950.00	$1,500
	D^O	P	416	1,000	1,500	2,000	2,500
	G^O	S	3,250	450.00	650.00	950.00	1,500
	M^O	C	14,400	450.00	650.00	950.00	1,500
	O^A	E	1,131	3,500	5,000	6,500	8,000
1871	C^N	P	3,046	450.00	650.00	950.00	1,500
	D^O	P varieties:	1,073	1,000	1,500	2,000	2,500
		1 over 0; normal date.					
	G^O	S	19,650	450.00	650.00	950.00	1,500
	M^O	M	21,014	450.00	650.00	950.00	1,500
	O^A	E	1,591	3,500	5,000	6,500	8,000
	Z^S	H	1,000	4,000	6,000	7,500	9,000
1872	CH	M	995	450.00	650.00	950.00	1,600
	C^N	P	972	450.00	650.00	950.00	1,500
	D^O	P^T			Rare		
	G^O	S	18,250	450.00	650.00	950.00	1,500
	M^O	M varieties:	11,100	450.00	650.00	950.00	1,500
		2 over 1; normal date.					
	O^A	E	255	4,000	6,000	7,500	9,000
1873	CH	M	950	450.00	650.00	950.00	1,600
	C^N	P	1,317	450.00	650.00	950.00	1,500
	G^O	S	7,000	450.00	650.00	950.00	1,500
	M^O	M	5,600	450.00	650.00	950.00	1,500
1874	CH	M	1,116	450.00	650.00	950.00	1,600
	C^N	P		450.00	650.00	950.00	1,500
	G^O	S		450.00	650.00	950.00	1,500
	H^O	R			Rare		
	M^O	M 4 over 2		450.00	650.00	950.00	1,500
		B 4 over 2		500.00	800.00	1,100	2,000
1875	CH	M	750	450.00	650.00	950.00	1,600

GOLD 20 PESOS

Date	Mint	Assayer	Quantity Minted	F	VF	EF	Unc.
	C^N	P		$450.00	$650.00	$950.00	$1,500
	G^O	S		450.00	650.00	950.00	1,500
	H^O	R			Rare		
	M^O	B		450.00	650.00	950.00	1,500
	Z^S	A		4,000	6,000	7,500	9,000
1876	A^S	L	276		Rare		
	CH	M	600	550.00	850.00	1,200	1,800
	C^N	P		450.00	650.00	950.00	1,500
		G		450.00	650.00	950.00	1,500
	D^O	M		1,000	1,500	2,000	2,500
	G^O	S		450.00	650.00	950.00	1,500
	H^O	F			Rare		
	M^O	B		450.00	650.00	950.00	1,500
1877	A^S	L	166		Rare		
	CH		55		Rare		
	C^N	G	*167*	550.00	950.00	1,250	1,750
	D^O	P	*94*	1,500	2,250	2,750	3,250
	G^O	S	⎫		Rare		
		M over S	⎬ 15,100		Rare		
		R	⎭	450.00	650.00	950.00	1,500
	M^O	M	*2,000*	450.00	650.00	950.00	1,500
1878	C^N		*842*		Rare		
	D^O		*258*		Rare		
	G^O	M		650.00	1,250	2,000	2,500
	G^O	S	*13,015*	450.00	650.00	950.00	1,500
	M^O	M	*7,000*	450.00	650.00	950.00	1,500
	Z^S	S	441	4,000	6,000	7,500	9,000
1879	G^O		*8,202*	550.00	800.00	1,000	2,000
	M^O	M		450.00	650.00	950.00	1,500
1880	M^O	M		450.00	650.00	950.00	1,500
	G^O	S	*7,375*	450.00	650.00	950.00	1,500
1881	C^N	D	*2,039*	450.00	650.00	950.00	1,500
	G^O	S	*4,909*	450.00	650.00	950.00	1,500
	M^O	M *varieties:* 11,000		450.00	650.00	950.00	1,500
		1 over 0; normal date.					
1882	CH	M	*1,758*	450.00	650.00	950.00	1,600
	C^N	D 2 over 1	*736*	550.00	950.00	1,250	1,750
	G^O	S	*4,020*	450.00	650.00	950.00	1,500
	M^O	M *varieties:* 5,800		450.00	650.00	950.00	1,500
		2 over 1; normal date.					
1883	CH	M	161	600.00	950.00	1,400	2,000
	C^N	M	*1,836*	450.00	650.00	950.00	1,500
	G^O	B	*3,705*	450.00	650.00	950.00	1,500
	M^O	M	*4,000*	450.00	650.00	950.00	1,500
1884	CH	M	496	450.00	650.00	950.00	1,600
	C^N	M		450.00	650.00	950.00	1,500
	G^O	B	*1,798*	450.00	650.00	950.00	1,500
	M^O	M *varieties:*		450.00	650.00	950.00	1,500
		4 over 3; normal date.					
1885	CH	M	122	600.00	950.00	1,400	2,000
	C^N	M	*544*	450.00	650.00	950.00	1,500
	G^O	R	*2,660*	450.00	650.00	950.00	1,500
	M^O	M	*6,000*	450.00	650.00	950.00	1,500
1886	C^N	M	882	450.00	650.00	950.00	1,500

GOLD 20 PESOS

Date	Mint	Assayer	Quantity Minted	F	VF	EF	Unc.
	G^O	R	1,090	$450.00	$650.00	$950.00	$1,500
	M^O	M	10,000	450.00	650.00	950.00	1,500
1887	C^A	M	550	450.00	650.00	950.00	1,600
	C^N	M	837	450.00	650.00	950.00	1,500
	G^O	R	1,009	450.00	650.00	950.00	1,500
	M^O	M	12,000	450.00	650.00	950.00	1,500
1888	A^S	L	——		Rare		
	C^A	M	351	450.00	650.00	950.00	1,600
	C^N	M	473	450.00	650.00	950.00	1,500
	G^O	R	1,011	450.00	650.00	950.00	1,500
	H^O	G	——		Rare		
	M^O	M	7,300	450.00	650.00	950.00	1,500
	O^A	E	170	4,000	6,000	7,500	9,000
	Z^S	Z	50		Rare		
1889	C^A	M	464	450.00	650.00	950.00	1,600
	C^N	M	1,376	450.00	650.00	950.00	1,500
	G^O	R	956	550.00	800.00	1,100	1,750
	M^O	M	6,477	450.00	650.00	950.00	1,500
	Z^S	Z	640	4,000	6,000	7,500	9,000
1890	C^A	M	1,209	450.00	650.00	950.00	1,600
	C^N	M	——	450.00	650.00	950.00	1,500
	G^O	R	879	550.00	800.00	1,100	1,750
	M^O	M	7,852	450.00	650.00	950.00	1,500
1891	C^A	M	2,004	400.00	600.00	950.00	1,600
	C^N	M	237	550.00	950.00	1,250	1,750
	G^O	R	818	550.00	800.00	1,100	1,750
	M^O	M *varieties:* 1 over 0; normal date.	8,725	450.00	650.00	950.00	1,500
1892	C^N	M	526	450.00	650.00	950.00	1,500
	G^O	R	730	550.00	800.00	1,100	1,750
	M^O	M	10,750	450.00	650.00	950.00	1,500
1893	C^A	M	418	450.00	650.00	950.00	1,600
	C^N	M	2,062	450.00	650.00	950.00	1,500
	G^O	R	3,343	450.00	650.00	950.00	1,500
	M^O	M	14,787	450.00	650.00	950.00	1,500
1894	C^N	M	4,516	450.00	650.00	950.00	1,500
	G^O	R	6,734	450.00	650.00	950.00	1,500
	M^O	M	13,909	450.00	650.00	950.00	1,500
1895	C^A	M	133	600.00	950.00	1,400	2,000
	C^N	M	3,193	450.00	650.00	950.00	1,500
	G^O	R *varieties:* 5 over 3; normal date.	7,118	450.00	650.00	950.00	1,500
	M^O	M	12,873	450.00	650.00	950.00	1,500
1896	C^N	M	4,072	450.00	650.00	950.00	1,500
	G^O	R	9,219	450.00	650.00	950.00	1,500
	M^O	B	14,365	450.00	650.00	950.00	1,500
1897	C^N	M *varieties:* 7 over 6; normal date.	959	450.00	650.00	950.00	1,500
	G^O	R	6,781	450.00	650.00	950.00	1,500
	M^O	M	12,397	450.00	650.00	950.00	1,500
1898	C^N	M	1,660	450.00	650.00	950.00	1,500
	G^O	R	7,710	450.00	650.00	950.00	1,500

GOLD 20 PESOS

Date	Mint	Assayer	Quantity Minted	F	VF	EF	Unc.
	M^O	M	19,682	$450.00	$650.00	$950.00	$1,500
1899	C^N	M	⎫ 1,243	450.00	650.00	950.00	1,500
		Q	⎭	550.00	950.00	1,250	1,750
	G^O	R	8,527	450.00	650.00	950.00	1,500
	M^O	M	23,320	450.00	650.00	950.00	1,500
1900	C^N	Q	1,558	450.00	650.00	950.00	1,500
	G^O	R	4,512	450.00	650.00	950.00	1,500
	M^O	M	20,859	450.00	650.00	950.00	1,500
1901	C^N	Q	1,496	450.00	650.00	950.00	1,500
	M^O	M	28,713	450.00	650.00	950.00	1,500
1902	C^N	Q	1,059	450.00	650.00	950.00	1,500
	M^O	M	38,341	450.00	650.00	950.00	1,500
1903	C^N	Q	1,121	450.00	650.00	950.00	1,500
	M^O	M *varieties:* 31,256		450.00	650.00	950.00	1,500
		3 over 2; normal date.					
1904	C^N	H	4,646	450.00	650.00	950.00	1,500
	M^O	M	51,513	450.00	650.00	950.00	1,500
1905	C^N	P	1,738	550.00	950.00	1,250	1,750
	M^O	M	9,757	450.00	650.00	950.00	1,500

6

ESTADOS UNIDOS MEXICANOS — THE UNITED STATES OF MEXICO

MODERN COINAGE 1905 TO DATE

By the end of the 19th century the coinage of Mexico was entirely inadequate for a developing nation. The copper centavo was awkward to handle and expensive to produce; in 1899 there was introduced in its place the small bronze centavo which was to serve for half a century. Minor silver was not fiduciary and consequently suffered the same difficulties as the peso in a time of fluctuating silver prices. Gold coinage no longer had any fixed relationship to silver, regardless of the denominations stated on the coins. Furthermore, the system bore no relation to the coinages of other countries. The use of the silver standard confused foreign trade. The coins themselves were struck to ancient and curious alloys: 902.7 thousandths for the silver as against the British sterling of 925 or the American and Latin Monetary Union of 900, and 875 thousandths for the gold against the universal use of 900.

In 1905 the entire system was altered. Not until that year was it possible to retire all the outstanding private mint contracts and finally close all the mints outside México, a process that had begun with Oaxaca and San Luis Potosí in 1893. Now the entire coinage was to be concentrated at the México mint, which would call on foreign mints to help with the burden when necessary. Under the watchful eye of the authorities in México the new coinage could proceed to be struck.

Physical properties of the reform coins are indicated below under each denomination. The smallest denominations, 1¢, 2¢, and 5¢ became completely fiduciary, while the 10¢, 20¢, and 50¢ silver were reduced in fineness to 800 thousandths in order to make them more attractive as coin than as bullion. The peso ceased to be struck, but was reinstated in 1908. Gold coins of $5 and $10 were much smaller than before, but raised in alloy to 900 thousandths fine.

Since 1905 the price of silver has fluctuated, and Mexico's position in foreign commerce has altered considerably. As a consequence of both, the peso has been devalued on several occasions and the coinage has been suitably modified. For details see the Introduction, pp. 9-11, and the descriptions of the individual issues. The general trend has been toward the elimination of fractional silver coin, the lowering of the fine silver content of the peso (with the final .100 fine alloy replaced by copper-nickel in 1970), and the introduction of ever higher denominations as the price level rises.

1 CENTAVO
Regular Bronze Coinage 1905-1915

The monetary reform of March 25, 1905 redefined the entire coinage save for the silver 1 peso. On all other denominations the obverse legend now read ESTADO UNIDOS MEXICANOS and the eagle was redesigned. The new 1 centavo issues were otherwise similar to the small bronze introduced in 1899, with slight reverse modification.

Fifty million pieces of the new type were struck in England at The Mint, Birmingham, Ltd. during 1906-1907. These are all dated 1906, bear the México mint mark, and are identical to the México mint issues.

For many dates there exists a number of die varieties showing wide, narrow and irregular spacing of numerals in the date. Such varieties are particularly evident in 1906 and 1911.

1 CENTAVO

1905-1914: diameter 20 mm; weight 3 grams; composition .950 copper, .040 tin, .010 zinc; edge: plain.
1914-1915: diameter 20 mm; weight 3 grams; composition .950 copper, .025 tin, .025 zinc; edge: plain.

Date	Quantity Minted	F	VF	EF	Unc.
1905	6,040,000	$3.50	$5.50	$8.50	$100.00
1906	67,505,000	.35	.75	1.25	12.00
1910	8,700,000	1.50	2.50	7.00	70.00
1911	16,450,000	.50	1.00	2.50	20.00
1912	12,650,000	.60	1.25	3.50	32.50
1913	12,850,000	.60	1.25	2.50	30.00
1914	17,350,000	.50	1.00	2.50	15.00
1915	2,276,947	8.50	17.00	55.00	300.00

Reduced Size Coinage 1915

This issue was struck while Mexico City was under the control of the *Convención*, represented militarily by the forces of Zapata. A decree of June 29, 1915, signed by the President of the *Convención* authorized the coinage of 1 and 2 centavos pieces identical to those already in circulation but of a smaller module. These pieces were struck during the month of July only.

The small 1 and 2 centavos did not circulate long, and were declared illegal by the opposing *Constitucionalista* government in notices of September 20 and October 6, 1916.

This particular coinage has been considered by some a revolutionary rather than a Federal coinage. However the political state of Mexico at this time was so chaotic that it would be difficult to justify as the "legal government" any of the factions engaged in what was in effect not a revolution but a civil war. At any rate the undersize issues of 1915 are issues of the México mint, bear the regular Federal design, and are listed in the mint report for the fiscal year 1915-16.[*]

Diameter 16 mm; weight 1.5 grams; composition .950 copper, .025 tin, .025 zinc; edge: plain.

1915	179,048	15.00	25.00	45.00	70.00

Regular Size Resumed 1916-1949

In 1916, coinage was resumed similar to the issues of 1905-1915, with a subsequent minor change of alloy in 1944.

*T.V. Buttrey, "The Status of the Mexican 1¢ and 2¢ of 1915," in *Plus Ultra* vol. 1 no. 7 (April 24, 1964), pp. 3-5, and no. 8 (May 22, 1964), pp. 3-4; reprinted in *The Numismatist* vol. 77 no. 7 (July, 1964), pp. 909-912.

1 CENTAVO

1916-1943: diameter 20 mm; weight 3 grams; composition .950 copper, .025 tin, .025 zinc; edge: plain.
1944-1949: diameter 20 mm; weight 3 grams; composition .950 copper, .010 tin, .040 zinc; edge: plain.

Date	Quantity Minted	F	VF	EF	Unc.
1916*	500,000	$35.00	$70.00	$175.00	$900.00
1920	1,433,000	12.50	25.00	75.00	425.00
1921	3,470,000	6.00	15.00	45.00	275.00
1922	1,880,000	5.00	10.00	45.00	350.00
1923	4,800,000	.75	1.00	2.00	14.00

1924,
4 over 3

Date	Quantity Minted	F	VF	EF	Unc.
1924 *varieties:*	2,000,000				
4 over 3		37.50	70.00	150.00	400.00
normal date		4.50	7.50	22.50	225.00
1925	1,550,000	5.00	11.00	22.50	210.00
1926	5,000,000	.75	2.00	4.50	25.00
1927	6,000,000	.50	1.25	3.50	20.00
1927/6		20.00	35.00	60.00	125.00
1928	5,000,000	.50	1.00	3.00	15.00
1929	4,500,000	.75	1.00	2.00	18.00
1930	7,000,000	.30	.60	2.00	20.00
1933	10,000,000	.15	.25	.75	15.00
1934	7,500,000	.25	.50	2.00	25.00
1935	12,400,000	.15	.20	.35	10.00
1936	20,100,000	.15	.20	.25	9.00
1937	20,000,000	.10	.15	.20	2.00
1938	10,000,000	.10	.15	.30	2.25
1939	30,000,000	.10	.15	.20	1.25
1940	10,000,000	.15	.25	.40	6.50
1941	15,800,000	.15	.25	.35	2.25
1942	30,400,000	.15	.20	.30	1.25
1943	4,310,000	.25	.50	.75	8.00
1944	5,645,000	.15	.25	.50	7.50
1945	26,375,000	.10	.15	.25	1.00
1946	42,135,000	.10	.15	.20	.45
1947	13,445,000	.10	.15	.20	.50
1948	20,040,000	—	.10	.15	1.00
1949	6,235,000	—	.10	.20	1.25

*Beware of altered dates.

1 CENTAVO
Brass Coinage 1950-1969

In 1950, the size of the 1 centavo was reduced as a result of the peso devaluation of 1949. The obverse carries a modified hooked neck eagle facing left, and inscription. The reverse has the denomination, date, and mint mark between three sheaves of wheat.

Diameter 16mm; weight 2.0 grams; composition .850 copper, .150 zinc; edge: plain.

Date	Quantity Minted	F	VF	EF	Unc.
1950	12,815,000	$ .10	$ .15	$ .30	$1.50
1951	25,740,000	.10	.15	.25	.75
1952	24,610,000	—	.10	.15	.40
1953	21,160,000	—	—	.10	.50
1954	25,675,000	—	—	.15	.60
1955	9,820,000	.10	.15	.25	.85
1956	11,285,000	—	.10	.15	.50
1957	9,805,000	—	.10	.15	.75
1958	12,155,000	—	.10	.15	.50
1959	11,875,000	—	.10	.15	.50
1960	10,360,000	—	—	.10	.20
1961	6,385,000	—	—	.10	.45
1962	4,850,000	—	—	.10	.40
1963	7,775,000	—	—	.10	.25
1964	4,280,000	—	—	.10	.15
1965	2,255,000	—	.10	.15	.20
1966	1,760,000	—	.10	.15	.20
1967	1,290,000	—	.10	.15	.40
1968	1,000,000	—	.10	.15	.75
1969	1,000,000	—	.10	.15	.70

Brass Coinage 1970-1973

In 1970 the size of the 1 centavo was again reduced, and the obverse eagle revised to the schematic design which was introduced on all denominations in 1970-1971.

Diameter 13 mm; weight 1.5 grams; composition .850 copper, .150 zinc; edge: plain.

1970	1,000,000	—	.10	.20	1.25
1972	1,000,000	—	.10	.20	1.50
1973	1,000,000	1.00	1.50	3.00	5.50

2 CENTAVOS

Regular Bronze Coinage 1905-1906

Under the monetary reform of 1905, a bronze 2 centavos coin was issued. Its main devices include the Mexican coat of arms on the obverse and the value as a monogram on the reverse. This design is identical to the 1 centavo pieces issued during the same years.

The Mint, Birmingham, Ltd. in England struck five million 2 centavos coins in 1906-1907. All are dated 1906 and are identical to those struck at the México mint. The 1906 coinage shows variation between wider and narrower spacing of the numerals in the date, but these varieties cannot be attributed definitely to one or the other of the two units.

Diameter 25 mm; weight 6 grams; composition .950 copper, .040 tin, .010 zinc; edge: plain.

Date	Quantity Minted	F	VF	EF	Unc.
1905*	50,000	$100.00	$200.00	$375.00	$1,250
1906	9,998,400	5.00	10.00	20.00	80.00
1906/inverted 6		10.00	20.00	40.00	175.00

*Beware of altered dates.

Reduced Size Coinage 1915

These smaller 2 centavos pieces were struck on flans appropriate to the regular 1 centavo, by order of the *Convención*. See the note on the reduced-size 1 centavo, page 171.

Diameter 20 mm; weight 3 grams; composition .950 copper, .025 tin, .025 zinc; edge: plain.

1915	486,980	5.00	7.50	10.00	50.00

Regular Sized Resumed 1920-1941

In 1920, coinage of the 2 centavos was resumed similar to the 1905-06 issues, except for a slight change of alloy.

The 2 centavos coins has been issued to facilitate small daily transactions. However, they proved to be unpopular and unnecessary. They were demonetized on December 31, 1942, and retired completely from circulation by May 31, 1943.

2 CENTAVOS

Diameter 25 mm; weight 6 grams; composition .950 copper, .025 tin, .025 zinc; edge: plain.

Date	Quantity Minted	F	VF	EF	Unc.
1920	1,325,000	$7.50	$15.00	$35.00	$225.00
1921	4,275,000	2.50	4.50	10.00	100.00
1922*	—	500.00	800.00	1,500	3,500
1924	750,000	8.00	20.00	40.00	450.00
1925	3,650,000	1.00	3.25	5.00	35.00
1926	4,750,000	1.25	2.75	5.50	30.00
1927	7,250,000	.75	1.00	2.25	22.50
1928	3,250,000	.75	1.50	4.00	27.50
1929	250,000	22.50	50.00	350.00	900.00
1935	1,250,000	5.00	9.50	25.00	175.00
1939	5,000,000	.40	.75	1.50	20.00
1941	3,550,000	.35	.50	1.50	17.50

*Beware of altered dates.

5 CENTAVOS

Pure Nickel Coinage 1905-1914

A pure nickel coinage of the 5 centavos was introduced in 1905. The obverse carries the standing eagle typical of the 1905 monetary reform. The value, date, and mint mark M are enclosed in a border on the reverse.

Planchets for this nickel coinage were supplied in part by the Scovill Manufacturing Company of Waterbury, Connecticut and the Coe Brass Manufacturing Company of Torrington, Connecticut. The Arthur Krupp Company of Berndorf, Austria, supplied planchets for the 1913 and 1914 coinage.

The larger part of the coinage of 1906 and 1911, and all of 1907-1910 was executed at The Mint, Birmingham, Ltd. (Heaton mint) in England.* All coins are identical to the issues of the México mint.

Diameter 20 mm; weight 5 grams; commercially pure nickel; edge: plain.

*The Heaton mint appears to have struck 5,000,000 pieces in 1914, but the Mexican Mint Report makes no mention of their having been received.

5 CENTAVOS

Date	Quantity Minted	F	VF	EF	Unc.
1905	1,420,000	$5.00	$10.00	$25.00	$135.00
1906	10,614,560	.75	1.25	3.25	45.00
6 over 5		10.00	17.50	45.00	Rare
1907	4,000,000	.75	3.50	11.00	150.00
1909	2,051,600	3.50	9.00	50.00	275.00
1910	6,181,200	.75	1.25	4.75	90.00
1911	4,486,925	.75	1.25	5.00	80.00
1912 *varieties:*	420,000				
large mint mark		40.00	80.00	160.00	500.00
small mint mark		50.00	90.00	150.00	500.00
1913	2,035,000	1.50	4.50	10.00	90.00
1914	2,000,000	1.00	2.00	4.00	50.00

Bronze Coinage 1914-1935

Because of the authorities' wish to produce both flans and finished coins in Mexico, and the coincidental impossibility of obtaining additional nickel planchets from Krupp with the outbreak of World War I, the 5 centavos piece was changed to a larger-size bronze coin during 1914. The design of this new piece shows the obverse eagle and reverse monogram as the main devices, similar in all respects to the other bronze issues.

This 5 centavos bronze coinage was demonetized in August of 1936 and finally withdrawn from circulation by March of 1937.

Diameter 28 mm; weight 9 grams; composition .950 copper, .025 tin, .025 zinc; edge: plain.

1914	2,500,000	7.50	20.00	45.00	240.00
1915	11,423,940	1.50	5.50	15.00	150.00
1916	2,860,000	15.00	35.00	185.00	650.00
1917	800,000	75.00	150.00	350.00	800.00
1918	1,332,000	30.00	80.00	225.00	625.00
1919	400,000	120.00	200.00	400.00	950.00
1920	5,920,000	3.50	7.50	45.00	300.00
1921	2,080,000	10.00	25.00	75.00	400.00
1924	780,000	40.00	90.00	225.00	650.00
1925	4,040,000	4.00	10.00	40.00	125.00
1926	3,160,000	5.00	12.00	45.00	250.00
1927	3,600,000	3.00	7.50	25.00	225.00

5 CENTAVOS

Normal date   Small 928 in date

Date	Quantity Minted	F	VF	EF	Unc.
1928 *varieties*	1,740,000				
normal date		$7.50	$15.00	$70.00	$250.00
small 928 (2¢ punches)		15.00	30.00	80.00	300.00
1929	2,400,000	5.00	10.00	30.00	150.00

Normal 0   Small squared 0

		F	VF	EF	Unc.
1930 *varieties:*	2,600,000				
normal round 0 in date		5.00	8.00	30.00	175.00
small squared 0 in date		40.00	80.00	175.00	500.00
1931*	—	500.00	750.00	1,200	3,000
1933	8,000,000	1.25	2.00	3.00	25.00
1934	10,000,000	1.00	1.50	2.25	22.50
1935	21,980,000	.50	1.00	1.50	17.50

*Beware of altered dates.

Copper-nickel Coinage 1936-1942

After more than twenty years the bronze 5 centavos was terminated and a new copper-nickel coinage inaugurated. The obverse hooked neck eagle and the reverse border, taken from the Aztec Calendar stone, recall the types of the gold $20 first struck in 1917. (For historical notes on the Calendar stone, see page 217.)

Since 1936 the hooked neck eagle has been introduced as the obverse design for each new type or denomination.

Diameter 20.5 mm; weight 4 grams; composition .800 copper, .200 nickel; edge: plain.

5 CENTAVOS

Date	Quantity Minted	F	VF	EF	Unc.
1936	46,700,000	$ .25	$ .40	$ .90	$6.00
1937	49,060,000	.25	.40	.90	5.00
1938	3,340,000	3.00	4.00	6.00	40.00
1940	22,800,000	.40	.80	1.25	7.00
1942	7,100,000	.75	1.00	2.25	18.00

Bronze Coinage 1942-1946

In 1942, for the first time in the history of Mexico, a woman was honored by having her effigy placed on a coin of the realm. This unusual person was Josefa Ortiz de Domínguez, wife of the Spanish-Colonial Governor of Mexico at the time when insurrection broke out against Spain.

Both she and her husband were in sympathy with the independence movement. Even when he was finally forced to act against the revolutionists in 1810, she managed to notify the rebel leader Hidalgo and others of the impending danger to themselves and their plans. She was subsequently arrested and tried a number of times, and imprisoned until June 17, 1817 when a new governor granted her a pardon. She died alone and forgotten, in extreme poverty, in 1829.

For many years her acts of heroism remained ignored. In fact, it was not until 1894 that Doña Josefa was given the honor she so richly deserved from a belatedly grateful country.

This 5 centavos coin, popularly nicknamed the "Josefita," was authorized by presidential decree on December 28, 1942. Actual striking began on December 19, ten days before the coin was authorized.

Diameter 25.5 mm; weight 6.5 grams; composition .950 copper, .010 tin, .040 zinc; edge: plain.

1942	900,000	6.00	20.00	65.00	300.00
1943	54,660,000	.30	.50	.75	3.00
1944	53,463,120	.10	.15	.20	.75
1945	44,262,000	.15	.25	1.00	3.25
1946	49,054,000	.30	.50	.90	2.00

5 CENTAVOS
Copper-nickel Coinage 1950

After a four-year hiatus, a new 5 centavos coinage of smaller size was authorized on December 29, 1949. The obverse bears a hooked neck eagle, and the reverse carries a redesigned bust of Josefa Ortiz de Dominguez facing right.

This issue was very short-lived, as coinage was suspended by a decree of December 29, 1950.

Diameter 20.5 mm; weight 4 grams; composition .750 copper, .250 nickel; edge: plain.

Date	Quantity Minted	F	VF	EF	Unc.
1950	5,700,000	$ .50	$ .75	$1.25	$5.00

Bronze Coinage Resumed 1951-1955

In 1951, coinage identical in type to the issues of 1942-1946 was resumed. There is a slight difference in metallic composition from earlier issues.

Diameter 25.5 mm; 6.5 grams; composition .950 copper, .050 zinc; edge: plain.

1951	50,758,000	.50	.75	1.00	3.25
1952	17,674,000	.75	1.25	2.50	9.00
1953	31,568,000	.25	.50	1.00	2.75
1954	58,680,000	.25	.50	1.00	2.75
1955	31,114,000	.75	1.25	2.00	11.00

Brass Coinage 1954-1969

No provision was made for the striking of this brass 5 centavos coin until 1955, but a small amount was coined the previous year in anticipation of authorization. Subsequently, the coins were hastily withdrawn and replaced with the larger bronze pieces.

The obverse is almost identical to the 1950 issue; the reverse design is similar except that the denomination is written out around the head, and the date and mint mark are to the right.

5 CENTAVOS

Diameter 20.5 mm; weight 4 grams; composition .850 copper, .150 zinc; edge: plain.

Date	Quantity Minted	F	VF	EF	Unc.
1954 w/o dot	—	$4.00	$8.00	$15.00	$175.00
1954 Dot		4.00	8.00	17.50	200.00
1955	12,136,000	.50	.80	1.50	10.00
1956	60,216,000	.10	.15	.20	.90
1957	55,288,000	.10	.15	.20	.90
1958	104,624,000	.10	.15	.20	.40
1959	106,000,000	.10	.15	.20	.90
1960	99,144,000	—	.10	.15	.30
1961	61,136,000	—	.10	.15	.45
1962	47,232,000	—	.10	.15	.35
1963	156,680,000	—	—	.10	.15
1964	71,168,000	—	—	.10	.15
1965	155,720,000	—	—	.10	.15
1966	124,944,000	—	—	.10	.35
1967	118,816,000	—	—	.10	.25
1968	189,588,000	—	—	.10	.25
1969	210,492,000	—	—	.10	.25

Brass Coinage 1970-1976

A decree of December 30, 1969 redefined the elements of all coins up to the denomination of $5. The brass 5¢ was reduced in size and struck with a newly designed hooked neck eagle obverse in which all the elements are represented two-dimensionally, without any relief, in the manner of a pre-Columbian illustration.

The reverse of the reduced 5¢ piece bears the same elements as those of the preceding issue, with mint mark and date rearranged.

Diameter 18 mm; weight 2.75 grams; composition .850 copper, .150 zinc; edge: plain.

1970	163,368,000	—	—	.10	.35
1971	198,844,000	—	—	.10	.15
1972	225,000,000	—	—	.10	.15

5 CENTAVOS

Date	Quantity Minted	F	VF	EF	Unc.
1973 flat top 3 595,070,000		—	—	$ .10	$ .30
1973 round top 3 ....Inc. Ab.		—	—	—	.15
1974 401,584,000		—	—	.10	.20
1975 342,308,000		—	—	.10	.20
1976 ....367,524;000		—	—	.10	.20

Bronze Coinage 1973

1973	—	—	—	—

10 CENTAVOS

.800 Silver Coinage 1905-1914

An entirely new issue of 10 centavos coins bégan in 1905. The obverse shows the standing eagle typical of coinage introduced under the 1905 reform. The reverse has the value, date, and mint mark M in a partial wreath, with rayed liberty cap above. This design became standard for all silver denominations by 1918.

The silver content is lower than that of the preceding issue (see coinage of 1869-1897). All 10 centavos coins were made at the México mint after 1905.

Diameter 18 mm; weight 2.5 grams; composition .800 silver, .200 copper; edge: reeded.

1905 3,920,000	4.00	6.00	7.50	28.00
1906 8,410,000	2.00	4.00	6.00	15.00

1907, 7 over 6   1910, 1 over 0

1907 *varieties:* 5,950,000				
7 over 6	15.00	25.00	50.00	100.00
normal date	3.00	5.00	7.50	25.00
1909 2,620,000	5.00	9.00	12.00	85.00

10 CENTAVOS

Date	Quantity Minted	F	VF	EF	Unc.
1910 *varieties:* 3,450,000					
1 over 0		$5.00	$9.00	$15.00	$80.00
normal date		4.00	6.00	9.00	20.00
1911 2,550,000		4.00	6.00	9.00	35.00
1912 1,350,000		5.00	9.00	14.00	125.00
1913 *varieties* 1,990,000		4.00	6.00	10.00	35.00
3 over 2; normal date.					
1914 3,110,000		2.00	4.00	6.00	12.00

Reduced Size .800 Silver Coinage 1919

In 1919, the size and weight of the silver 10 centavos coin were reduced. The coinage of 1919 is otherwise similar in design to the preceding issue.

Diameter 15 mm; weight 1.8125 grams; composition .800 silver, .200 copper; edge: reeded.

1919 8,360,000		4.00	8.00	17.50	100.00

Large Bronze Coinage 1919-1921

Rising silver prices in 1919 forced silver coins out of circulation. To remedy this situation, a 10 centavos issue in bronze was begun in October of that year.

The design conforms in all respects to the bronze coinage of lower denominations, showing the eagle on the obverse and value as a monogram on the reverse.

Diameter 30.5 mm; weight 12 grams; composition .950 copper, .025 tin, .025 zinc; edge: plain.

1919 1,232,000		20.00	35.00	80.00	500.00
1920 6,612,000		7.50	15.00	45.00	350.00
1921 2,255,000		15.00	30.00	75.00	675.00

.720 Silver Coinage 1925-1935

A silver 10 centavos was reintroduced in 1925. It is of the same diameter as the 1919 issue, though reduced in weight and silver content. The design is also simi-

10 CENTAVOS

lar to the 1919 coinage. The only modification is the annotation of the new fineness, "0.720," on the obverse.

Diameter 15 mm; weight 1.666 grams; composition .720 silver, .280 copper; edge: reeded.

Date	Quantity Minted	F	VF	EF	Unc.
1925	5,350,000	1.25	2.50	4.00	27.50
1925/15 or 1825/19		6.00	12.50	25.00	75.00
1925/3		10.00	20.00	35.00	95.00
1926	2,650,000	1.50	3.00	7.00	40.00
1927	2,810,000	1.25	2.25	3.50	17.00
1928	5,270,000	1.00	1.50	2.50	10.00
1930	2,000,000	1.50	3.00	6.00	20.00
1933	5,000,000	.75	1.25	2.00	7.00
1934	8,000,000	.50	1.00	1.75	6.00
1935	3,500,000	1.00	2.00	5.00	14.00

Bronze Coinage Resumed 1935

In 1935, the large bronze 10 centavos coin reappeared as a result of unsteady silver prices. It is similar in all respects to the earlier bronze coinage of 1919-1921.

By March of 1936, the bronze 10 centavos coins were scheduled for gradual retirement as the newly authorized copper-nickel issue replaced them.

1935	5,970,000	8.00	15.00	30.00	120.00

Copper-nickel Coinage 1936-1946

A new copper-nickel 10 centavos issue was authorized on March 26, 1936. Coinage began in May of that year.

The design is similar to its companion 5 centavos coin. Obverses show a hooked neck eagle facing left, and reverses have the value and mint mark M in the center. An ornate border taken from the Aztec Calendar stone surrounds the value and mint mark (see note on the gold 20 pesos).

10 CENTAVOS

Diameter 23.5 mm; weight 5.5 grams; composition .800 copper, .200 nickel; edge: plain.

Date	Quantity Minted	F	VF	EF	Unc.
1936	33,030,000	.20	.40	.90	7.00
1937	3,000,000	1.25	2.50	15.00	20.00
1938	3,650,000	.75	1.50	3.00	45.00
1939	6,920,000	.30	.75	1.75	20.00
1940	12,300,000	.20	.40	.90	5.00
1942	14,380,000	.20	.60	1.25	7.00
1945	9,557,500	.20	.35	.60	3.50
1946	46,230,000	.15	.25	.50	2.25

Bronze Coinage 1955-1967

After a nine-year lapse in coinage, a newly designed bronze 10 centavos issue began in 1955. The obverse shows a modern hooked neck eagle, and the reverse bears a portrait of Benito Juárez was a full-blooded Zapotec Indian who gained the post of Minister of Justice in 1857. He became President of the Republic, and occupied that position during the French intervention. After the withdrawal of the French forces and the capture and execution of Maximilian in 1867, Juárez was twice re-elected President. He died in office in 1872.

Diameter 23.5 mm; weight 5.5 grams; composition .950 copper, .050 zinc; edge: plain.

1955	1,817,500	.60	1.00	3.50	20.00
1956	5,255,000	.20	.50	2.00	17.50
1957	11,925,000	.15	.20	.50	3.50
1959	26,140,000	.10	.15	.20	.40
1966	5,872,500	—	.10	.15	.40
1967	32,317,500	—	.10	.15	.35

10 CENTAVOS
Copper-nickel Coinage 1974-1980

Coinage of small sized 10 centavos pieces commenced in 1974; for some reason the pieces were not officially released to circulation until February 1977. The obverse is the revised version of 1970-1971. The reverse shows an ear of ripened corn in the center. This is now Mexico's lowest denomination coin in circulation.

Diameter 15 mm; weight 1.485 grams; composition 75% copper, 25% nickel; edge: paired reeding.

   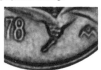

Variety I
5 full rows of kernels,
pointed stem

Variety II
5 full, plus 1 partial row of kernels,
blunt stem

Date	Quantity Minted	F	VF	EF	Unc.
1974	6,000,000	—	—	.10	.35
1975	5,550,000	—	.10	.15	.35
1976	7,680,000	—	.10	.20	.45
1977 pointed stem	144,650,000	—	—	.10	.25
1977 blunt stem	Inc. Ab.	—	—	.10	.20
1978 pointed stem	271,870,000	—	—	.10	.25
1978 blunt stem	Inc. Ab.	—	—	.10	.25
1979	375,660,000	—	—	.10	.25
1980	21,290,000	.50	.75	1.50	3.50

20 CENTAVOS
.800 Silver Coinage 1905-1914

The 20 centavos issue beginning in 1905 is reduced in weight and silver content from the previous coinage (see issue of 1898-1905). Its design is similar to the 10 centavos coin of the same years. Obverses show the typical standing eagle of the 1905 monetary reform. Reverses have the value, date, and mint mark in a partial wreath, with rayed liberty cap above.

The only issue of foreign coinage ever struck at the New Orleans, Louisiana, mint took place in 1907, when 5,434,619 pieces of 20 centavos were produced. The México mint mark was placed on the coins, which are therefore identical to the México issues.

Diameter 22 mm; weight 5 grams; composition .800 silver, .200 copper; edge: reeded.

20 CENTAVOS

Date	Quantity Minted	F	VF	EF	Unc.
1905 2,565,000		5.00	10.00	17.50	150.00
1906 6,860,000		3.50	7.00	11.00	75.00

Straight 7   Curved 7

	Quantity Minted	F	VF	EF	Unc.
1907 *varieties:* 9,434,699					
straight 7		3.00	6.00	8.00	50.00
curved 7		3.00	6.00	8.00	50.00
1908* 350,000		35.00	75.00	150.00	600.00
1910 1,135,000		5.00	10.00	17.50	75.00
1911 1,150,000		6.00	12.00	20.00	125.00
1912 625,000		17.50	35.00	85.00	325.00
1913 1,000,000		7.00	14.00	22.50	80.00
1914 1,500,000		5.00	10.00	15.00	50.00

*Beware of altered dates.

Reduced Size .800 Silver Coinage 1919

A rise in the price of silver caused a reduction in size and weight of the 20 centavos piece in 1919. The design remained similar to the issues of 1905-1914.

Diameter 19 mm; weight 3.625 grams; composition .800 silver, .200 copper; edge: reeded.

	Quantity Minted	F	VF	EF	Unc.
1919 4,155,000		12.50	25.00	60.00	225.00

Large Bronze Coinage 1920

Because of rising silver prices, a bronze 20 centavos issue was made in 1920 to replace the vanishing silver coins. The design is similar in all respects to the smaller bronze denominations issued since 1905. Obverses show a standing eagle, and reverses have the denomination as a monogram.

The bronze 20 centavos coins were made for six months, after which a silver 20 centavos of lower silver content appeared.

Diameter 32.5 mm; weight 15 grams; composition .950 copper, .025 tin, .025 zinc; edge: plain.

20 CENTAVOS

Date	Quantity Minted	F	VF	EF	Unc.
1920 4,835,450		12.50	35.00	95.00	450.00

.720 Silver Coinage 1920-1935

Silver 20 centavos coinage of lower weight and silver content was begun during the latter part of 1920. The size and design remained similar to the silver issue of 1919.

Diameter 19 mm; weight 3.333 grams; composition .720 silver, .280 copper; edge: reeded.

1920 3,710,000	2.50	5.00	12.00	125.00
1921 6,160,000	2.50	5.00	12.00	85.00
1925 1,450,000	4.50	9.00	22.50	120.00
1926 1,465,000	2.50	5.00	10.00	100.00
1926/5	6.00	9.00	17.50	135.00
1927 1,405,000	2.00	4.00	7.50	110.00
1928 3,630,000	1.50	2.50	3.50	15.00
1930 1,000,000	2.00	3.50	7.00	25.00
1933 2,500,000	1.25	2.25	3.25	12.00
1934 2,500,000	1.25	2.25	3.25	12.00
1935 2,460,000	1.25	2.25	3.25	10.00

Bronze Coinage Resumed 1935

The bronze 20 centavos coins made a brief reappearance in 1935, again because of fluctuations in the price of silver. This issue is similar in all respects to the bronze coinage of 1920.

By 1937, silver prices had stabilized. The bronze pieces were retired from circulation as silver coinage was resumed that year.

20 CENTAVOS

Date	Quantity Minted	F	VF	EF	Unc.
1935 20,000,000	2.50	5.00	7.50	60.00

.720 Coinage Resumed 1937-1943

Silver coinage of the 20 centavos was resumed in 1937. Design, weight, and silver content remained similar to the issues of 1920-1935.

Date	Quantity Minted	F	VF	EF	Unc.
1937 10,000,000	.75	1.00	2.00	4.50
1939 8,800,000	.75	1.00	1.75	4.00
1940 3,000,000	.75	1.00	1.75	4.00
▶ 1941 5,740,000	.75	1.00	1.50	3.00
1942 12,460,000	.75	1.00	1.50	3.00
1943 3,955,000	.75	1.00	1.50	3.00

Bronze Coinage 1943-1955

A completely new 20 centavos issue of bronze was introduced in 1943. The obverse carries the hooked neck eagle with inscription above. An attractive reverse shows two volcanoes, Popocatepetl on the right and Ixtaccihuatl on the left. (These are memorialized in Indian myth as a prince and princess, respectively, who came from different tribes. They fell in love, eloped, and were exiled. Now they are said to be eternally asleep, personified by the mountains bearing their names.)

Between these two mountains is the Pyramid of the Sun at Teotihuacán, the place name inscribed on the base in very small letters. In place of the traditional brances of oak and laurel, an organ pipe cactus is at the lower left, and leaves of a prickly-pear tree at the right. Above the mountains and pyramid are the value, mint mark and Liberty cap; the date and CENTAVOS are below.

This design was prepared by Manuel L. Negrete, chief engraver of the México mint, assisted by Francisco Rivera Paniagua.

Diameter 28.5 mm; weight 10 grams; composition .950 copper, .010 tin, .040 zinc; edge: plain.

20 CENTAVOS

In 1951, there was a change of alloy. Tin was completely omitted from the composition of the coin.

Composition .950 copper, .050 zinc.

Date	Quantity Minted	F	VF	EF	Unc.
1943	46,350,000	.30	.60	3.00	18.00
1944	83,650,000	.25	.50	.75	9.00
1945	26,800,500	.20	.40	1.75	9.00
1946	25,695,000	.25	.45	1.25	6.00
1951	11,385,000	1.25	2.50	5.00	70.00
1952	6,559,500	1.00	1.50	3.50	20.00
1953	26,947,500	.20	.30	.50	6.00
1954	40,108,000	.20	.30	.50	9.00
1955	included below	1.25	3.00	6.50	70.00

Redesigned Eagle 1955-1971

During 1955, the obverse eagle was redesigned. Both the older and newer style eagle are found that year. The reverse is identical to the preceding issue.

Date	Quantity Minted	F	VF	EF	Unc.
1955	both types 16,950,000	.40	.75	1.75	10.00
1956	22,431,000	.15	.25	.35	3.00
1957	13,455,000	.20	.50	1.00	9.00
1959	6,016,500	2.00	4.00	8.00	60.00
1960	39,756,000	.10	.15	.20	.45
1963	11,869,000	.10	.20	.30	.70
1964	28,653,500	—	.10	.15	.35
1965	74,161,500	—	.10	.15	.35
1966	43,744,500	.10	.15	.20	.45
1967	46,486,500	.10	.15	.20	.35
1968	15,477,000	.10	.15	.25	.75

20 CENTAVOS

Date	Quantity Minted	F	VF	EF	Unc.
1969	63,646,500	.10	.15	.25	.75
1970	76,287,000	.10	.15	.20	.45
1971	49,891,500*	.10	.25	.35	1.25

Redesigned Eagle 1971-1974

The schematic obverse first introduced to the coinage in 1970 was not applied to the 20 centavos until the following year, so that both old and new obverses occur with the date 1971. The types and physical characteristics of the denomination remained otherwise unchanged.

1971	included above	.10	.15	.25	.75
1973	78,398,000	—	.10	.15	.45
1974 bronze	34,200,000	.10	.20	.30	1.00

Copper-nickel Coinage 1974-1983

The rising price of copper compelled the abandonment of the large bronze 20 centavos which had been struck for more than thirty years. In 1974 a copper-nickel piece of the same denomination was struck to a much smaller module. The reverse bears a portrait of President Francisco I. Madero.

Diameter 20 mm; weight 3 grams; composition .750 copper, .250 nickel; edge: paired reeding.

1974	112,000,000	—	—	.10	.25
1975	611,000,000	—	.10	.15	.25
1976	394,000,000	—	.10	.15	.25
1977	394,350,000	—	.10	.15	.30
1978	527,950,000	—	.10	.15	.25
1979	524,615,000	—	—	.10	.25
1980	326,500,000	—	.10	.20	.40

*This figure is the combined total for both types, old obverse and new obverse.

20 CENTAVOS

Date	Quantity Minted	F	VF	EF	Unc.
1981 open 8	106,205,000	—	.10	.30	.60
1981 closed 8	248,500,000	—	.10	.25	.75
1982	286,855,000	—	.10	.25	1.00
1982/1	Inc. Ab.	Rare			
1983	100,875,000	—	.10	.25	1.00

Bronze Coinage 1983-

The continuing depreciation in the value of the peso compelled the introduction of a new 20 pesos issue made of bronze, rather than copper-nickel, as it could be produced more inexpensive. The obverse introduced a newly modelled rendering of the traditional eagle and snake design, while the reverse features a sculptured Indian face.

Diameter 20 mm; weight 3.04 grams; composition .950 copper, .050 zinc; edge: reeded.

1983	260,000,000	—	.10	.25	1.00
1984	180,320,000	—	.10	.25	1.50

25 CENTAVOS

Base Silver Coinage 1950-1953

The 25 centavos was struck in 1950 after a lapse of 58 years. The obverse carries a modern hooked neck eagle, with inscription above. The reverse closely resembles the balance scale type that preceded it, with major differences only in the inscription.

Diameter 21.5 mm; weight 3.333 grams; composition .300 silver, .500 copper, .100 nickel, .100 zinc; edge: reeded.

1950	77,060,000	—	BV	.50	1.50
1951	41,172,000	—	BV	.50	1.25
1952	29,264,000	—	BV	.60	1.50
1953	38,144,000	—	BV	.50	1.25

25 CENTAVOS
Copper-nickel Coinage 1964-1966

After an 11-year hiatus, Mexico again tried to circulate the 25 centavos denomination. This later issue bears the Mexican eagle on the obverse and a facing bust of Francisco I. Madero (president 1911-13) on the reverse.

Diameter 23 mm; weight 5.50 grams; composition .750 copper, .250 nickel; edge: reeded.

Date	Quantity Minted	F	VF	EF	Unc.
1964	20,686,000	—	—	.10	.25
1966	180,000	.25	.50	1.00	2.50

50 CENTAVOS
.800 Silver Coinage 1905-1918

A new 50 centavos coin appeared as part of the monetary reform of 1905. The design is completely uniform with the lower silver denominations of the same years. Obverses show the Mexican coat of arms with inscription above. Reverses have the rayed cap, date, value, and mint mark M.

In 1906, the San Francisco mint produced 3,800,000 of these coins. In 1907, this mint struck 8,642,000 pieces, and the Denver mint made 6,199,239 of the same coins. No special mark was placed on these issues, which are identical to the México mint coinage.

Although the diameter remained the same, both the weight and fine silver content were reduced from the previous issue.

Diameter 30 mm; weight 12.5 grams; composition .800 silver, .200 copper; edge: lettered INDEPENDENCIA Y LIBERTAD.

1905	2,446,000	7.50	15.00	22.50	175.00
1906	16,966,000	4.00	6.00	10.00	27.50

50 CENTAVOS

 Straight 7    Curved 7

Date	Quantity Minted	F	VF	EF	Unc.
1907 *varieties:*	33,761,239				
straight 7		3.50	6.00	8.00	25.00
curved 7		3.00	5.00	7.50	25.00
1908*	488,000	45.00	75.00	170.00	550.00
1912	3,736,000	4.50	9.00	12.50	35.00

1913, 13 over 07   1913, 3 over 2

1913 *varieties:*	10,510,000				
13 over 07		15.00	25.00	40.00	175.00
3 over 2		7.50	12.50	25.00	50.00
normal date		3.00	5.00	9.00	27.50
1914	7,710,000	3.00	5.00	10.00	27.50
1916*	480,000	30.00	50.00	90.00	200.00
1917	37,112,000	3.00	5.00	7.00	20.00
1918*	1,320,000	60.00	120.00	160.00	350.00

*Beware of altered dates.

Reduced Size .800 Silver Coinage 1918-1919

Because of a sharp rise in the price of silver, the 50 centavos coin was further reduced in the course of 1918. The design remained identical with the previous issue, but diameter and weight were diminished.

Diameter 27 mm; weight 9.0625 grams; composition .800 silver, 200 copper; edge: lettered INDEPENDEN-CIA Y LIBERTAD.

50 CENTAVOS

Date	Quantity Minted	F	VF	EF	Unc.
1918	2,760,000	10.00	20.00	50.00	225.00
1919	29,670,000	5.00	10.00	20.00	100.00

.720 Silver Coinage 1919-1925

Further rise in silver prices caused a reduction in silver content of the 50 centavos coin from .800 to .720. This new issue of 50 centavos was begun on October 27 of 1919, and was the only coin made with the lower silver content that year.

The design is similar to the previous issues. The only change is the addition of the fine silver content expressed as "0.720" to the obverse.

Diameter 27 mm; weight 8.333 grams; composition .720 silver, .280 copper; edge: lettered INDEPENDEN-CIA Y LIBERTAD.

Date	Quantity Minted	F	VF	EF	Unc.
1919	10,200,000	4.00	8.00	17.50	90.00
1920	27,166,000	3.00	6.00	9.00	60.00
1921	21,864,000	3.00	6.00	9.00	50.00
1925	3,280,000	6.00	10.00	25.00	125.00

.420 Silver Coinage 1935

On May 22, 1935, an issue of 50 centavos coins was authorized to be struck in base silver, only .420 fine. Instability of silver prices earlier in the year made this action necessary.

A large number was struck, at the México mint as well as in all three U.S. mints then in operation (Denver, 17,000,850 pieces; Philadelphia, 25,000,000; San Francisco, 18,000,000). All the coins are similar in every respect, including the mint mark M.

The design is identical to previous issues except that the legend "0.720" is eliminated from the obverse because of the reduction in silver content.

Total circulating life of these coins was only fifteen months. They were demonetized by decree on August 28, 1936, and removed from circulation soon afterwards.

Diameter 27 mm; weight 7.973 grams; composition .420 silver, .580 copper; edge: lettered INDEPENDEN-CIA Y LIBERTAD.

50 CENTAVOS

Date	Quantity Minted	F	VF	EF	Unc.
1935 70,800,000		BV	1.50	2.00	4.00

.720 Coinage Resumed 1937-1945

In 1937, 50 centavos coinage of .720 fine silver content was resumed. In all respects this issue is similar to the 1919-1925 coinage.

Date	Quantity Minted	F	VF	EF	Unc.
1937 20,000,000		BV	3.00	4.00	6.00
1938* 100,000		25.00	50.00	80.00	225.00
1939 10,440,000		—	BV	2.50	5.00
1942 800,000		—	BV	3.00	6.00
✔ 1943 41,512,000		—	BV	2.00	4.50
1944 55,806,000		—	BV	2.00	4.50
1945 56,766,000		—	BV	2.00	4.50

*Beware of altered dates. For an example see page 251.

.300 Silver Coinage 1950-1951

In 1950, a new type of 50 centavos was struck. It has on the obverse a modern hooked neck eagle, with inscription above. On the reverse is a three-quarter bust of the Aztec leader Cuauhtémoc facing right, with surrounding date, mint mark, and value.

Cuauhtémoc, the last Aztec emperor, tried unsuccessfully to unite the Indian city-states against the Spanish Conquistadores. After a courageous defense of the capital city Tenochtitlán, he was captured in 1521. By order of Cortées, he was subsequently hanged for treason.

Because of the severe devaluation of the peso in 1949, this coinage shows a general reduction in all of its physical properties in comparison with previous issues.

50 CENTAVOS

Diameter 26 mm; weight 6.666 grams; composition .300 silver, .500 copper, .100 nickel, .100 zinc; edge: reeded.

Date	Quantity Minted	F	VF	XF	Unc.
1950	13,570,000	BV	$1.00	$1.25	$2.50
1951	3,650,000	BV	1.00	2.00	3.50

Bronze Coinage 1955-1959

In 1955 a new coinage of 50 centavos coins in bronze was issued, and for the first time silver was eliminated as a coinage metal for this denomination.

The obverse design shows a modern hooked neck eagle, and the reverse carries a redesigned head of Aztec chieftain Cuauhtémoc with war headdress, facing left. This bust is similar to that used on the 5 pesos silver coins in 1947 and 1948.

Diameter 33 mm; weight 14 grams; composition .950 copper, .025 tin, .025 zinc; edge: reeded.

1955	3,502,000	.50	1.00	2.00	20.00
• 1956	34,643,000	.25	.50	1.00	2.50
1957	9,675,000	.20	.30	.50	3.25
1959	4,540,000	.10	.20	.30	1.00

Copper-nickel Coinage 1964-1969

A new copper-nickel type was issued to replace the large bronze pieces in 1964. The new coin proved more practical for this popular denomination because of its convenient size and more attractive color. The design is basically the same as the previous issue, although the lettering, arms and bust are proportionally larger and there are no beads around the rim.

50 CENTAVOS

Diameter 25 mm; weight 6.50 grams; composition .750 copper, .250 nickel; edge: reeded.

Date	Quantity Minted	F	VF	XF	Unc.
1964	43,806,000	—	—	$ .10	$ .25
1965	14,326,000	—	—	.10	.30
1966	1,726,000	$ .10	$ .20	.40	1.20
1967	55,144,000	—	—	.10	.50
1968	80,438,000	—	—	.10	.50
1969	87,640,000	—	.10	.20	.90

Redesigned Eagle 1970-1983

In accord with the decree of December 30, 1969, the obverse design of the 50 centavos was modified. Although the hooked neck eagle was retained, it appears here in a more stylized form derived from native Indian art. Neither the reverse design nor the physical specifications were changed.

1970	76,236,000	—	.10	.15	.90
1971	125,288,000	—	—	.10	.75
1972	16,000,000	.20	.45	1.25	3.25
1975	177,958,000	—	.10	.15	.40
1976	37,480,000	—	.10	.15	.40
1977	12,410,000	1.00	2.50	3.50	10.00
1978	85,400,000	—	.10	.15	.50
1979 round 2nd 9	229,000,000	—	.10	.15	.50
1979 square 9's	Inc. Ab.	—	.10	.15	.50
1980 narrow date	89,978,000	—	—	.10	.50
1980 wide date	178,188,000	—	—	.10	.50
1981 rectangular 9	142,212,000	—	—	.10	.50
1981 round 9	Inc. Ab.	—	—	.10	.50
1982	49,053,500	—	.10	.40	1.50
1983	90,318,000	—	.10	.50	2.00

Stainless Steel Coinage 1983

Early in 1983, as a stopgap measure, faced with continued depreciation in the value of the peso, the production of the Cuauhtemoc 50 centavos of the type introduced in 1970, struck of copper-nickel and featuring the stylized eagle obverse design, was switched to a stainless steel composition.

Diameter 25 mm; weight 6.61 grams; composition: stainless steel; edge: reeded.

Date	Quantity Minted	F	VF	XF	Unc.
1983		—	Not Confirmed		

Stainless Steel Coinage 1983-

In response to the rapidly depreciating value of the peso, late in 1983 the government introduced a new 50 centavos design, struck of steel, that was significantly smaller and less than two-thirds the weight of the preceding copper-nickel issue. The obverse introduced a newly modelled rendering of Mexico's traditional eagle and snake symbol. The reverse introduced a new design featuring an Indian portrait, that of Palenque.

Diameter 21.9 mm; weight 4.2 grams; composition: stainless steel; edge: plain.

Date	Quantity Minted	F	VF	XF	Unc.
1983	66,148,000	—	—	.10	1.00
1984	33,392,000	—	—	.10	.25

1 PESO

Coinage of the Liberty cap peso, which had been struck from 1898 to 1905, was resumed in 1908 and 1909. Plans for a new design were being developed as early as 1907, but the resulting coin was not struck until 1910. Additional pesos were much in demand by the end of 1907, however, and the 1905 monetary law called for no changes in physical standards of this denomination. Therefore the reissue of the old type with its obsolete legend REPUBLICA MEXICANA appears to have been a simple matter of expediency. The 1908-09 pesos are listed with other dates of the same type on page 155.

Silver Coináge 1910-1914

The 1 peso coinage beginning in 1910 was commemorative in nature. It was released to coincide with the centennial of Father Hidalgo's "Grito de Dolores" — the cry that catapulted Mexico into revolution against Spanish rule in 1810.

1 PESO

Date	Quantity Minted	F	VF	XF	Unc.
1912 322,000		50.00	100.00	175.00	350.00
1913 varieties: 2,880,000					
3 over 2		22.50	32.50	70.00	200.00
normal date		22.50	35.00	75.00	200.00
1914* 120,000		600.00	850.00	1200.	2500.

*Beware of altered dates.

.800 Silver Coinage 1918-1919

The 1 peso coinage beginning in 1918 was issued in conformity with the lower silver denominations. The obverse shows an eagle on cactus, and the reverse has the cap and rays, denomination, date, and mint mark.

This issue is reduced in all of its physical properties from the previous peso coinage.

Diameter 34 mm; weight 18.125 grams; composition .800 silver, .200 copper; edge: lettered INDEPENDEN-CIA Y LIBERTAD.

1918 3,050,000		20.00	35.00	90.00	3000.
1919 6,151,000		12.50	20.00	35.00	2000.

.720 Silver Coinage 1920-1945

Further reduction in the weight and silver content of the 1 peso coin was necessary in 1920 because of rising silver prices. The new silver content of .720 is shown on the obverse, split to the left and right of the eagel's head. The types are otherwise identical to the 1918-19 issues.

Diameter 34 mm; weight 16.66 grams; composition .720 silver, .280 copper; edge: lettered INDEPENDEN-CIA Y LIBERTAD.

1 PESO

Date	Quantity Minted	F	VF	XF	Unc.
1920 varieties:	8,830,000				
2 over 1		$20.00	$30.00	$50.00	$250.00
normal date		4.00	6.00	12.50	100.00
1921	5,480,000	4.00	6.00	12.50	100.00
1922	33,620,000	—	BV	5.00	22.50
1923	35,280,000	—	BV	5.00	22.50
1924	33,060,000	—	BV	5.00	22.50
1925	9,160,000	BV	5.00	10.00	35.00
1926	28,840,000	—	BV	5.00	22.50
1927	5,060,000	BV	4.00	8.00	35.00
1932	50,770,000	—	BV	4.00	6.00
1933	43,920,000	—	BV	4.00	6.00
1934	22,070,000	—	BV	4.00	8.00
1935	8,050,000	—	BV	6.00	12.00
1938	30,000,000	—	BV	3.50	7.00
1940	20,000,000	—	BV	3.50	6.00
1943	47,662,000	—	BV	3.50	5.00
1944	39,522,000	—	BV	3.50	5.00
1945	37,300,000	—	BV	3.50	5.00

.500 Silver Coinage 1947-1949

A reduction of the 1 peso coin and a new type combined for the issue of 1947-49. The obverse shows a hooked neck eagle, with inscription above. The reverse carries a portrait of Morelos, with surrounding value, date, mint mark and silver content. The portrait had first appeared on a pattern coin in 1936 (see Pattern 122), and was adopted with a few small changes in 1947.

José Morelos y Pavón was a leader of the revolutionists fighting Spain for their independence. He was also a priest, as was his great teacher Hidalgo.

Morelos headed the insurgent army that fought in the southern Mexican provinces from 1811 to 1814. He was finally captured in November of 1815, tried before the Inquisition, and executed in December of that year. Morelos is well known in Mexican numismatic history. He is responsible for issuing a large series of coins, mostly copper, during the time his roving army was engaged in combat.

1 peso coins dated 1949 were not released to circulation because of a severe peso devaluation which took place that year. As in most cases of this kind, a very small number did escape the melting pot and have found their way on the market.

1 PESO

This coinage is reduced in all of its physical properties from the preceding issue.

Diameter 32 mm; weight 14 grams; composition .500 silver, .400 copper, .060 nickel, .040 zinc; edge: reeded.

Date	Quantity Minted	F	VF	XF	Unc.
1947	61,460,000	—	BV	$2.00	$4.00
1948	22,915,000	—	BV	3.00	6.00
1949*	4,000,000	$500.00	$800.00	1500.	2500.
					Proof 4000.

*Beware of altered dates and counterfeits.

.300 Silver Coinage 1950

In 1950 a new coinage of the 1 peso appeared which was reduced in weight and silver content from the preceding issue.

The design of the 1950 peso is also considerably different. A more schematized hooked neck eagle appears on the obverse, and a three-quarter bust of Morelos facing left is on the reverse.

Diameter 32 mm; weight 13.333 grams; composition .300 silver, .500 copper, .100 nickel, .100 zinc; edge: reeded.

1950	3,287,000	—	BV	1.50	4.00

1 PESO

.100 Silver Coinage

Juárez-Constitution Centennial 1957

This 1 peso coin was the lowest of three denominations issued in honor of the centenary of the Mexican constitution. The series was designed by Manual L. Negrete. Benito Juárez, who had been Minister of Justice when the constitution of 1857 was adopted, is shown in profile on the reverse.

The 1 peso was made in very base silver, only .100 fine. To provide a silver sheen for a coin of such base metal, the planchets were dipped in a pure silver bath before striking. Uncirculated examples will preserve their appearance of a high silver alloy, while circulated pieces take on the yellow or brassy color of billon.

Diameter 34.5 mm; weight 16 grams; composition .100 silver, .700 copper, .100 nickel, .100 zinc; edge: lettered INDEPENDENCIA Y LIBERTAD.

Date	Quantity Minted	F	VF	EF	Unc.
1957	500,000	1.25	2.00	3.50	16.00

Regular Coinage 1957-1967

Regular coinage of a new 1 peso issue began in 1957. The reverse device is a restyled bust of Morelos; the obverse is identical to the 1957 Constitution commemorative.

Diameter 34.5 mm; weight 16 grams; composition .100 silver, .700 copper, .100 nickel, .100 zinc; edge: lettered INDEPENDENCIA Y LIBERTAD.

1 PESO

Date	Quantity Minted	F	VF	EF	Unc.
1957	28,273,000	—	BV	.60	2.50
1958	41,899,000	—	BV	.80	2.00
1959	27,369,000	—	BV	1.50	4.00
1960	26,259,000	—	BV	.80	3.00
1961	52,601,000	—	BV	.80	2.50
1962	61,094,000	—	BV	.60	1.50
1963	26,394,000	—	BV	.60	1.50
1964	15,615,000	—	BV	.60	1.25
1965	5,004,000	—	BV	.60	2.00
1966	30,998,000	—	BV	.60	1.50
1967	9,308,000	—	BV	.60	3.00

Copper-nickel Coinage 1970-1985

The redesigned 1 peso of 1970 was the first regular issue of its denomination in Mexican history to contain no silver at all. The obverse bears the schematized type introduced on other denominations as well in 1970; the reverse, a rather youthful and idealized portrait of Morelos.

Diameter 29 mm; weight 9 grams; composition .750 copper, .250 nickel; edge: reeded.

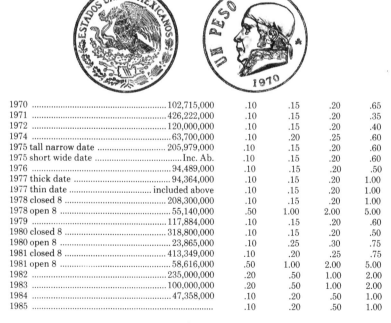

1970	102,715,000	.10	.15	.20	.65
1971	426,222,000	.10	.15	.20	.35
1972	120,000,000	.10	.15	.20	.40
1974	63,700,000	.10	.20	.25	.60
1975 tall narrow date	205,979,000	.10	.15	.20	.60
1975 short wide date	Inc. Ab.	.10	.15	.20	.60
1976	94,489,000	.10	.15	.20	.50
1977 thick date	94,364,000	.10	.15	.20	1.00
1977 thin date	included above	.10	.15	.20	1.00
1978 closed 8	208,300,000	.10	.15	.20	1.00
1978 open 8	55,140,000	.50	1.00	2.00	5.00
1979	117,884,000	.10	.15	.20	.60
1980 closed 8	318,800,000	.10	.15	.20	.50
1980 open 8	23,865,000	.10	.25	.30	.75
1981 closed 8	413,349,000	.10	.20	.25	.75
1981 open 8	58,616,000	.50	1.00	2.00	5.00
1982	235,000,000	.20	.50	1.00	2.00
1983	100,000,000	.20	.50	1.00	2.00
1984	47,358,000	.10	.20	.50	1.00
1985		.10	.20	.50	1.00

1 PESO

Stainless Steel Introduced 1984-

The fifth Morelos peso type was introduced in 1984. The obverse presented a
newly modelled rendering of Mexico's traditional eagle and snake symbol, while
the reverse introduced a right facing three-quarters portrait bust of Morelos
remindful of a similar left facing bust represented on the 1950 issue. This issue is
significantly reduced in size, and about one-third lighter, than the copper-nickel
issue it was designed to replace.

Diameter 24.5 mm; weight 6.07 grams; composition: stainless steel; edge: plain.

1984	722,802,000	—	—	.10	.25
1985	935,580,000	—	—	.10	.25

1936

2 PESOS

Centennial of Independence 1921

As part of the celebration of the centennial of independence from Spain, a 2
pesos silver coin was issued in 1921. The obverse carries a hooked neck eagle and
mint mark in a wreath, with surrounding inscription. The two dates 1821-1921
are at the bottom in Roman numerals.

The reverse shows a winged angel of Victory holding an olive branch (peace)
and a broken chain (end of bondage). In the background are shown the two legendary mountains, Ixtaccihuatl and Popocatepetl (see note on the 20 centavos
1943-1955). Value and silver content are to the left and right of Victory, respectively. Because of the reverse design, the coins were popularly called "Victorias."

Three million pieces were authorized, but less than half of that quantity was
coined. The designer was Emilio del Moral.

Diameter 39 mm; weight 26.666 grams; composition .900 silver, .100 copper; edge: reeded.

2 PESOS

Date	Quantity Minted	F	VF	EF	Unc.
1921	1,277,500	22.50	37.50	65.00	450.00

5 PESOS
Regular Coinage 1947-1948

The first coinage of a silver 5 pesos coin took place in 1947. The obverse shows a hooked neck eagle, with inscription above. The reverse carries a portrait of the Aztec chieftain Cuauhtémoc in war headdress facing left, with surrounding value, date, mint mark, and silver content.

Diameter 40 mm; weight 30 grams; composition .900 silver, .100 copper; edge: reeded.

1947	5,110,000	—	BV	8.50	12.00
1948	26,740,000	—	BV	8.00	10.00

Railroad Commemorative 1950

A 5 pesos coin was struck in 1950 to commemorate the completion of the Southeast Railroad between Coatzacoalcos and Campeche, making rail traffic possible between México and Mérida, capital of the state of Yucatátan. The obverse shows the Mexican coat of arms, with inscription, date, and mint mark. The reverse carries a steam locomotive in amazing detail, rayed sun above with the date 1950, and surrounding inscription.
This design is by Manuel L. Negrete.

Diameter 40 mm; weight 27.777 grams; composition .720 silver, .280 copper; edge: lettered AGRICULTURA INDUSTRIA COMERCIO.

5 PESOS

Date	Quantity Minted	F	VF	EF	Unc.
1950 200,000		17.50	27.50	45.00	65.00

Regular Coinage 1951-1954

A regular issue of the 5 pesos coin began in 1951. The obverse is similar to the previous issue except for date. The main reverse device is a bust of Hidalgo facing left.

Miguel Hidalgo y Costilla, first patriot and leader to be honored on Mexican coinage, is revered as the originator of the spirit which rose up to free Mexico from Spanish rule. He was a parish priest, dedicated toward bettering the lot of his poor parishioners in the little town of Dolores.

In 1810, Hidalgo became very active as a conspirator against the Spanish regime. His strong sermon of September 16 of that year, now known as the "Grito de Dolores" (the Cry of Dolores), was the spark that ignited the revolution. He himself was ambushed and captured in 1811, and was executed by the Spanish.

Numismatically, Hidalgo will be remembered for organizing the first rebel mint, that at Guanajuato, in 1810. His appearance on the 5 pesos silver coin of 1951 is the first time he is shown on any coinage other than the modern gold pieces.

Diameter 40 mm; weight 27.777 grams; composition .720 silver, .280 copper; edge: lettered AGRICULTURA INDUSTRIA COMERCIO.

5 PESOS

Date	Quantity Minted	F	VF	EF	Unc.
1951 4,958,000		—	BV	6.00	8.00
•1952 9,595,000		—	BV	6.00	8.00
• 1953 20,376,200		—	BV	5.50	7.50
1954* 30,000		15.00	35.00	70.00	100.00

*Beware of altered dates.

Hidalgo Bicentennial 1953

In honor of the 200th anniversary of the birth of Hidalgo, a 5 pesos silver coin was issued in 1953. The obverse is similar to the regular coinage beginning in 1951. The reverse shows a facing bust of Hidalgo, with the cathedral of the town of Dolores in the background, and appropriate inscription.

The coin was designed by Manuel L. Negrete.

Diameter 40 mm; weight 27.777 grams; composition .720 silver, .280 copper; edge: lettered AGRICULTURA INDUSTRIA COMERCIO.

• 1953 1,000,000		—	,BV	8.00	12.00

Reduced Size Coinage 1955-1957

A 5 pesos coin reduced in size was introduced in 1955. The obverse bears a small hooked neck eagle and national legend in almost the same size as the obverse type of the new 10 centavos of 1955, surrounded by a second inscription. The reverse has a bust of Hidalgo facing left, similar to that used on the regular issues of 1951-1954.

The popular name given to this small-size 5 pesos is "Hidalgo Chico."

Diameter 36 mm; weight 18.055 grams; composition .720 silver, .280 copper; edge: reeded.

5 PESOS

Date	Quantity Minted	F	VF	EF	Unc.
1955	4,271,000	—	BV	4.00	6.00
• 1956	4,596,000	—	BV	4.00	6.00
1957	3,464,000	—	BV	4.00	6.00

Juárez-Constitution Centennial 1957

Similar to the 1 and 10 pesos coins struck for the Constitutional celebration, this 5 pesos issue has the bust of Juárez on the reverse combined with an eagle on the obverse.

The percentage of silver in the alloy of the 5 pesos is higher than that of the 1 peso, and lower than that of the 10 pesos.

Diameter 36 mm; weight 18.055 grams; composition .720 silver, .280 copper; edge: lettered INDEPENDEN-CIA Y LIBERTAD.

Date	Quantity Minted				
◣ 1957	200,000	5.00	6.50	10.00	17.50

Carranza Centennial 1959

In 1959, the centennial of the birth of Mexican President Venustiano Carranza was commemorated with a 5 pesos issue. Governor, revolutionist, and finally President of Mexico, Carranza fought fiercely against General Huerta during the revolution of 1910-1917. He was elected to the highest office in 1917, and served as President until his assassination in 1920.

The reverse of this coin shows a bust of Carranza facing left, with inscription above the dates 1859-1959 below. The obverse has the typical coat of arms, and the edge is plain.

This coin was designed by Manuel L. Negrete.

Diameter 36 mm; weight 18.055 grams; composition .720 silver, .280 copper, edge: plain.

5 PESOS

Date	Quantity Minted	F	VF	EF	Unc.
‣ 1959	1,000,000	BV	$4.00	$6.00	$12.00

Copper-nickel Coinage 1971-1978

The first non-silver coinage of the 5 pesos denomination appeared in 1971. The obverse carries the redesigned eagle, the reverse a military bust of Vicente Guerrero. Guerrero was one of the major heroes of the war for independence, fighting the Spanish with great success from the earliest days of the resistance. When the struggle had been almost extinguished by the execution of Morelos, it was Guerrero who kept military opposition to the regime alive, and ultimately aligned with Iturbide to establish the Mexican Empire. After the collapse of the Empire, in part engineered by Guerrero in disillusionment, the general became a major political figure, serving as vice-president, then as president 1829-1831. His execution in 1831 was an act of political vengeance by Santa Ana.

The Mexican state of Guerrero is named in his memory.

Diameter 33 mm; weight 15 grams, composition .750 copper, .250 nickel; edge: lettered INDEPENDENCIA Y LIBERTAD.

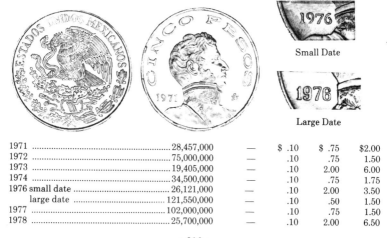

Small Date

Large Date

1971	28,457,000	—	$ .10	$ .75	$2.00
1972	75,000,000	—	.10	.75	1.50
1973	19,405,000	—	.10	2.00	6.00
1974	34,500,000	—	.10	.75	1.75
1976 small date	26,121,000	—	.10	2.00	3.50
large date	121,550,000	—	.10	.50	1.50
1977	102,000,000	—	.10	.75	1.50
1978	25,700,000	—	.10	2.00	6.50

5 PESOS
Copper-nickel Coinage 1980-1984

The 5 pesos issue was substantially reduced in size and reintroduced into circulation in 1980, at which time a new design was introduced. The obverse features a new modelled rendering of Mexico's eagle and snake symbol. Carried on the reverse is a representation of an Aztec sculpture of the head of the god Quetzalcoatl.

Diameter 27.1 mm; weight 10.36 grams; composition .750 copper, .250 nickel; edge: lettered INDEPENDENCIA Y LIBERTAD.

Date	Quantity Minted	F	VF	EF	Unc.
1980	276,900,000	—	.10	.20	1.75 ₄
1981	30,500,000	—	.10	.20	2.25
1982	20,000,000	—	.10	.25	3.25
1984	16,300,000	—	—	.20	2.50
1985	76,900,000	—	—	.20	2.50

Brass Coinage 1985-

The continuing depreciation in the value of the peso led to the introduction of a very small format 5 peso coin in mid-1985. The obverse features a modelled rendering of Mexico's eagle and snake design similar to that represented on the issue that it replaces. The reverse presents a simple design "$5" representing the denomination of the piece.

Diameter 17 mm; weight 3.12 grams; composition: aluminum-bronze; edge: reeded.

1985	25,000,000	—	—	.10	.20

10 PESOS
Regular Coinage 1955-1956

The first silver 10 pesos coin was released as a regular issue in 1955, together with a 5 pesos coin of similar design. It shows the Mexican coat of arms on the ⸱

10 PESOS

e, combined with the bust of Hidalgo on the reverse.
 ... popular name given to this coin is "Hidalgo Grande."

Diameter 40 mm; weight 28.888 grams; composition .900 silver, .100 copper; edge: reeded.

Date	Quantity Minted	F	VF	XF	Unc.
1955	584,500	—	BV	8.00	14.00
1956	3,535,000	—	BV	7.00	11.00

Juárez-Constitution Centennial 1957

The second issue of a 10 pesos silver coin took place in 1957. It is the highest of the three denominations issued for the Constitutional celebration that year. The design is similar to the 1 and 5 pesos, showing the bust of Juárez on the reverse and the coat of arms on the obverse.

The silver content of the 10 pesos is higher than either of the others struck for this occasion.

Diameter 40 mm; weight 28.888 grams; composition .900 silver, .100 copper; edge: lettered INDEPENDEN-CIA Y LIBERTAD.

1957	100,000	10.00	15.00	25.00	45.00

10 PESOS

Hidalgo-Madero Commemorative 1960

The 10 pesos coin issued in 1960 is a double commemorative. The portraits of two famous Mexican patriots, Hidalgo and Madero, are carried on the reverse. At Hidalgo's left is the date 1810, the year in which he gave his sermon that started Mexico's war for independence (see note on 5 pesos 1951-1954). At Madero's right is the date 1910, the beginning of the modern revolutionary period. The upper and lower legends of the reverse were slogans of Hidalgo and Madero respectively.

Francisco I. Madero published a book in 1910 that was severely critical of the regime of President Porfirio Diaz. The book made Madero famous, and helped to fan the flames of revolt against Diaz. Madero was elected president in 1911 but was unable to carry out his reforms. Revolutionary warfare continued against his government. Madero fell to a military coup in 1913 and was executed.

This coin was designed by Manuel L. Negrete.

Diameter 40 mm; weight 28.888 grams; composition .900 silver, .100 copper; edge: reeded.

Date	Quantity Minted	F	VF	EF	Unc.
◄ 1960	 1,000,000	—	BV	$8.00	$11.00

Copper-nickel Coinage 1974-1982

The continuously rising price of silver forced cessation of precious metal coinage in the 10 pesos denomination after the issue of 1960. For more than a decade both the 5 pesos and 10 pesos denominations were served only by paper currency. In 1974, however, a new copper-nickel 10 pesos piece was struck, on an unusual heptagonal flan with slightly bowed sides. The reverse portrait of Hidalgo is similar to that already familiar from previous coinage.

Although the initial coinage was dated 1974, this issue was first released to circulation in 1976.

Diameter 30.4 mm; weight 10 grams; composition .750 copper, .250 nickel; edge: plain.

1905 to Date

10 PESOS

Date	Quantity Minted	F	VF	EF	Unc.
1974	3,900,000	—	—	1.75	3.75
1975	1,000,000	—	1.00	3.50	6.75
1976	74,500,000	—	—	.75	1.75
1977	79,620,000	—	—	1.00	2.25
	Thick Flan Introduced				
1978	124,850,000	—	.10	1.75	2.75
1979	57,200,000	—	.10	1.00	2.00
1980	55,200,000	—	.10	.20	2.25
1981	222,767,990	—	.10	.20	2.25
1982	151,770,000	—	.10	.20	2.75
1982	1,000	—	—	Proof Issue	
1985	57,900,000	—	.10	.20	2.00

Stainless Steel Coinage 1985-

In response to the continuing depreciation in value of the peso, late in 1985 the government introduced a new 10 pesos issue, struck of steel, that was greatly reduced in size and weight from its predecessor. The obverse presents the modern modelled rendering of Mexico's traditional eagle and snake symbol. Like its predecessor, this issue presents a portrait of Miguel Hidalgo y Costilla, but facing rather than in profile, the denomination is also indicated thereon in Braille.

Diameter 19 mm; weight 3.84 grams; composition: stainless steel; edge: plain.

1985	255,350,000	—	—	.10	.25

20 PESOS

Copper-nickel Coinage 1980-1984

The 20 pesos value was reintroduced to Mexican coinage in 1980, following a lapse of nearly 60 years following the discontinuance of gold coinage in this denomination, as a replacement for the circulation of notes of the same denomination. The obverse design features a traditional modelled rendering of Mexico's

20 PESOS

familiar eagle and snake symbol. The reverse features a representation of an ancient Mayan sculptor or astronomer within a circle.

Diameter 32 mm; weight 15.14 grams; composition: copper-nickel; edge: lettered INDEPENDENCIA Y LIBERTAD.

Date	Quantity Minted	F	VF	EF	Unc.
1980	84,900,000	—	.10	.50	1.25
1981	250,573,396	—	.10	.50	.125
1982	236,892,000	—	.10	.50	1.25
1984	55,000,000	—	.10	.50	3.00

Brass Coinage 1985

Depreciation in the value of the peso led to the introduction of a new 20 pesos issue of greatly reduced size and weight in 1985. The obverse design features a modelled rendering of Mexico's traditional eagle and snake symbol similar to that presented on the predecessor issue. The reverse presents a facing portrait of G. Victoria; the denomination is also indicated thereon in Braille.

Diameter 21 mm; weight 5.96 grams; composition: aluminum-bronze; edge: reeded.

1985	5,750,000	—	—	.10	.30

25 PESOS

Olympic Commemorative 1968

The nineteenth modern Olympic Games were held in México in October, 1968, and a commemorative coin was designed for the event. Because the value of silver had risen greatly in the eight years since the last issue of large silver coins, a new denomination of 25 pesos was created. Although slightly smaller, lighter and

25 PESOS

of lower fineness than the earlier 10 pesos, its intrinsic value was still around 60 per cent of face value at the time of issue.

On the obverse is the traditional rendition of the Mexican eagle, but the denomination is in a stylized form intended to suggest the shield worn on Olympic uniforms. The reverse shows a pre-Columbian Mayan handball player against a plan view of an early playing court, with the official Olympic symbol of five linked rings at the bottom. The design was the work of sculptor Lorenzo Rafael.

Production actually began in October, 1967. On the first few trial pieces the three upper rings of the Olympic emblem were arranged in a slight arc to follow the curvature of the coin's rim. A corrected design was actually put into production, however, showing the three rings in horizontal alignment. When it proved impossible to recover and destroy all pieces of the first variety, it was decided to coin a large quantity of them, thus avoiding the creation of a rare variety.

Diameter 38 mm; weight 22.50 grams; composition .720 silver, .280 copper; edge: lettered INDEPENDENCIA Y LIBERTAD.

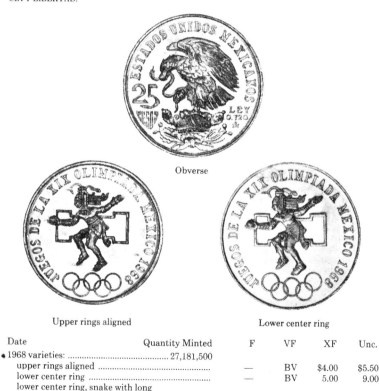

Obverse

Upper rings aligned   Lower center ring

Date	Quantity Minted	F	VF	XF	Unc.
♦ 1968 varieties: 27,181,500					
upper rings aligned		—	BV	$4.00	$5.50
lower center ring		—	BV	5.00	9.00
lower center ring, snake with long					
curved tongue		—	BV	9.00	14.00

25 PESOS

Regular Coinage 1972

A second type of this denomination bears the revised obverse introduced in 1970 and a reverse portrait of President Juárez. The unusual half-facing bust is reminiscent of (and perhaps a deliberate imitation of) the portrait of Juárez on a rare Revolutionary 5 centavos of Oaxaca struck in 1915 (Wood 168). The physical characteristics of the coin remain unchanged from the Olympic issue.

Diameter 38 mm; weight 22.50 grams; composition .720 silver, .280 copper; edge: lettered INDEPENDEN-CIA Y LIBERTAD.

Date	Quantity Minted	F	VF	XF	Unc.
✓ 1972	2,000,000	—	BV	4.50	7.50

Soccer Commemorative 1985

A pair of 25 pesos silver commemoratives were struck in 1985 to commemorate Mexico's hosting of the 1986 World Cup Soccer Championship games. The first issue, struck in both uncirculated (.720 fine silver) and proof (.925 fine silver) editions, on its reverse carries a representation of a soccer ball in flight, along with the "Mexico 86" games symbol. The second issue, struck only in a .925 fine silver version, on its reverse carries representations of a pre-Columbian "geroglyph" and a traditional Mexican window, known as "ojo de buey," conjoined with a soccer ball. The obverses of both pieces present a representation of the traditional eagle and snake design.

Diameter 24 mm; weight 7.775 grams; composition (uncirculated) .720 silver, .280 copper; edge: plain.

Diameter 26 mm; weight 8.406 grams; composition (proof) .925 silver, .075 copper; edge: plain.

First issue   Second issue

25 PESOS

Date	Quantity Minted	Unc.	Proof
1985 Soccer Ball In Flight		8.00	16.00
1985 Soccer Ball and two objects		—	16.00

50 PESOS
Copper-nickel Coinage 1982-1984

Introduced as a coin of commerce in 1982, the 50 pesos coin was a crown size issue with a value equivalent to about $1 U.S. at the time of its release; a devaluation of the Mexican peso two days later dropped its exchange value to just 62.5 cents U.S. The obverse of the issue features a modelled rendering of Mexico's traditional eagle and snake emblem, while the reverse depicts a representation of the dismembered body of the Aztec moon goddess Coyolxauqui, this depiction being based on a colossal carved stone disc uncovered in Mexico City in the late 1970s.

Diameter 36 mm; weight 19.63 grams; composition: copper-nickel; edge: reeded.

1982	219,311,000	—	.25	1.00	3.25
1983	45,000,000	—	.25	1.25	3.50
1984	73,537,000	—	.25	1.25	3.50

Copper-nickel Coinage 1984-

The continuing depreciation in the value of the peso led to the introduction of a greatly reduced size 50 peso issue late in 1984. The eagle and snake rendering on the obverse of this issue is similar to that employed on the predecessor issue. The reverse presents a portrait of Benito Juarez; the denomination is also indicated thereon in Braille.

Diameter 23.6 mm; weight 8.55 grams; composition: copper-nickel; edge: reeded.

50 PESOS

Date	Quantity Minted	F	VF	XF	Unc.
1984	94,216,000	—	.25	1.25	2.00
1985	293,782,000	—	.25	1.00	1.50

Soccer Commemorative 1985

A pair of silver 50 pesos commemoratives were issued in 1985 to commemorate Mexico's hosting of the World Cup Soccer Championship games in 1986. The first issue, struck in both uncirculated (.720 fine silver) and proof (.925 fine silver) editions, on its reverse carries a focused representation of the feet of a soccer player dribbling a soccer ball, along with the "Mexico 86" games symbol. The second issue, struck only in a .925 fine silver version, on its reverse carries a representation of a pre-Columbian athlete engaged in playing "pot a pok" or "tlachco," along with the "Mexico 86" games symbol. The obverses of both pieces present a representation of the traditional eagle and snake design.

Diameter 32 mm; weight 15.552 grams; composition (uncirculated) .720 silver, .280 copper; edge: plain.

Diameter 32 mm; weight 16.813 grams; composition (proof) .925 silver, .075 copper; edge: plain.

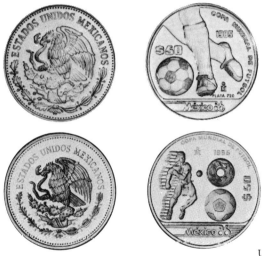

	Unc.	Proof
1985 Soccer Ball and Feet	11.00	24.00
1985 Pre-Columbian Athlete	—	24.00

100 PESOS

Regular Coinage 1977-1979

In 1977 there was issued a silver crown-size 100 pesos coin, thus continuing Mexico's tradition of producing large silver coins for circulation. The 100 pesos

100 PESOS

denomination is the highest ever used for any coinage in Mexico, and is a direct result of the peso devaluation of 1976.

The design of the reverse features a facing portrait of Morelos, a leader of the revolutionists fighting Spain in the early part of the 19th century (for more details on Morelos see notes on the 1 peso, page 199).

Diameter 39 mm; weight 27.77 grams; composition .720 silver, .280 copper; edge: reeded.

Date	Quantity Minted	F	VF	EF	Unc.
• 1977 low 7's in date, sloping shoulder 5,225,000		—	BV	5.00	8.00
1977 high 7's in date, sloping shoulder .... Inc. Ab.		—	BV	5.00	8.00
1977 level 7's in date, blocked shoulder ..... Inc. Ab.		—	BV	5.00	8.00
• 1978 9,879,000		—	BV	5.00	8.00
• 1979 783,500		—	BV	6.00	9.00

Aluminum-bronze Coinage 1984-

Following a four year suspension of coinage, the 100 peso denomination was returned to production, with the former .720 fine silver content giving way to an aluminum-bronze alloy. The obverse of this issue features a modelled rendering of Mexico's traditional eagle and snake emblem, while the reverse carries a portrait of Venustiana Carrenza. An additional feature of the reverse design is the incorporation or a representation of the demoninational value in Braille.

Diameter 26.5 mm; weight 11.97 grams; composition: aluminum-bronze; edge: alternating reeded and plain segments.

100 PESOS

Date	Quantity Minted	F	VF	XF	Unc.
1984 227,809,000	—	.50	1.00	2.75
1985 377,423,000	—	.50	.75	2.00

Soccer Commemorative 1985

A pair of 100 pesos silver commemoratives were struck in 1985 to commemorate Mexico's hosting of the 1986 World Cup Soccer Championship games. The first issue, struck in both uncirculated (.720 fine silver) and proof (.925 fine silver) editions, on its reverse carries a rather intricate Aztec design in combination with a soccer ball that's represented to be in motion. The second issue, struck only in a .925 fine silver version, carries on its reverse a representation of the head of a soccer player heading a soccer ball behind a net, along with the "Mexico 86" games symbol. The obverses of both pieces present a representation of the traditional eagle and snake design.

Diameter 38 mm; weight 31.103 grams; composition (uncirculated) .720 silver, .280 copper; edge: plain.

Diameter 38 mm; weight 33.625 grams; composition (proof) .925 silver, .075 copper; edge: plain.

100 PESOS

Date	Quantity Minted	Unc.	Proof
1985 Intricate Aztec Design		16.50	35.00
1985 Player Heading Soccer Ball		—	35.00

200 PESOS

175th Anniversary of Independence Commemorative 1985

The first 200 peso denomination coinage of Mexico was a 1985 commemorative issue circulated in observance of the 175th anniversary of the country's independence. The obverse presents a modelled rendering of Mexico's traditional eagle and snake symbol, similar to that introduced to all new coinage types of the 1980s. The reverse provides a representation of Mexico City's "Winged Victory" surmounted Independence column, facing which are the conjoined portraits of four heroes of the war for independence — Allende, Hidalgo, Morelos and Guerrero — with appropriate commemorative wording below.

Diameter 29.6 mm; weight 17.19 grams; composition: copper-nickel; edge: lettered INDEPENDENCIA Y LIBERTAD.

		EF	Unc.
1985 ....75,000,000 — —	.50	1.00

75th Anniversary of the Mexican Revolution 1985

Design identical to 500 peso, except for the indication of denomination.

Diameter 29.6 mm; weight 17.19 grams; composition: copper-nickel; edge: lettered INDEPENDENCIA Y LIBERTAD.

1985 98,590,000	.50	1.00

500 PESOS

75th Anniversary of the Mexican Revolution 1985

Diameter 38.1 mm; weight 33.45 grams; composition: .925 silver; edge: plain.

		Proof
1985 40,000	36.00

SILVER BULLION PIECES

1 Onza Troy de Plata 1949-1980

This crown-size piece was originally struck at the México mint in 1949. It is popularly called the *Onza* because of the reverse inscription UNA ONZA TROY = 480 GRANOS DE PLATA PURA (*One Troy Ounce = 480 Grains of Pure Silver*). The gross weight of the piece is somewhat more than an ounce, however, because of its copper content. The fineness of .925 (sterling silver) is higher than that used for any Mexican coin. In 1978 the issue was reintroduced into production on an annual basis, at which time the obverse design was modified slightly.

Although the Onza is not a coin, it is included in many collections of modern Mexican coins because of its similarity in style and size to the silver crowns, and because of its portrayal of coinage themes. The obverse is inscribed CASA DE MONEDA DE MÉXICO (*The México Mint*) and bears the familiar M° mint mark. Depicted on this side is the earliest coining press used at the mint. Dating from the early eighteenth century, the hand-operated screw press is still in existence. On the reverse is a suspended balance scale.

One of the original reasons for striking the Onzas was to demonstrate the high quality work of which the México mint was capable. It was hoped that other countries would submit orders for coinage as a result. A second reason was that the government wished to dispose of a large amount of silver bullion. The pieces were issued through commercial and financial organizations in various parts of the world at an initial price of one dollar each.

Diameter 41 mm; weight 33.625 grams; composition .925 silver, .075 copper; edge: reeded.

Date	Quantity Minted	F	VF	EF	Unc.
✦ 1949 1,000,000		10.00	12.50	17.50	30.00
✦1978 wide spaced DE MONEDA 280,000		—	BV	9.00	15.00
1978 close spaced DE MONEDA ....Inc. Ab.		—	BV	8.00	11.00
1979 pan points to U in UNA 4,508,000		—	BV	9.00	15.00
₊1979 pan points bet. U and N in UNA ....Inc. Ab.		—	BV	8.00	10.00
✦ 1980 6,104,000		—	BV	8.00	10.00
1980/70 ....Inc. Ab.		—	BV	9.00	14.00

Libertad Series 1982-

Starting with a 1982 dated issue, the Mexico City Mint introduced the production of a pure silver bullion issue. A modelled rendering of Mexico's traditional eagle and snake symbol, similar to that widely employed on the country's coinage issues of the 1940s and 1950s, is presented on the obverse. The reverse of this piece depicts Mexico's "Winged Victory" from atop the Independence column in Mexico City, in a rendering similar to that employed on the country's gold "Centenarios" 50 pesos which was minted from 1921 through 1947.

Diameter 41 mm; weight 31.10 grams; composition .999 fine silver; edge: lettered INDEPENDENCIA Y LIBERTAD.

1 ONZA

Date	Quantity Minted	F	VF	EF	Unc.
1982	1,049,680	—	—	—	11.00
1983	1,268,000	—	—	—	9.25
1984	1,014,000	- -	—	—	8.75
1985	2,017,000	—	—	—	8.75

GOLD 2 PESOS 1919-1948

The 2 pesos gold coin was introduced in 1919. Its design consists of the standing eagle on the obverse typical of the period, and the value in a wreath on the reverse.

The popular name given to this coin is the "Quinto Hidalgo," or one-fifth of a "Hidalgo," the 10 pesos gold coin.

Diameter 13 mm; weight 1.666 grams; composition .900 gold, .100 copper; edge: reeded.

Date	Quantity Minted	F	VF	EF	Unc.
1919	1,670,000	—	BV	22.50	30.00
1920	4,282,418	—	BV	22.50	30.00
1944	10,000	25.00	35.00	50.00	65.00
1945*	140,000	—	—	BV	+ 25% *
1946	167,500	30.00	50.00	65.00	110.00*
1947	25,000	25.00	40.00	55.00	80.00
1948†	45,000		no specimens known		

*During 1951-1972, 4,590,493 pieces were restruck, probably with the 1945 date.
†The $2 gold of 1948 is attested in the mint report but seems to be unknown. Since the $2½ gold dated 1948 does exist, the $2 piece as well was presumably struck from currently dated dies but never issued.

GOLD 2½ PESOS 1918-1948

The 2½ pesos gold coin with the bust of Hidalgo on the reverse was first issued in 1918. The obverse carries the standing eagle similar to other coinage made under the reform of 1905.

GOLD 2½ PESOS

The popular name of this coin is the "Quarto Hidalgo," or one-fourth of the 10 pesos "Hidalgo."

Diameter 15.5 mm; weight 2.083 grams; composition .900 gold, .100 copper; edge: reeded.

Date	Quantity Minted	F	VF	EF	Unc.
1918	1,704,000	—	BV	25.00	35.00
1919	984,000	—	BV	30.00	40.00
1920 *varieties:*	607,060				
2 over 1		—	BV	65.00	100.00
normal date		—	BV	25.00	35.00
1944	20,000	30.00	40.00	50.00	90.00
1945*	180,000	—	—	BV +	18%
1946	163,000	30.00	40.00	50.00	75.00
1947		200.00	275.00	350.00	550.00
1948	63,000	30.00	40.00	50.00	80.00

*During 1951-1972, 5,025,087 pieces were restruck, probably with the 1945 date.

GOLD 5 PESOS 1905-1955

As early as 1862, the idea of placing the bust of Hidalgo on Mexican gold coinage was seriously discussed. In the first attempt to carry out this idea, pattern 10 and 20 pesos gold (patterns 106-107) were struck at the México mint in 1892, with the great patriot shown on the reverse. For unknown reasons they were rejected, and it was not until the monetary reform of 1905 that Hidalgo's portrait appeared on regular issues of gold coinage.

The obverse of the 5 pesos coin beginning in 1905 shows the typical standing eagle of the 1905 reform. The reverse has a bust of Hidalgo facing left, with surrounding denomination, date, and mint mark. This piece came to be known popularly as the "Medio Hidalgo."

Four million pieces were struck at the Philadelphia mint in 1906. These are identical to the coinage of the México mint.

Diameter 19 mm; weight 4.166 grams; composition .900 gold, .100 copper; edge: lettered INDEPENDEN-CIA Y LIBERTAD.

1905	18,076	100.00	200.00	300.00	700.00
1906	4,638,000	—	BV	45.00	60.00
1907	1,088,000	—	BV	45.00	60.00

GOLD 5 PESOS

Date	Quantity Minted	F	VF	EF	Unc.
1910	100,000	BV	50.00	70.00	90.00

1918,
8 over 7

1918 *varieties:*	609,000				
8 over 7		45.00	55.00	65.00	90.00
normal date		—	BV	45.00	60.00
1919	506,000	—	BV	45.00	60.00
1920	2,384,598	—	BV	45.00	60.00
1955*	48,000	—	—	BV	+ 11%

*During 1956-1972, 1,767,645 pieces were restruck, probably with the 1955 date.

GOLD 10 PESOS 1905-1959

The 5 and 10 pesos gold coins issued under the monetary reform of 1905 constitute the first Republican Mexican coinage to bear the portrait of a famous patriot. The obverse of the 10 pesos shows the usual standing eagle, while the reverse bears Hidalgo's portrait facing left. The popular name given to this coin is the "Hidalgo."

One million pieces were coined at the Philadelphia mint in 1906. These are identical to the México mint issues.

Diameter 22.5 mm; weight 8.333 grams; composition .900 gold, .100 copper; edge: lettered INDEPENDENCIA Y LIBERTAD.

1905	38,612	100.00	125.00	150.00	250.00
1906	2,949,000	—	BV	85.00	110.00
1907	1,589,000	—	BV	85.00	110.00
1908	890,000	—	BV	90.00	115.00
1910	451,000	—	BV	90.00	115.00
1916	26,000	100.00	135.00	175.00	300.00
1917	1,966,500	—	BV	85.00	110.00
1919	266,000	—	BV	90.00	115.00
1920	11,603	175.00	300.00	450.00	750.00
1959*	50,000	—	—	BV	+ 10%

*During 1961-1972, 954,983 pieces were restruck, probably with the 1959 date.

GOLD 20 PESOS 1917-1959

The 20 peso denomination was reintroduced in 1917, struck to the weight and fineness appropriate to the Reform of 1905. The hooked neck eagle here made its first appearance on the regular coinage since 1825. The reverse illustrates the so-called Aztec Calendar stone. This giant stone is three feet thick and twelve feet in diameter, and weighs thousands of pounds. It is believed that when Corteés conquered México in 1521 the Calendar stone resided in the great central temple of the city. Thrown down and buried when the Spanish destroyed the temple, it was re-discovered in 1790 and is now displayed in the National Museum of Anthropology. While not a calendar proper, it takes its name from the circle of the twenty days symbols which rings the facing head of the Sun God.

The coin, whose popular name is the "Azteca," was designed by Jorge Encisco.

Diameter 27.5 mm; weight 16.666 grams; composition .900 gold, .100 copper; edge: lettered INDEPENDENCIA Y LIBERTAD.

Date	Quantity Minted	F	VF	EF	Unc.
1917	852,000	—	BV	175.00	200.00
1918	2,830,500	—	BV	175.00	200.00
1919	1,093,500	—	BV	175.00	200.00
1920 *varieties:*	462,198				
2 over 1		—	BV	190.00	225.00
normal date		—	BV	175.00	200.00

1921,
2 over 1

1921 *varieties:*	921,500				
2 over 1		—	BV	190.00	225.00
normal date		—	BV	175.00	200.00
1959*	12,500	—	—	BV	+ 7%

*During 1960-1970, 1,158,414 pieces were restruck, probably with the 1959 date.

GOLD 50 PESOS 1921-1947

The 50 pesos gold coin was first struck in 1921 as part of the centennial celebration of independence from Spain. The obverse carries the typical Mexican coat of arms, and the reverse bears the symbolization of winged Victory, with the legendary mountains Ixtaccihuatl and Popocatepetl in the background (see note on 20 centavos 1943-1955). The reverse design is similar to the silver issue of 1921.

Originally made for the 1921 celebration, the 50 pesos gold piece was coined regularly for a number of years afterwards.

The popular name given to this coin is the "Centenario." The design is by Emilio del Moral.

Diameter 37 mm; weight 41.666 grams; composition .900 gold, .100 copper; edge: lettered INDEPENDENCIA Y LIBERTAD.

Date	Quantity Minted	F	VF	EF	Unc.
1921	180,400	—	BV	475.00	650.00
1922	462,600	—	—	BV	450.00
1923	431,800	—	—	BV	450.00
1924	439,400	—	—	BV	450.00
1925	716,000	—	—	BV	450.00
1926	600,000	—	—	BV	450.00
1927	606,000	—	—	BV	450.00
1928	538,000	—	—	BV	450.00
1929	458,000	—	—	BV	450.00
1930	371,600	—	—	BV	450.00
1931	136,860	—	BV	450.00	600.00

Denomination Omitted 1943 Only

GOLD 50 PESOS

Date	Quantity Minted	F	VF	EF	Unc.
1943	89,400	—	—	BV	450.00

Denomination "50 Pesos" Reinstated 1944-1947*

1944	592,900	—	—	BV	450.00
1945	1,012,299	—	—	BV	450.00
1946	1,587,600	—	—	BV	450.00
1947	309,200	—	—	BV	+ 4%

*During 1949-1972, 3,975,654 pieces were restruck from predated dies.

GOLD 250 PESOS

Soccer Commemorative 1985

The first 250 pesos denomination coins minted in Mexico were struck of gold in 1985 to commemorate the country's hosting of the 1986 World Cup Soccer Championship games. The reverse of the first issue, minted in both an uncirculated condition edition bearing an "ORO 900" fineness statement, and a proof edition without the indication of fineness, depicts a soccer ball backdropped by a wall bearing Aztec designs, with a representation of the "Mexico 86" games symbol below. The second issue, minted only in proof, and without any indication of metal content, presents a rendering of Mexico's classic one peso "Caballito" design of "Liberty on horseback," as originally rendered on the silver peso issue of 1910-14, set against the background of a soccer ball. Encircling this design is a legend which also provides commemoration of the 450th anniversary of the establishment of the Mexico City Mint, while the "Mexico 86" games symbol is reproduced below. The obverses of both pieces present a representation of the traditional eagle and snake design.

Diameter 23 mm; weight 8.64 grams; composition .900 gold, .100 copper; edge: plain.

	Unc.	Proof
1985 Soccer Ball and Aztec Wall	170.00	225.00
1985 "Caballito" Design	—	225.00

GOLD 500 PESOS
Soccer Commemorative 1985

The first 500 pesos denomination coins minted in Mexico were struck of gold in 1985 to commemorate the country's hosting of the 1986 World Cup Soccer Championship games. The reverse of the first issue, minted in both an uncirculated condition edition bearing an "ORO 900" fineness statement, and a proof edition without the fineness statement, depicts a soccer player in action against a backdrop of an Aztec calendar stone, with a representation of the "Mexico 86" games symbol below. The second issue, minted only in proof, and without any indication of metal content, presents a representation of a soccer ball superimposed over the likeness of a Charles I one real reverse as minted during the period 1536-72. Encircling this design is a legend which also provided commemoration of the 450th anniversary of the establishment of the Mexico City Mint, while the "Mexico 86" games symbol is reproduced below. The obverses of both pieces present a representation of the traditional eagle and snake design.

Diameter 29 mm; weight 17.28 grams; composition .900 silver, .100 copper; edge: plain.

Date	Quantity Minted	Unc.	Proof
1985 Aztec Calendar Stone		335.00	450.00
1985 Soccer Ball and One Real Coin		—	450.00

GOLD BULLION ISSUES

The basic design of Mexico's modern gold bullion issues series is an adaptation of the classic "Winged Victory" sculpture which surmounts the Independence column in Mexico City. The rendering is similar to that first employed on the country's gold "Centenarios" 50 pesos which were minted bearing dates from

1921 through 1947. A statement of the pure gold weight, as applicable, is incorporated in the design of each piece.

1/4 ONZA 1981

Diameter 23 mm; weight 8.6396 grams; composition .900 gold, .100 copper; edge: lettered INDEPENDENCIA Y LIBERTAD.

Date	Quantity Minted	F	VF	EF	Unc.
1981 312,850		—	—	BV + 11%

1/2 ONZA 1981

Diameter 29 mm; weight 17.2792 grams; composition .900 gold, .100 copper; edge: lettered INDEPENDENCIA Y LIBERTAD.

1981 192,850		—	—	BV + 8%

1 ONZA 1981-

Diameter 34.5 mm; weight 34.5585 grams; composition .900 gold, .100 copper; edge: lettered INDEPENDENCIA Y LIBERTAD.

1 ONZA

Date	Quantity Minted	F	VF	EF	Unc.
1981	596,000	—	—	BV	+ 5%
1985		—	—	BV	+ 5%

PROOF SET 1982-83

The sets, authorized by the Banco de Mexico, are the first proof sets struck at the Mexico mint to be offered to the public in the mint's 450-year history.

They consist of eight coins with legal-tender status: 1982 five peso, 1982 10 peso, 1982 20 peso, 1983 20 centavo, 1983 50 centavo, 1983 one peso, 1983 50 peso, and 1983 Libertad.

The three 1982 dates were included apparently because the 10 peso was not struck in 1983 and dies for the five peso and 20 peso had not been prepared yet. One thousand Libertads, out of the 1 million authorized, were recalled and struck as proofs for inclusion in the sets.

Date	Quantity Minted	
1982-83	1,000	Issue Price $495.

7 | NON-CIRCULATING ISSUES

PATTERNS

NOTE: Because so many listings have been added to the Patterns section since the previous edition, the entire group has been completely renumbered.

The First Empire

1 8 Reales (1822), México. Silver.

This is presumably a pattern, less likely a trial strike for variety 3B of the 1822 Iturbide 8 Reales. The imperial portrait and eagle on *nopal* are exquisitely cut, but the dies used for this impression have no legends on either face.

2 8 Escudos (1822), México. Silver.

A second impression, again without legends, pairs the obverse of No. 1 above with a reverse not found in the regular coinage. The eagle is in cartouche upon crossed arms, but the cartouche is almost square, gently arched above. The pattern is presumably for the 8 Escudos, given the reverse type.

The Republic

Although the types of the regularly issued Republican coinage were persistently conservative for the first seventy-five years (until in this century a new conception of the possibilities and opportunities in coin designs evolved), there have been attempts in the past to alter or redesign the standard figures. A good many of these Mexican patterns are known today. They are here arranged chronologically, except for the 1831-1833 Durango issues which are considered as a group.

Unfortunately the origin of these patterns is usually not attested documentarily, and we frequently cannot even be certain whether the piece is of public or private origin. It follows that there is no necessary implication that the pattern was struck at the mint whose mint mark it bears. By law all Federal-type dies or matrices had to emanate from the mint in México; the branch mints were not permitted to design their own, although they sometimes did so. Further, most of the branches had neither the expertise nor the equipment to produce fine patterns. Most of the patterns attributed to the branch mints were therefore not actually struck there, and very likely were not even struck in Mexico.

It should be emphasized that the many base metal imitations of all denominations of the nineteenth century coinage, which are frequently taken to be patterns, are merely contemporary counterfeits.

State and Federal Coppers

3 ¼ Real 1828, Guanajuato. Copper.

This earliest pattern of the state coinage of Guanajuato bears the designs of the regular issue of the same year. It is struck with a plain edge and a raised border, however, and there are no stars beside the date as on the pieces struck for circulation. The pattern is probably a product of the Soho mint of Birmingham, England. Some examples may be restrikes made subsequent to the closing of the mint and the sale of its equipment in 1848.

4 ¼ Real 1836, Guanajuato. Copper.

This pattern bears no mint mark and has been attributed to México, but that it was struck at (or at least *for*) Guanajuato is suggested by the design and style. The obverse eagle is rather thin and its wings slightly convex, characteristic of the obverse in use at Guanajuato in the 1830's and 1840's. The reverse type of Liberty cap within a ring of clouds with rays beyond had been the regular reverse type of the Guanajuato state copper since 1828, and in fact the type is an exact duplication, with the addition of the legend, of the reverse of the 1828 pattern ¼ *real,* even to the same number punches. The origin of the pattern is unknown. It occurs on both thick and thin planchets.

| Obverse | No. 5 | No. 7 |

5 ¼ Real 1838, Chihuahua. Brass.

6 As above, silver.

7 ¼ Real 1838, Durango. Brass. See discussion following No. 15.

No. 8   No. 9

8 ¼ Real 1838, Guadalajara. Brass.

9 ¼ Real 1838, Guanajuato. Brass. See discussion following No. 15.

No. 10

10 ¼ Real 1838, México, with reverse wreath. Brass.

11 ¼ Real 1838, México, no reverse wreath. Brass.

12 ¼ Real 1838, México, flying eagle above column within reverse wreath. Brass. See discussion following No. 15.

No. 12   No. 13   No. 14

13 ¼ Real 1838, San Luis Potosí. Brass.

14 ¼ Real 1838, Zacatecas. Brass.

15 As above, silver.

For the first time on the Republican coinage the obverse bears a human head, the head of Liberty whose name appears on the hair band. The two obverse dies of these patterns (Nos. 5-9, 11-14; and No. 10), though of one type, vary considerably in style and in the form of the letter and number punches. On the reverse are the denomination and mint mark within a wreath or decorative border, the form of the reverse varying with the mint. These pieces are probably not products of any of the regular Mexican mints.

16 ¼ Real 1838, Chihuahua. Copper.

The obverse die is that of the preceding number, but the reverse carries the regular Chihuahua design showing a standing Indian. The flan is very squarely struck, with a high, sharp edge from having been struck in a collar, unlike the regular issues of this state.

17 ¼ Real 1838, Tuxtla. Copper.

This piece belongs with the preceding state patterns although it was struck in the name of a local district, that of Tuxtla (presumably Tuxtla Gutierrez in the state of Chiapas).

18 ¼ Real 1861, Culiacán. Copper.

Like the regular issues of the state of Sinaloa, this piece bears no mint mark. It differs from the normal type most noticeably in the omission of the obverse wreath and in the excellent style.

19   ⅛ Real 1863, México. Copper.

Although this piece is of the regular types of the 1841-1861 ⅛ *real* (see page 52) it cannot have been a regular issue, since decimal copper had already been introduced at the México mint when it was struck.

Real/Escudo Silver and Gold

20   8 Reales 1823 JM, México. Silver.

The earliest Mexican Republican pattern was struck in the first year of the nation's existence, an experimental 8 *reales* with facing eagle in place of the hooked neck eagle of the regular coinage. On the reverse a very individualistic Liberty cap is set within, rather than upon, a burst of rays. This reverse type was never taken up on the Mexican coinage but is a feature of several patterns. LIBERTAD upon the cap is spelled out in block letters rather than script; otherwise the legends are regular for 1823. The pattern is presumably the product of the México mint.

21 8 Reales 1823 JM, México. Silver.

Another experimental piece dated 1823 bears many features of the adopted design. The obverse is similar to the circulation strike, but with a more finely modeled eagle and wreath. The reverse bears a small cap inscribed with incuse LIBERTAD, upon a burst of closely spaced rays. Legends on both sides are normal for the México mint.

22 8 Reales 1824 JM, México. Silver, uniface plates.

A further peso experiment bears an elegant facing eagle of a style which was not adopted at the time, but was perhaps the precursor of the eagle which appeared on the México copper of 1829-1837.

23 8 Reales 1825 JM, Tlalpam. White metal, uniface.

One of the handsomest of the Mexican patterns, this piece was designed, in the opinion of Dr. Pradeau, by José Guerrero. The obverse type, of a vigorous style, is enclosed in a very precise border of pearls. On the reverse the legend which normally falls under the cap is distributed around the perimeter of the coin. The mint mark M̃ suggests that the pattern was executed at the México mint, for the Estado de México mint at Tlalpam.

No. 26

24 8 Reales 1826 WW, Guanajuato. Sterling silver.
25 8 Escudos 1826 WW, Guanajuato. Gold. See below.
26 8 Reales 1827 WW, Guanajuato. Sterling silver.

The great British engraver William Wyon was commissioned by the Anglo-Mexican Company to provide new dies for the coinage of the Guanajuato mint, whose lease it held. Although dies for all denominations in gold and silver were to be created, such records as survive at the Royal Mint in London suggest that only the 8 *reales* and *escudos* dies were actually completed. Specimens were struck from them in London, and the dies and coins were sent to Mexico in 1827. They were seized by customs agents at the port of Veracruz, however, because they were in violation of the regulation that only the central mint at México could provide dies and matrices to the branch mints. The examples known of the 8 *reales* pattern are probably survivals from the lot seized at Veracruz. (No. 62 below suggests that dies were preserved as well.) It is attested that Wyon finished the dies for his Guanajuato pattern of 8 *escudos,* and that examples were struck from them, apparently in 22 carat gold. No example of the 8 *escudos* appears to be known today.

The plain edge 8 *reales* pattern is one of the finest attempts at rendering the standard Mexican types. The obverse eagle is a fine and lively conception. The reverse rays are an ingenious elaboration of differing planes, and the lettering is small and delicate.

27 8 Reales 1827 S^A, San Luis Potosí. Silver.

Distinctive features of this piece include the use of the denomination 8 R^S (used on regular issues of this mint into the 1830's) rather than the customary 8 R, and the abbreviation S^A in place of JS for assayer Juan N. Sanabria.

28 8 Reales 1829 JS, San Luis Potosí. Silver.

29 As above, bronze.

30 As above, overstruck on British 1797 copper "cartwheel" penny of George III.

The types of this pattern are those of the regular issue, but the workmanship is very fine. No documentary information is available concerning its origin. However the matrices and punches are still to be found in the museum of the Royal Mint, London, so that they must have been manufactured there. The engraver is unknown.

No. 38

31 8 Escudos 1831 MJ, Guanajuato. Silver.

32 As above, copper.

This pattern is probably a product of the Soho mint in Birmingham, England. The fine style suggests a European source, and the eagle with slightly concave wings is to be found on the later 8 reales attributed to that mint, Nos. 50-57 below.

33 8 Reales 1832 JS, San Luis Potosí. Lead, uniface reverse.

The design is that of the regular issue, but the letter and number punches are drawn from a font of rather squarish design, comparable but not the same as that of the Durango patterns of 1831-1833, Nos. 34-44 below.

34 ½ Real 1833 RL, Durango. Silvered.

35 As above, silver.

36 1 Real 1833 RL, Durango. Silvered.

37 2 Reales 1832 RL, Durango. Silvered.

38 8 Reales 1831 RL, Durango. Silvered. See discussion following No. 44.

39 As above, bronzed. Possibly white metal underneath.

No. 43

40 ½ Escudo 1833 RL, Durango, 3 over 2. Gilded.

41 1 Escudo 1831 RL, Durango. Gilded.

42 2 Escudos 1832 RL, Durango. Gilded.

43 4 Escudos 1832 LR *(sic)*, Durango. Gilded.

44 8 Escudos 1832 RL, Durango. Gilded.

In the early 1830's dies of extremely fine execution were cut for the mint at Durango in the five denominations of gold and four of the five of silver (omitting the 4 *reales*). Their style is entirely unlike that of the dies then being produced at México. A large quantity of dies or matrices was manufactured; some were still being used in the 1850's. According to the 1849 *Memoria* their origin was Paris, contrary to law (see Patterns 25-26 above).

The dies of the various denominations are identical in style. The obverse eagle sits rather high above a wreath of elaborate detail. His wings are unusually high, giving the impression of hunched shoulders. On the reverse of the silver the rays are thick, and the lettering of both gold and silver is quite precise.

All the denominations for which these dies were cut were first struck off as patterns. It is doubtful that they were struck in the very years whose dates they bear. That the assayer is given as R.L. suggests that they must be earlier, since in the regular issues R.L. did not appear after 1829; and on these dies as employed for the ordinary coinage R.L. is regularly recut to the proper R.M. Further, while the pattern of the new style 1 *real* is dated 1833, regular production of this denomination in this style had already begun in 1832. Therefore it is probable that the dates of the patterns were meant only to be illustrative and do not indicate the year of their production.

The patterns of gold and silver are of brass and white metal respectively, often gilded or silvered. A silver strike of the ½ *real* is known in circulated condition.

45 1 Real 1834 OM, Zacatecas. Silver.

This pattern revives the hooked neck eagle which had gone out of use after 1825, and had never been struck at Zacatecas at all. The numeral 1 of 1R is cut over 8, and the necessary lapping of the die accounts for the weakness of the reverse. The initials are appropriate to the date, but the reeded edge, as well as the style and fabric which are much superior to the ordinary run of Mexican coinage at the time, suggest a foreign origin for the piece.

46 8 Reales 1834 OM, Zacatecas. Copper.

This peculiar pattern is struck from the same pair of dies as the 1 *real* of the same year and mint described above, even to the size of the flan, 19 mm. However the denomination of this tiny piece is given in the legend in its original state as "8 R."

47 (8 Reales 1834 OM, Zacatecas?). Silver.

This 8 *reales* pattern is very close in design, style, and in the reeded flan to the tiny 8 *reales* of Zacatecas just described. However the strike is very weak and no legend can be discerned on either side of the coin. It seems reasonable to include the piece at this point until a fully legible example can be found.

48   8 Reales 1840 OMC, Durango. Silver.

49   As above, white metal.

A pattern of unknown origin. The peculiarity of the letter A preceding the mint mark remains unexplained; Dr. Pradeau's suggestion, *annum dominationis* would convert the mint mark into the Latin word, which seems unlikely given the otherwise regular form of the reverse legend.

50   8 Reales 1843 PM, Guanajuato. Silver.

51   8 Reales 1843 MM, México. Silver.

52   As above, copper.

53   8 Reales 1843 OM, Zacatecas. Silver.

54   8 Reales 1844 PM, Guanajuato. Copper.

55   8 Reales 1844 MM, México. Copper.

56   8 Reales 1844 OM, Zacatecas. Copper.

57   8 Reales 184–. Copper.

The types and legends of these pieces conform to those of the 8 *reales* being struck for circulation in 1843, but the relief is high, the style fine, and the coins carefully struck. On the obverse the wreath is handled with great care, and the *nopal* shows far more spiny detail than on the regular dies. The Liberty cap of the reverse is elaborately modeled, the rays large and spread. No. 57 was struck before the die was completed, and lacks mint mark, assayer's initial, and the last digit of the date.

All these patterns clearly derive from the same source, probably the Soho mint in Birmingham, England. The mints of Guanajuato and Zacatecas were at the time under contract to the firm of Manning and Marshall, and the eagle of the patterns has the same slightly concave wings characteristic of the Guanajuato coinage. The same firm was to have secured new equipment for the México mint at about this time. It can be supposed that the patterns were produced as samples of their work.

58   (4 Reales size — 31mm) ca. 1850. Copper.

These strikes (and those of the similar 8 *reales*) were prepared by Eugène Kurtz, presumably in Paris, on the occasion of his supplying new machinery for the México mint. They bear no mark of value and should be considered specimens of his equipment's capabilities, rather than proposed coinage types.

59   (8 Reales size — 37mm) ca. 1850. Silver.

60   As above, copper.

61   As above, brass.

Kurtz' 8 *reales* pattern is identical with his 4 *reales*, save for a slight alteration in the reverse legend: "Eugène" is abbreviated as "EU^E" and mint mark P is given below the wreath.

62   8 Reales 1882 JA, Hermosillo. Silver.

Dies for this piece are those of the 8 *reales* designed by William Wyon for the Guanajuato mint in 1827 (No. 26). The reverse legend, however, is of a late nineteenth century style of letter and number punch, and the initials are appropriate to the late date — in fact, the Hermosillo mint was not in existence when Wyon cut the dies. One can only conclude that at least one of Wyon's reverse dies was sent to Mexico in 1827 with no legend incised, and that this die was for some reason preserved with an obverse for over half a century and then resuscitated to be cut for Hermosillo. Since the reverse punches are official, the pattern strike may also have been.

63   8 Escudos 1851 CE, Culiacán. Gilded.

The types of the pattern are standard for the denomination, but the narrow, square lettering and large interpuncts mark it as an essay.

Decimal System

64   1 Centavo 1841, México. Copper.

Luciano Rovira designed the first pattern centavo. The obverse is identical to that of the ⅛ *real* introduced in the same year; the reverse is similar to the ⅛ *real,* merely stating the denomination, date and mint mark, all within wreath. The edge is lettered REPUBLICA MEXICANA. The purpose of the pattern is unclear since the centavo was not a denomination commensurate with the monetary system of *reales* and *escudos.*

65 1 Peso 1842 ML, México. Silver.

In 1842 Rovira designed a second decimal pattern, of unique types. The obverse eagle on *nopal* occupies the entire field, and is unaccompanied by wreath or legend save for the engraver's name below. The reverse bears the Liberty cap on pole, within a wreath of olive and oak (left and right respectively, the reverse of the normal usage on Mexican coins). Above, REPUBLICA MEXICANA; below M T.A.1842.M^O .FL. The assayer's initials ML, which frame the legend, are appropriate for the year, but T.A. and F remain unexplained. In the center, 1 PESO / 903 M^S (milésimos, thousands), the silver fineness expressed decimally. The pattern was struck at the México mint.

66 1 Centavo 1862, México. Copper.

67 As above, silver.

68 As above, silvered copper.

The second centavo pattern was cut by Paredes. Two varieties are known, with and without the engraver's name below the reverse wreath. The eagle obverse was apparently unacceptable for some reason, for when the centavo was first struck for circulation in 1863 the obverse was Rovira's seated Liberty, even though Paredes' name appeared as engraver.

69 5 Centavos 1863, México. Silver.

70 10 Centavos 1863, México. Silver.

These first silver decimal coins of Mexico, although struck in the year in which they were authorized, probably should be considered patterns. They are very rare and apparently are not found in circulated condition. The design, a continuation of that used for the standard *real* silver, was regularly struck for the 5 and 10 centavos denominations of México and San Luis Potosí after the reestablishment of the Republic in 1867 until the complete decimalization of the coinage in 1869.

A71 50 Centavos 1866, Mexico. Silver, smaller shield than regular issue.
71   1 Peso 1866, México. Silver.
72   As above, silvered copper.
73   As above, copper-nickel.
74   As above, copper.

The pattern 1 peso of Maximilian bears the regular design, but with the obverse legend cut in smaller characters and minor differences in the reverse arms. The coin is scarce, but the allegations that only 36 were struck, that the die mysteriously shattered at this point, and that this was the emperor's age when executed, are all a myth.

No. 75   No. 76   No. 77

75   1 Centavo 1868, México. Copper.
76   5 Centavos 1868 C, México. Silver.
77   10 Centavos 1868 C, México. Silver.

Except for the date, the pattern strikes of the 1, 5, and 10 centavos of 1868 are identical with those struck for circulation in 1869 and thereafter.

78   20 Pesos 1868 CH, México. Gold.

A fancy pattern for the new decimal series was designed by Sebastián Navalón, who had joined in engraving the handsome coins of Maximilian. On the obverse the eagle above the wreath is enclosed in a frame upon various Indian arms. The reverse bears a head of Liberty. The fineness .875 is the decimal equivalent of 21 carats, the legal fineness of the escudo system gold.

79   10 Pesos 1869 C, México. Copper.

This pattern for the regular series which began in 1870 is, like Nos. 75-77, identical in design to the pieces struck for circulation.

No. 80

Reverse of No. 82

80   (25 Centavos) ca. 1885. Tin.

81   As above, brass.

82   (1 Peso) ca. 1885. Copper. See discussion following No. 84.

Obverse of Nos. 82-83   Reverse of No. 83

83 (1 Peso) ca. 1885. Copper.

84 As above, brass.

These three types were struck as machine trials by the firm of Mennig Frères of Brussels, during the preparation of presses for the mint of San Luis Potosí. The smaller measures 27 mm, the diameter of the 2 *reales* (which was still in circulation) instead of the 25 mm of the silver 25 centavos; the larger trials are 39 mm in diameter, the legal module of the 8 *reales*.

85 1 Peso "1810" (1887) M H, México. Silver.

In style the piece is an anticipation of the patterns of 1889 (see Nos. 86-93) and the regular silver peso first issued in 1898. The date is presumably a whimsy on the part of the engraver, Emilio del Moral, though 1810 was a pivotal year in Mexican history, the year of the "Grito de Dolores" and the opening of the war for independence.

86 1 Centavo 1889, México. White metal. See discussion following No. 93.

No. 89

87 5 Centavos 1889 AM, México. White metal.

88 20 Centavos 1889 AM, México. White metal. Like No. 105.

89 50 Centavos 1889 AM, México. White metal.

90 1 Peso 1889 AM, México. White metal.

91 2½ Pesos 1889 AM, México. White metal.

92 10 Pesos 1889 AM, México. White metal.

93 20 Pesos 1889 AM, México. White metal.

A series of 1889 patterns from the 1 centavo through the 20 pesos preserved the modules of all the pieces except the 25 centavos then in circulation, but introduced a redesigned eagle on the obverses. Reverses of all denominations bore the cap and rays, although this design was never employed for regular issues of copper or gold. Only one of these patterns came to be used, the redesigned peso first struck for circulation in 1898, but the obverse eagle was used on all values.

Obverse of Nos. 94-103　　　Typical reverse Nos. 94-102　　　Reverse of No. 103

94　2 Centavos 1890, Campeche. Bronze.

95　2 Centavos 1890, Coahuila. Bronze.

96　2 Centavos 1890, México. Bronze.

97　2 Centavos 1890, Nuevo León. Bronze.

98　2 Centavos 1890, Puebla. Bronze.

99　2 Centavos 1890, Querétaro. Bronze.

100　2 Centavos 1890, Sans-Luis *(sic)* Potosí. Bronze.

101　2 Centavos 1890, Tlaxcala. Bronze.

102　2 Centavos 1890, Zacatecas. Bronze.

103　(2 Centavos) 1890, 80th Anniversary of Independence. Bronze.

　　The firm of L. Chr. Lauer in Nürnberg, Germany, struck a series of ten unofficial 2 centavos bronze patterns in 1890. A Liberty head appears throughout the series on the obverse. On the reverse, nine of the ten pieces bear the name of a Mexican state; the tenth bears the inscription 15 SETIEMBRE / INDEPENDENCIA / 1810-1890 upon a field of rays.

104　2 Centavos 1890, Republic of North Mexico. Bronze.

　　An additional fantasy of 1890 is the 2 centavos struck privately for the nonexistent Republic of North Mexico. The influence of the U.S. bronze 2 cents is clear.

105 20 Centavos 1892 AM, México. Silver. Like No. 88, except for fineness.

This pattern was struck in accordance with the legislation of 1892 which suspended the production of the 25 centavos, substituting the 20. The cap and rays type had been officially abandoned since 1869, in fact since the last 2 *reales* were struck at Alamos in 1872, but revived for the patterns of 1889 (see Nos. 86-93 above). Note the unique indication of fineness, ".903." The new design was not accepted and coinage of the 20 centavos silver for circulation did not actually begin until 1898.

No. 107

106 10 Pesos 1892 AM, México. Gold.

In 1892 a pattern with the head of Hidalgo was struck at the México mint. The obverse is very similar in style to the silver peso of 1898-1909. The reverse honors one of the great Mexican patriots on a 10 peso gold coin that already, legally, bore his name — the "Hidalgo." While the assayer's initials are correct for the year, the fineness of .900 is not that actually then in use for the gold coinage.

107 20 Pesos 1892 AM, México. Gold.

The "doble Hidalgo" or 2 Hidalgo piece, identical in type with the pattern 10 pesos gold of 1892.

108 5 Centavos 1897, México. Silver.
109 10 Centavos 1897, México. Silver.
110 20 Centavos 1897, México. Silver.
111 1 Peso 1897, México. Silver.

The above four patterns all have the restyled eagle design finally adopted in 1898 after over a decade of experimentation with it.

112   1 Peso 1898, México. Bronze.

A pattern peso bears the regular type of facing eagle on the obverse; on the reverse, an Indian-Liberty head left. At the left, UN PESO Mᴼ; at the right, H • 902,7 • The flan is of the regular 39 mm peso diameter with a broad edge.

113   50 Centavos 1907, México. Silver.

Designed by Charles Pillet of Paris, this type was to come into use on the 1 peso of 1910-1914, but the 50 centavos pattern was never used. The word ESSAI *(Pattern)* appears to the right of both eagle and horse. The edge occurs plain, or with the legend INDEPENDENCIA Y LIBERTAD incuse or raised.

114   50 Centavos 1908, México. Silver. Same type as No. 113.

115   1 Peso 1908, México. Silver.

116   1 Peso 1909, México. Silver.

117   As above, reverse die only, date incomplete. Bronzed lead.

The 1 peso Pillet patterns are similar in all respects to the 50 centavos pattern of 1907, save that the word ESSAI appears to the left of the eagle on the obverse. On the reverse the lowest ray at the left is cut short to allow for the artist's signature; on the coin as struck for circulation the name did not appear but the ray remained short on the pesos of 1910 and some of 1911. The edge occurs plain, or with the legend INDEPENDENCIA Y LIBERTAD incuse or raised.

118   1 Peso 1911, México. Silver.

119   As above, bronze.

120   As above, brass.

121   20 Pesos 1916, México. Copper.

The $20 gold pattern of 1916 introduced experimentally the style of obverse with compact lettering which would first appear in the regular coinage on the reduced size 50¢ of 1918. The reverse illustrates the Aztec calendar stone completely surrounded by legend. For some reason the proposed gold content (16.7185 grams 90% pure = 15.047 grams pure gold) exceeds by about three-tenths of 1% that warranted by the proportionate weights of the already existing $5 and $10 gold coins.

122 1 Peso 1936, México. Silver.

The obverse type of this pattern, produced at the México mint, is identical with the hooked neck eagle introduced in 1936 for the 5 and 10 centavos copper-nickel. The reverse introduces the bust of Morelos to the Mexican coinage. The type was not accepted in 1936, but it served for the new peso of 1947 when the reverse was adjusted to accommodate a more conventional legend and the fineness was lowered from .720 to .500.

No. 123   No. 124

123 1 Peso 1947, México. Silver.

A smaller pattern, similar to the peso of 1936 but with a more conventional legend, was struck in 1947 to the fineness of .720. The regular peso of the same year, however, was larger and of poorer alloy.

124 1 Peso 1947, México. Silver.

In conjunction with the Morelos pattern, a similar piece portraying Juárez was designed. The module, alloy and obverse type are identical with the preceding.

No. 125

125 5 Pesos silver 1947, México. Silver.

In its flan and in the obverse design this pattern is identical with the Cuauhtémoc 5 pesos silver struck regularly in 1947 and 1948. The reverse bears the same information as the Cuauhtémoc reverse, but the type is a handsome repetition of the balance, scroll, sword, and Liberty cap of the peso of 1869-1873.

126 Onza 1947, México. Silver.

The piece is identical to the regular issue of 1949, save for the date.

No. 127

127 5 Pesos silver 1950, México. Silver.

The obverse of this pattern is the regular obverse of 1950, cut for the 5 pesos silver commemorating the Southeast Railroad. The reverse bears a version of the Hidalgo type which was not regularly issued until 1951. The salient difference between the pattern and the type struck for circulation is in the extent of the wreath, which on this piece completely encircles the portrait.

128 5 Pesos silver 1950, México. Silver.

As above, with the shorter wreath as issued regularly from 1951.

No. 129

129 50 Centavos 1955, México. Bronze.

In 1955, the first year of issue of the bronze 50 centavos, a pattern was struck of the same type and metal as the regular issue, but with smaller lettering and on a smaller flan. The planchet measures 30.5 mm., weighs 11.65 grams, and is reeded.

130 1 Peso 1955, México. Copper-nickel.

The obverse of this pattern bears the regular hooked neck eagle first introduced in 1936. On the reverse the bust of Morelos in military uniform is surmounted by the legend UN PESO Mo. 1955. The portrait is virtually that adopted for the billon peso of 1957 and following.

131 10 Centavos 1970, México. Bronze.

The obverse bears the redesigned eagle which appears on other denominations regularly issued in 1970. On the reverse is a bust of Ignacio Allende facing right.

132 10 Pesos 1980, Mexico. Bronze. 30 mm.

TRIAL AND PRESENTATION STRIKES

All mints regularly test their dies for strength, sharpness of detail, setting, etc., by striking trial pieces before undertaking the regular issues. Some off-metal strikes are also intended as presentation pieces or as a record of the fact of an issue. The following trials of the Mexican Republic have been recorded; doubtless others survive. The proper metal of the issue as intended for circulation is indicated in parentheses.

		Official Metal	Metal of Trial Strike

State and Federal Coppers

Durango	⅛ Real 1824	(copper)	silver
Guanajuato	⅛ Real 1829	(copper)	silver
	⅛ Real 1856	(copper)	white metal
	¼ Real 1828	(copper)	silver
Jalisco	⅛ Real 1856	(copper)	silver
	⅛ Real 1857	(copper)	silver
Occidente	⅛ Real 1828	(copper)	gold
San Luis Potosí	¼ Real 1828	(copper)	silver
	¼ Real 1862	(copper)	silver
Zacatecas	⅛ Real 1825	(copper)	silver
	⅛ Real 1832	(copper)	silver
	⅛ Real 1833	(copper)	silver
	⅛ Real 1846	(copper)	silver
	⅛ Real 1862	(copper)	silver
	¼ Real 1832	(copper)	silver
	¼ Real 1833	(copper)	silver
	¼ Real 1846	(copper)	silver
México	¼ Real 1834	(copper)	silver (overstruck on 2 reales 1801 Ṁ FT)

Real/Escudo Silver and Gold

8 Reales	1822Ṁ JM Iturbide small head	(silver)	lead
	183- Ǥ PJ	(silver)	copper
	1836 Ǥ MJ	(silver)	copper
	1844 Ǥ PM	(silver)	copper
½ Escudo	1856 Ṁ GF	(gold)	silver
	1860 Ṁ FH	(gold)	copper
1 Escudo	1857 Zˢ OM	(gold)	silver
2 Escudos	1848 Ṁ GC	(gold)	copper
4 Escudos	1835 Ṁ ML, 5 over 4	(gold)	copper
8 Escudos	1823 Ṁ JM	(gold)	silver
	1831 Ǥ MJ	(gold)	copper
	1854 C CE	(gold)	copper
	1861 Ṁ CH	(gold)	silver
	1865 Ȟ FM over PR	(gold)	silver
	1869 Ṁ CH	(gold)	copper

TRIAL STRIKES

		Official Metal	Metal of Trial Strike

Decimal Coinage 1863-1905

1 Centavo	1863 M̊, round 3	(copper)	lead
	1863 M̊	(copper)	silver
	1864 M, Maximilian	(copper)	silver
	1869 M̊	(copper)	silver-plated copper
	1883	(copper-nickel)	bronze, uniface obverse & reverse
2 Centavos	1883	(copper-nickel)	bronze, uniface obverse & reverse
5 Centavos	1869 M^O C	(silver)	copper
	1883	(copper-nickel)	bronze, uniface obverse & reverse
	1883	(copper-nickel)	white metal, uniface obverse
10 Centavos	1871 M^O M	(silver)	copper
20 Centavos	1901 C^N Q	(silver)	bronze
25 Centavos	1869 M^O C	(silver)	copper
	1871 M^O M	(silver)	copper
50 Centavos	1869 M^O C	(silver)	copper
	1870 M^O M, 70 over 69	(silver)	copper
1 Peso	1866 M^O, Maximilian	(silver)	copper, lead
	1904 Z^S FZ	(silver)	aluminum
1 Peso	1872 M^O M	(gold)	silver
	1888 P^I R	(gold)	silver
	1896 G^O R	(gold)	silver
	1897 C^N M	(gold)	silver
2½ Pesos	1888 P^I R	(gold)	silver
5 Pesos	1873 M^O M	(gold)	copper
	1888 P^I R	(gold)	silver
10 Pesos	1879 A^S L	(gold)	silver
	1888 P^I R	(gold)	silver, gold
20 Pesos	1866 M^O, Maximilian	(gold)	copper
	1870 M^O C	(gold)	copper, white metal
	1875 M^O B	(gold)	copper
	1884 CH. M	(gold)	copper
	1888 P^I R	(gold)	silver
	1898 C^N M	(gold)	silver

Modern Coinage

1 Centavo	1936	(bronze)	copper-nickel
2 Centavos	1906	(bronze)	silver
	1910*	(bronze)	bronze
5 Centavos	1962	(brass)	copper-nickel
25 Centavos	1970*	(copper-nickel)	copper-nickel
50 Pesos	(no date)	(gold)	gold

Note that base nineteenth century counterfeits of gold or silver denominations are frequently represented as trial strikes. These can usually be distinguished from genuine strikes by a careful examination of their style.

*Although these pieces were struck in the correct metal, there were no regular issues bearing these dates.